AN INTRODUCTION TO POLITICAL PHILOSOPHY

An Introduction to Political Philosophy

Alexander Moseley

continuum

Continuum International Publishing Group
The Tower Building   80 Maiden Lane
11 York Road   Suite 704
London SE1 7NX   New York
                                      NY 10038
www.continuumbooks.com

British Library Cataloguing-in-Publication Data
A catalogue record for this book is available from the British Library.

ISBN: 0–8264–8307–0 (hardback)
       0–8264–8306–2 (paperback)

ISBN-13: 9780826483072 (hardback)
         9780826483065 (paperback)

Library of Congress Cataloging-in-Publication Data

A catalog record for this book is available from the Library of Congress.

Typeset by Servis Filmsetting Ltd, Manchester
Printed and bound in Great Britain by
MPG Books Ltd, Bodmin, Cornwall

CONTENTS

CHAPTER 1

AN INTRODUCTION TO POLITICAL PHILOSOPHY

Political philosophy deals with the individual and his or her relationship with others. It asks questions such as what status does the individual possess relative to the society in which he or she lives? What rights, privileges, responsibilities or duties may be accorded either or both? Should there be a coercive authority to impose law or rules of behaviour? To what extent – if any – may it justly intervene in human affairs? Upon what principles should justice be founded? Should there to be any relationship between governments, and what manner ought it to take? In brief, political philosophy asks what kind of life is proper, good and just for a person amongst people.

Discourses concerning politics develop, broaden and flow from conceptions of human and social nature and conjectured answers to social and ethical problems such as the justification of authority over others. What distinguishes the theories that are fleshed out and investigated are the descriptions that writers give human nature (even if they eschew such a description); what status the individual is given relative to the group in which he lives; and what relations tend to, or necessarily, unfold between people. Theorists divide on what kind of state there should be, if there should be one at all, and what justifies or legitimizes that state. In turn, splits emerge on how the state should interact with other governments and peoples outside its jurisdiction.

Politics is the application of political philosophy – just as ethics is the application of the deeper considerations of morality. Daily, politicians and their policies exhaust much of the news headlines with proposals for the alleged benefit of the people or the world (we've yet to meet the arrogance of benefiting the universe). For some, politics is the proper method to make the world a better place; for others politics can only make life worse – and there are many proposals that lie in between these two positions. I will not be considering whether politics can or cannot make the world a better place – I shall leave the reader to judge if politics is at all appropriate, and if not why not, and if so under what circumstances. But I shall not avoid criticism where it is duly appropriate according to a theory's own ideals. In order to look at the deeper questions and ideas that politics uses (and sometimes abuses), we need to enter the world of philosophy, and in particular for this book, political philosophy.

We can begin political philosophy from several perspectives, and each has its advantages and disadvantages. The route I have chosen is to consider political ideas as they best present themselves, stripping proposals down to their essential ideas, from which we can then pursue their implications, regardless of whether particular thinkers or supporters applaud or avoid them. In everyday political life people typically espouse a mixture of ideals that reside, if looked at closely, uneasily with one another. This is either because they have not made the effort to examine their thoughts closely (and Socrates berated us that the unexamined life is not worth living), or because they seek power or consensual agreement over and above consistency, coherency or the principled life. Working out the contradictions should not, however, be left to professional philosophers. If we attempt to live a life immersed in the chaos of contradictory, inconsistent and uncollated thoughts, we leave ourselves open to challenges of hypocrisy and irrationalism, living life according to what presently captures our fleeting attention, rushing from job to job, cause to cause, pamphlet to pamphlet, increasingly vulnerable to any demagogue who may whip up our latest fancies into a concerted programme. While the psychology of political incompetence mounts daily, leaving the curious bemused and the indifferent bored, we should not be put off arming ourselves with theories by which to understand what our leaders and intellectuals espouse. This book provides food for thought as well as some intellectual weaponry to understand the present political morass.

CHAPTER 2

STATISM

The entire political establishment of the West is statist, and the political and cultural assumptions are rife with statism. All news items and common discussion imply a need not just for a state to exist but also for the government to 'do something' on practically every issue: to alleviate poverty, ignorance, sickness and unemployment; to reduce risk and encourage innovation; to embrace new technology and ensure its widespread application; to save the planet; to ensure a minimum standard of life for all. Government is also expected to cultivate certain political visions – a democratic society, a just society, a compassionate society, a tolerant society, etc.

The term 'statism' describes the collection of proposals that presume the need of a state to control and direct a proportion of the economy's wealth for political ends and the actions of the people for moral ends.

Political ends can be quite varied: they may range from ensuring redistribution of wealth from one class of citizens to another, to running specific industries. Motives may also differ and extend across that part of the philosophical spectrum supporting a role for the state from socialist idealism of equality of income, realist visions of military strength, libertarian acceptance of state ownership and control of the police, military and courts, to conservative and liberal acceptance of a minimum welfare state. Statism thus describes the broad justification of the mixed economy that goes under the names of democratic socialism, modern liberalism, the third way, the planned economy, communitarianism, or the welfare state. In terms of political economy, the philosophy extends from a small interfering state to the acceptance of directing most aspects of life short of full-blown socialism. They all have in common the presumption of state ownership and control of part of the economy by bureaucratic organs that in turn may or may not be accountable to higher political authorities or to democratic processes.

The moral ends can be derived from different ethical theories. Utilitarians (Bentham, J. S. Mill) will seek to harness the state's power to improve the welfare of the majority of the people – what determines happiness can be a mere play of opinion polls or it can be a reasoned moral programme devised by the great thinkers, the Platonic philosopher-kings (the majority not comprehending what would be in their interest). A prescribed programme of happiness may seem inconsistent for a utilitarian to espouse, but historically statists have often leant towards some form of social engineering designed to make the majority better off, and they do so according to a broadly utilitarian calculus in which some are destined to suffer, be persecuted or be driven from their homes, or even killed in order to secure the majority's welfare. Nonetheless, other utilitarians may rebut such moves and claim that since happiness is an inalienable and immeasurable individual possession it is illogical to seek the improvement of other people's happiness: they should be allowed to do what they will. A consistent utilitarian could not support state intervention as it is mainly counterproductive and violent.

Virtue theorists, by contrast, will seek to exploit the power of the state for making better, more virtuous citizens. They may define virtue culturally or rationally (i.e., the best kind of Englishman or all-round American, the true spirit of the Frenchman, etc.), or seek to cultivate those attributes deemed eternally and universally of the highest order: good breeding, intelligence, tolerance, etc.

The third main branch of modern ethics, deontology, demands that officials do their duty according to their position and not seek any private gain. But the prescriptive content of their programme is problematic to explain – after all, if it is one's duty to obey the law, then one must accept the law as it is and not seek to change it. If one's duty is to reason (regardless of tradition or present law), then the deontologist will claim that the law should be reasonable too: but if law and reason conflict, then the deontologist must reject the law in favour of reason, and rebel, withdraw from government, or seek reform.

Statists who seek to employ the force of government for specific ends certainly invoke morality, even if they do not do so explicitly. After all, if they claim that their policy will lead to a better life for all or for some, the comparison implies a moral claim. Similarly, if a statist argues that it is a moral duty of some social order or echelon to give money to the poor, the economic consequences of forcibly redistributing wealth must be accepted, as well as the implied morality of using force on one group of people in taking their property to benefit another. The interconnections between morality and economics are powerful and yet seldom expounded upon honestly or consistently (with great confusion promoted by equating traders with taxmen and robbers), and the ethic of forcibly taking from one to give to another is rarely questioned. Statists take it for granted that that is what government ought to do, and if it is not expropriating from some for the benefit of others, government, they add, should impose a set of values upon people different from what they themselves would freely choose: because the state's officials know better.

On that note, much statist political philosophy is accepted by mainstream commentators and the general public, and therefore is rarely justified properly. Even many philosophers, who pride themselves on questioning the legitimacy of authority, end up merely decrying the present officials in favour of another group: they rarely, unless they are consistent anarchists, reject authority *per se*. Alternative political philosophies must, on the other hand, by virtue of their exclusion from power, express in detail the logical arrangements of their programmes and explain clearly their political vision. But the incumbent tradition rarely needs to: the anarcho-communist needs to explain to us how resources are to be produced and distributed in the absence of property; the socialist has to justify the absolute dissolution of private property rights and answer the same question; the anarcho-libertarian how security will be provided in the absence of the state; the environmentalist must defend putting the earth first above mankind; the libertarian putting the individual first above society. The statist, however, typically enjoys the state's privileged incumbent position with very little opposition to the broad philosophy that supports it. A glance at the major political parties' stances will verify how little they seek to uproot statist traditions and expectations of government intervention. Statist politicians do not wish to remove the apparatus that provides them with position and power; similarly, few academics reject statism, especially when income and tenure are dependent upon direct or indirect government largesse. Economic incentives alone do not produce personal opinions, but they do act to entrench general trends by providing the easier option for people to follow, and it is these dispositions that statists invoke in their statistical (*statistic* from state) descriptions of human behaviour, which are then used to identify 'issues' for political action and 'goals' for the 'people as a whole'.

In effect, statism is the present dominant ideology for most political communities, and whereas the other political philosophies are ideals which proponents would like to effect, statism is firmly in place as political practice. However, it could be argued that the current affairs of any age are less the product of philosophy than the product of chance: the muddled outcome of political, economic, cultural and legal factors that are hardly the work of organized minds seeking definite outcomes. Certainly, there is much truth in asserting that chance plays a role in human and political affairs, but chance will impact upon and affect the course of lives and decisions in all political societies. What is important is the underlying, guiding ideal to which people revert in explaining why conditions and expectations are acceptable or not. In the current climate, the victory of the state is secure. Why it has become so requires a brief look at the historical and intellectual context of its recent triumphant growth.

THE RISE OF STATISM

Historically (and unsurprisingly) statism developed with the rise of the nation-state in the sixteenth and especially the seventeenth centuries. It corresponded with increased centralization in legal, constitutional and taxation apparatus, and the usurping of the wealth of growing and advancing economies in the eighteenth century. It was not long before the nation-state had entered the political consciousness of the West and men fought under the new banners of nationalism as proclaimed in song and painting and later in explicit indoctrination through state-owned schools. The history of the state's growth (at times accidental, at times encouraged and directed) is fascinating to read, but the relevant point that must be understood is that prior to the sixteenth century, people were more likely to give their allegiance to their locality or to the personage of the monarch or local prince: government was loosely connected to the lives of most and even up until the early nineteenth century it rarely impinged upon local affairs. The state as we're familiar with today did not exist – it is a *very modern creation*.

It is imperative to bear that in mind when reflecting upon political affairs in general: a shallow reading of history, a cursory glimpse of modern nations and their histories told through statist eyes, and a thoughtless acceptance of the status quo as paraded by superficial media analysis are liable to render the state eternally unassailable by new generations: a sure dimming of the intellect. For a philosopher, there should be no barriers to thinking: statism needs presenting in its best light certainly, but also it needs its opaque veil ripped away to show what it truly assumes and extols; to break through presumptions a more accurate assessment is demanded.

Since the First World War, statism has triumphed over all other contenders for the political mind. Initially, it could be argued, the statist 'middle' or 'third way' was claimed to be, and thereby justified as, the resolution required for the ideological forces pulling on the great economies of the first part of the twentieth century – Britain, France, America and Germany. The choice was touted as that between a world of free trade and a totalitarian world of complete state control over all aspects of life. Libertarianism (or what was then called liberalism) and totalitarianism were characterized as opposing extremes that must by all accounts be avoided. Libertarianism, it was argued, had scuppered its chances by bringing the disastrous Great War upon the world, and totalitarianism (in its communist, fascist and national socialist forms) was forging a new aggressive tyranny (although it must be said that proponents of both ideologies would deny these charges). Radicals pushed for the totalitarian vision as necessary for forging new, great societies, in which all would act in unison (socially engineered by the elite) for the benefit of their country, class, or race; whereas conservatives sought to hang on to the old freedoms and the class system of prewar times. Unsurprisingly, when opposing possibilities are presented, a synthesis of the two is inevitably attempted. Proponents of the third way sought to exploit the benefits of both totalitarianism and libertarianism, arguing that men could retain the majority of their freedoms while the harshness of poverty or the predilection for war was removed by benevolent state intervention and control.

The justifications for the middle way were – and remain – broad, coming as they do from a variety of arguments, all of which derived in some manner or form from the justification of state regulation and intervention in the economy and life. Some argue that economics (especially of the Keynesian variety) demands state intervention;

others that national security necessitates it; and still others that the state is needed for children's education. Democrats argue that the majority of citizens have a right to have a say in how a nation and its affairs should be run, or they follow Rawls and argue that people would accept statism if they were having to construct a society with no knowledge of personal or cultural affiliations (from the so-called 'original position'). Social democrats agree, but also press for a partial socialization of the economy's resources to effect a just distribution of wealth. Conservatives approve the putative solution in accepting the need to pander to the masses so as to avoid revolution and thereby acknowledge the need for a new contract with society in which the poor are accorded more economic and political rights. Statists of all brands – mercantilist, militarist, welfarist or environmentalist – proclaim that the state is not only more capable of directing the economy towards certain ends (stronger economy, mightier armies, health and education for all, a greener planet) but also add that it has a moral duty to do so. The statist collection of proposals and ideologies stretches across the recognizable Western political spectrum. Most, if not all, mainstream political critique and assessment takes place *within* statism.

Until the 1980s, the statist political pendulum swung to democratic socialism in which large sectors of the economy were to be taken over and held accountable (in some manner or form) to democratically elected bodies. Government was to socially engineer society in order to secure (usually) economic goals of technological and material progress; schools, universities, factories and utilities were to be harnessed by the elected elites (or at least by those in power if they were not elected) to drive the nation into a future vision of prosperity for all. As a result, freedom of exchange was gradually dropped by the major political parties of the West in favour of state intervention in domestic and international exchange to 'protect' producers; freedom of speech was gradually replaced by the advancement of government-based media, either monopolizing or controlling the newly developed technologies of film and radio broadcasting, to 'protect' readers and listeners; freedom of movement was replaced by passports and the requirement of internal identity cards to 'protect civilians'; freedom of association was replaced by race or gender employment quotas to 'protect' minorities. In many respects the desire to control and to direct, which had intellectually been defeated by the libertarian movement of the nineteenth century rode triumphantly back into the twentieth century, producing the social engineering experiments that characterized not just the obviously totalitarian countries but also the so-called free nations of the West.

By the 1980s, the socialist variety of statism was in retreat as politics swung right to a conservative-libertarian agenda of privatization and rolling back the frontiers of the state. The Thatcher–Reagan years are perennially enshrined in the popular imagination as destroying the socialist dream: an era which was capped by the collapse of the Soviet Union and the demise of communist-inspired totalitarianism. Yet the state did not stop growing – neo-conservative reforms left the welfarism intact both in terms of reach and expenditure and intellectually so; privatization did not lead to a rolling back of the state in other areas, although it indubitably supported the economic growth experienced in the 1980s and 1990s. In the twenty-first century, the social engineering experimentation of the state may seem irrelevant or nonexistent compared to the brutal and murderous versions imposed upon peoples around the world – in the Soviet Union, Nazi Germany, Maoist China, Khmer Rouge Cambodia, and so on, but interventionism remains embedded in political expectations. Today, it is not dragoons or tanks that marshal the people of the West into government-planned futures, but the relatively quieter officers of the courts and jails. The implied social engineering is still there, regardless of whether the representatives are elected or not, or whether they speak the language of freedom.

MAN

The statist distrusts the common man to look after his own life effectively or efficiently: he must be directed in some or all parts of his life by those who are deemed better able to know what is right for him. Hence the need to control, regulate, tax and direct him. Without taxes, the government could not defend the people from what Alexander Hamilton feared would be a state of 'continual plunder'; once the money is flowing into the state's coffers then other interventions can be paid for.

Metaphorically, proponents often refer to the ship analogy (first used by Plato) in which the community (state, society, culture, people) are all presumed to live on a common vessel requiring a common direction. If all people sought to pursue their own ends, the analogy goes, the ship would not get anywhere – so we depend on the ship's captain and crew to navigate us properly. That is, the individual, tempted by his self-interest and pursuit of happiness will not secure either his own happiness or his conjectured community's interests, and he therefore needs directing or controlling through forceful means. Or, at least, he needs manipulating through indirect means such as taxes or subsidies: raise alcohol taxes to deter consumption; make education compulsory up to a certain age; lower health-care costs to ensure greater demand, and so on.

This view of man is reminiscent of the conservative position, which accords a hierarchy of talent, and hence of social status, stemming from the lowest orders, who are presumed to possess little reasoning capacity, or who lack the prerequisite education to control their own lives. Those at the top are assumed to be most capable of controlling their own lives for they are better educated, and hence they are also assumed to be better at perceiving how others should live too. In contrast, the anarchist and libertarian would reject this description of man either totally or partially: communist anarchists deny that men are different, except in so far as the contrived circumstances of government and capitalism have made them so; libertarians accept such differences, but they do not justify the empowerment of one person over another. Liberals agree, but prescribe that children should be educated equally to avoid beginning their adult life with such handicaps.

The statist could also propose that all individuals are naturally morally weak and incapable of directing their own lives, never mind others', but that the evolution or contingent development of the state over the centuries has resulted in those institutional arrangements that ensure the best lives for all. Committed republicans as well as democrats accept the moral intemperance of man and the formation of government as his best means of security and direction. Republicans, those who reject monarchical, feudal or theological government in favour of government 'by the people, for the people', argue that constitutional arrangements can readily reflect the need for checks and balances that the core insufferable qualities of human nature demand; such arrangements evolve to reflect man's innate weakness, and a failure of government is merely a failure adequately to reflect or respond to the driving need to control the weaker or darker side of human nature. Democrats put their faith in the majority to decide the right course for all people, arguing implicitly or explicitly that while the individual cannot see what his true interests are or should be, a collective decision either does or tends sufficiently towards the common interest. For republican champions of the rule of constitutional arrangements or the democratic adherents to what the majority desire, individuals are viewed as weak and incapable of expressing the general interest, and hence they need to direct their egos through communal organs such as the ballot box or their representatives. Such statists can be conservative or reformist depending on their understanding of human nature and their reading of the will of the people; whereas elitist statists prefer to reject the input of the majority or 'the people', however considered or consulted, in favour of their own vision of how society should be and what economic or moral direction we all should be cajoled or pushed towards.

A pertinent question to raise is why is man considered so weak that he requires a state framework to ensure his happiness or basic welfare? The anarchist may retort that man lived for thousands of years without a state, and while life was rudimentary and harsh, there is no immediate justification for claiming that a more complex culture requires the imposition of force and violence on people's lives and choices. Such interference, the anarchist adds, is both simplistic and brutal and only effects disaster, displacement, disillusion and often death, despite statist assumptions to the contrary. Statists reply that there is every need for government intervention for supporting and directing life in a complex society, but the philosopher has to push the question further: why? Primarily, there are certainly theological variations on 'original sin', the claim man is innately weak and morally ineffectual. Such ideas, it can be argued, lag culturally behind the modern vision of man, yet their remnants affect much human thought, including the commonly held conception that if left alone, or in the absence of legal controls, most people would take advantage of their neighbours. Adults are thus held to be like children who would run riot or not look after themselves if left alone; their innocence must be protected or their disposition to sin must be restrained by formal arrangements of violent restraint and direction.

Moreover, statists argue that the expansion of society into increasingly complex forms demands a common legal framework in which all can secure their property, or be provided with a basic minimum income or education. The argument here taps into much cultural criticism of the open or capitalist society which holds that modern man is becoming increasingly alienated from his 'true' values, which typically imply a more communal existence and sense of solidarity. Alienation from the group begins, according to the Marxist-influenced statists (see Chapter 5 on socialism), with the division of labour into its market-driven specializations, and instead of securing the most natural development of the individual's talents, the price mechanism casts him adrift from his normal, traditional or natural support structures into the solipsist life that conservatives and socialists both condemn as contrived. The state on this argument is thus needed to reinstitute those structures in the form of universal welfare programmes, even if they distort the otherwise efficient workings of the market to produce and distribute goods.

Evidence, statists argue, supports the inherent moral incontinence of man. In disasters, men strive to preserve themselves, and while that disposition may or may not be eradicable in the long run through education, it is something that must be recognized and dealt with in the here and now. Some may claim that people are thus ruled by their instinct and emotions, but we have to ask: if this is true of all people, or only some; and if, presumably, it is only some (others may support reason over emotion), we must ask what separates one man from another? Is it breeding or training, luck or caste? The statist may not wish to deal with such a question, but his answer is implied in all that he prescribes – the majority (or all) of people are incapable of ruling themselves properly because the individuals that make up society are morally incompetent.

We can enquire whether people are deemed so incapable some of the time or all of the time? Answers may differ, but the answers then give us more insight into statist thinking. If people cannot rule themselves some of the time, we may enquire as to why; if given a satisfactory answer, we must be able to identify which times – e.g., disasters, wars or in conserving the environment for future generations. But, if that can be affirmed, the statist secondly needs to justify state intervention as being either necessary to avert a greater disaster or to promote a more efficient outcome for all. Critics may accept that humans run amok in testing times but reject government intervention as either illiberal and immoral or counterproductive (or a mixture of both). While disasters momentarily make headlines, such tumultuous affairs are not the standard for everyday life for most people. Where human settlement may encounter disasters, there is great incentive to migrate. Yet, ironically, much state intervention seeks to prohibit or raise the costs of migration (or subsidize habitation) thereby keeping people on lands that are subject to shocks natural and artificial. On the other hand, voluntary decisions to remain can also be said to reflect the worthiness of the risk to the inhabitants, a decision that libertarians and anarchists argue should be accepted and respected. But the statist presents this as the ultimate opportunity to show the *raison d'être* of the state: the emergency draws forth the best in the experts trained to deal with disasters, whose life-saving actions are to be heralded as heroic endeavours for all to congratulate and worship. The implication is that without the state many more would die.

If the state is to be justified only by the periodic disasters then its justification can be said to fail at all other times. There would be thus no need for a state, except for a minimum 'night-watchman state' existing in abeyance, prepared and trained for the unpredictable but not active or interfering in peaceful times. While this may appeal to the libertarian, it does not typically satisfy the demands of the statist, who prefers to see a more active state – not just manning the fire stations, but regulating people's lives and homes to avoid the outbreak of fires. If the periodic disaster scenario is rejected in favour of a permanent need for the state, then the justification must similarly explain the necessity of permanency – of not only a sleeping emergency service sector but as a constant intervention in life and choices.

But is man so in need of constant regulation and direction by authorities? Apparently so in the statist view: if we take the now dominant 'liberal' (i.e., modern liberal) vein running through statist thinking (as opposed to the earlier socialist variety), the absence of government is characterized by uncertainty and fear from predation. At the core, man cannot be trusted to live his own life as he sees fit – he must be restrained from lapsing into selfish pursuits, which are typically construed as immoral and detrimental to his neighbour. The 'liberal' statist stresses the 'rights' of the individual to pursue certain forms of life unmolested by others or authority, but this does not extend to trusting his manner of doing business with those not of his creed, or that of the majority's culture: he must be encouraged to drop his prejudices or be educated out of them to enjoy a better life of moral egalitarianism. The socialist statist rejects the rights of the individual in favour of the group's right to an equal distribution of resources and control over key industries that are deemed vital for general economic well-being. The good life, such redistributionists note, requires a minimum of wealth to ensure basic needs are met, without which the moral life cannot be pursued. This Aristotelian assumption stretches across the present political spectrum: without adequate access to physical resources, the individual cannot be free to enjoy his right to pursue happiness – and this is the argument that we hear most often in statist presentations on man.

SOCIETY

For the statist, society is often characterized as possessing a single overarching direction or system of priorities that all may or should recognize, or if they are deemed incapable of recognizing should bow to the authority of those who are so capable. The ship metaphor is highly useful both for encouraging statist thinking, as well as for understanding and therefore critiquing it. All members of society are on a ship: indeed, as environmentalism is making inroads into the political culture of the West, that ship is often seen as 'planet earth' taken as a whole and involving all life – human, animal and vegetable. But more often the ship holds a specific people – the English, the Catholics, the Africans, God's Chosen, or some other collective. Aboard the ship are the various strata of human society, usually described as a hierarchy reflecting status or talent, which may in turn be either shallow (in the more socialist readings) or deep (as in the more conservative readings), but in either case a pure equality is rejected in favour of some people gaining or being awarded the privilege of power to navigate the ship.

The authorities (representatives or the natural elite) then decide what direction society ought to be heading. In the modern world, the direction is often forward-looking – into a more technologically advanced future, whose path and direction reflect the vision of scientists; recently, it has taken on the green mantle of progress of environmentalist visions of clean technologies, sustainable production and recycling – all very much part of the earlier planning philosophy of the twentieth century but now rising to political and cultural primacy. Society is looked upon as a manipulable mass, into which individuals, despite any libertarian rhetoric to the contrary, are held to be of much less importance than the collective and its interests.

Statists across the political spectrum deploy aggregating statistics in their play for power and usually for more regulation – even those of a privatizing bias invoke fictitious abstracts such as GDP (gross domestic product) to assert the truths of their claims, and appropriately, statists often invoke utilitarian justifications of policy: the greatest happiness of the greatest number must be secured and that can only be enacted through the moulding of all to the public interest. Statists disregard the incommensurability of human happiness, clumping people's alleged interests together in categories that can change according to policy requirement or, in a nutshell, propaganda. Farmers are held as the bastion of nature one day, then slammed with regulations for being too close to nature the next; teachers seek to encourage individuality but then are told (if they are government-funded) to follow pre-set criteria and content. Lumping categories into statistical aggregates certainly jars against the libertarian conscience which is normally so concerned with the individual. Unsurprisingly, there have been recent attempts to merge the individualism of libertarian philosophy with collectivism: communitarian philosophers (e.g., Kymlicka) speak liberally of individuals, but remind them of their duties towards others of different cultural or religious persuasions and the common political and cultural institutions which all must support.

Politics for the statist thereby demands a political conscience on the part of all who are capable. The emphasis on the proper focus of political activity and conscience differs across the political spectrum: some prefer to underline the importance of local politics, while others stress national or even international politics. There is no true left-wing/right-wing split on this, for social democrats and statist conservatives may agree on the need to keep politics local or national; nevertheless, it is quite evident that Western governments have increasingly become removed from local control. What governs the focus of political thinking regarding political society depends for the most part on the dominant ideology as found in implied or explicated expectations. A quick reflection will elucidate the presumed proper or immediate political focus of attention: is it a supranational body, the nation-state, the provincial authorities, the locale, or kith and kin? Our attention is also helped, or diverted, depending on one's perspective, by the power to tax. The role of tax in human affairs cannot be ignored: most wars, civil and international, have been affected, if not caused, by taxation, often by states or authorities seeking to

AN INTRODUCTION TO POLITICAL PHILOSOPHY

secure lucrative tax-bases, and tax-bases in turn are imposed upon collectives of people – on farmers, the rich, the industrialists, the service sector, the workers, the middle class, and so on. The power to tax – such a vital ingredient for statism – has generally become highly centralized and disconnected from locality, a characteristic of modern politics that statist detractors (anarchists, environmentalists, some conservatives and libertarians) typically denounce, but which inevitably turns our attention from the antics of local politicians whose control over tax revenues pales meagrely in comparison with national and even supranational bodies (e.g., the European Union).

The society of which we then speak is governed by philosophical thinking (no matter how barren) but also pragmatically by the institutions that tax us and distribute its largesse; such institutions grew haphazardly as well as through design, but now impact on our critical assessment of politics. After all, without the European Union, for example, political attention would be fixed on the society of the national state, and in the absence of the national state, it would be focused on the society of the locality – of the city, the village, the county, or province. Each remove from the locality has required an incentive to alter political perception (tax) as well as an alteration in political thinking. Perhaps we can agree with several commentators that the heyday of nationalism is over – it climaxed in the Second World War, after which a concerted effort by intellectuals of many persuasions has acted to shift our political conception of society beyond our borders (or to exclude them as restraints on thinking) to embrace notions of people and culture independent of political borders, ultimately applauding the idea of 'one people, one world', which, if it were not for the world-government apparatus usually attached to such visions, would return us to the anarchist utopia of a radical absence of borders and controls.

GOVERNMENT

The state is the set of institutions by which the social elite, the elected representatives and/or experts run society. Through the apparatus of the state, the vision of advancement, stability, or even a return to a better past, is to be enacted. Such institutions depend on the exaction of tax from the citizenry, which is effected by the use or threat of force, and the visions are enacted into law, departure from which entails punishment of some form or other.

Whatever putative nobility the state possesses, its existence is dependent on force and violence: that is what the state is. Whenever we hear a cry for the government 'to do something' we must translate it into the imposition of force on some people; that is the irrefutable core of the demand and couching it in philosophically weasel words such as justifying it in the 'name of the people' or as 'supporting democracy and freedom' or 'peace and security' does not alter the imposition or threat of violence. Everything about the state opposes voluntary, peaceful interaction: when a committee sits, it draws funds from taxation; when a piece of legislation is passed, it is enforced by state courts and infringement punished by the policing agencies; when welfare is doled out to targeted groups, that money has been forcefully expropriated from its owners; when money is printed by the state's central bank, this indirect form of taxation causes a redistribution of wealth to the recipients of the new money. Its more obvious effects on society – police and army activity – are readily visible as naked power deployed, but the broader, more indirect expenditure and programmes that attract votes (or keep hordes of people from revolting against tax burdens) also rely on the threat of violence.

In a philosophical introduction to politics, such thoughts have to be amplified to raise an awareness of the nature of *what is*, just as in epistemology philosophers get us to question the validity of our senses or reasoning (or generally speaking our preconceptions) in order to sharpen our thoughts. Consider: the activities of government have expanded over the past century beyond the remit of an agency protecting life and property to include funding for education, universities, arts, media, scientific and technological experiments, child care, health-care, environmental protection, unemployment insurance, sickness benefits, building houses, roads, taking direct or indirect control of railways, roads, waterways and airports, electricity production, libraries, sports centres, steel and iron production, removals, telecommunications, astronomical and geological societies, mail delivery, investing in business, savings accounts. More indirectly, its regulations now typically extend from driving a car to painting a house, employing or firing a person, to cutting down or even planting a tree, using fuels to heat homes and building a house according to state-approval dimensions or quality. The present state is omnipresent (often being the largest employer in a nation) – it is very difficult to avoid – and behind its every move and word is violence or its threat.

Such is the institution of government, but how do statists justify it? Mostly they have recourse to Hobbes's philosophy: in the state of nature, in which humanity is without government, life would be 'solitary, poore, nasty, brutish, and short'. This is quite true, if we consider life for prehistoric man, but Hobbes's thought does not seek an empirical grounding. Instead the state of nature is presented as a model of life without government, which may or may not have been true in the past and which can always be true today or in the future should we abandon government. We meet the same fearful expectation of violence in the realist, the conservative, and to some extent the libertarian; only the anarchist rejects the model and points in contrast to the everyday peaceful cooperation taking place far beyond, or even without, the state's knowledge – such as my writing this book, trading with the local stores, serving my clients, conversing with neighbours. But statist proponents can retort that evidence of such peace implies that the state has been successful: the fact that I walk around safely is because of the implied recognition of the consequences of rule-breaking. They can also point to the fact that there is little clamour for radical change, except in publications such as this which present alternative viewpoints and visions, or in the provocative musings on university campuses; but generally speaking, the existence of government is accepted as necessary for peace.

The common statist thesis is that the actuality of fear or danger – or its implied and potential threat – in the absence of government drives men to form a protective agency to secure their lives and liberty. The Hobbesian thesis dominates statist thinking, but it is not the only justification for forming a government. Reverting to the ship analogy, others note how society is similar to a household in that it needs direction – a captain at the helm to secure not just safe passage but also to implement a vision for all to aim at. So, even in the absence of external threats to life and limb, a state may be required to enforce a common vision, without which (as we have seen above) all would seek his or her own direction and cause cultural, economic, and hence political, mayhem. Such freedom of personal direction cannot be accepted by the statist; or only certain kinds of freedoms may be permitted. Typically, social democrats lean towards a moral permissiveness but would impose restrictions on commercial exchange; whereas conservatives extol the benefits of commercial freedom but not personal morality. Critics note how this split assumes a duality of body and mind, both sides expressing confidence in the freedom of one aspect but not the other.

The statist's moral, political and cultural vision may be the product of a single man (a president) or a parliament. The visionary authority may derive from a personal belief in the nation's greatness or from the people. In the latter case, democracy – as understood as the rule of the ballot box – is the great director of human affairs, something critics from the Greeks down to the present day worry about. For if society's direction is to be governed by what the majority want, a series of concerns arises: who constitutes the majority can always change, thereby disrupting consistency; similarly, what the majority of people decide upon, aggregated together through the ballot box, is not necessarily what each would agree to independently of the force of numbers. The majority's attention may thus be fickle, so one year it might clamour for peace, the next for war. The majority may also turn its myopic distrust against minorities and pass persecutory legislation. Overall a majority vote is not necessarily a guarantee of moral truth or a protection of otherwise sacrosanct freedoms. Would it be better, therefore, to place political trust in a single individual? Monarchy or dictatorship has often been turned to when majority rule has led to strife and chaos, as the only solution to allow clarity of purpose and direction, and there is a great deal of cultural momentum to look to the wise or powerful leader for direction, even today when the economy has developed greatly beyond the small tribal affair of production and distribution by the leaders. But what we now see in leadership contests is far removed from the first half of the twentieth century in which figures such as Hitler, Roosevelt, Churchill, de Gaulle, Mussolini, Lenin and Stalin focused their nation's attention upon themselves and fostered personality cults.

On the one hand, the leader must bend society to his or her will: all must bow to the greatness and clear vision the leader presents. Such leaders are often presented as *Übermenschen*, and thereby accorded due status as gods on earth to be depicted in large murals and idealized, oversized statues exuding their heroism and clarity of purpose. On the other hand, the leader depicts himself or herself as the voice of the people, forever assessing what the majority wants, tempering perhaps dangerously myopic calls for immediate action in favour of cool-headed responses designed to 'listen to the people' and 'to understand their concerns' but also to guide them wisely, rationally and properly; such a leader seeks to forge a balance between the imperious dictator and the unruly mob, recognizing that the masses hold the key to power and must be acknowledged and appeased if necessary, while never permitting them full control over their own lives. The conservative philosophy dovetails nicely into such thinking, but so too does much malleable social democrat ideology, and in Western constitutions the inherent tendency for a leader to impose his or her will on the nation is tempered by the complexity of state and extrastate relations and institutions and the ballot box: accordingly, he or she acts as a 'representative' of the people.

The representative is the modern version of Plato's philosopher-king – able and adroit at understanding what the people want and rising to give them direction while not promoting himself into a deity. Yet whom does the representative represent? Ideally, him or herself. Edmund Burke famously argued that he was elected to parliament, not as a mouthpiece for a vocal minority or voting majority, but as his own man: politics produces few such capably independent men or women. An overview of any government recognizes that there are, beyond the obvious constituency, several extragovernmental lobbying groups who may press for the representative's ear – some critics of government keep a sharp eye out for sponsorship, which is acceptable or not depending on social expectations of influence. Public choice theory, which assesses the implicit economic and political incentives that politicians and officials face, clarifies much political behaviour (especially in terms of the broad direction and incentives faced), but we must remember that material incentives alone are not sufficient explanations of human action – an individual struggles to better his conditions as he sees them, and what constitutes a betterment is a subjective understanding and prioritization of facts and beliefs. A lobby group may offer a politician a good deal of money and yet he or she may reject it – we may call that politician virtuous; but then again, if we stand outside the framework and presumptions of statism, we may point out the hypocrisy of gleefully and triumphantly doling out the largesse that has been expropriated through taxation and not received from voluntary donations.

Beyond the extrastate lobby groups, whose ability to influence debate and hence legislation should not be underestimated (as a close reading of political history will demonstrate), the representative typically belongs to a party that demands his or her obedience in the legislative chamber. Such parties are either loosely or tightly controlled, depending again on cultural expectations and personalities. In a tightly controlled party, the representative loses the connection with the constituency he or she represents in obeying the grand mandate that the party upholds nationally (or provincially); the party believes it has a right to impose what in the United Kingdom is known as the 'whip' on its members to vote with the party – regardless sometimes of conscience and constituents' interests. Such is the stuff of domestic statism – the stories, dilemmas, revolts, shifting allegiances, clandestine support and networking that make up the modern state – but as philosophers we must see through the headlines and the collective triumphs of parties, presidents or parliaments to examine the ideology that all participants uphold as being normal and right. This politicking takes place at extraordinary cost to human endeavour, liberty and even, at times, life; this is more evident when we turn to statism in international relations.

INTERNATIONAL AFFAIRS

States regard each other as individuals on the international stage, claimed Christian Wolff at the dawn of the era of modern nationalism – that is, the vast and complex institutions that lie behind the word 'state' should be personified. States thus are said to act, to think, to believe, to desire – all logical nonsense, but how quickly and easily does the grammar of collective entities slip into political conscience in asserting such notions as 'France seeks to break deadlock in the Middle East', or 'Germany acts to relieve immigration problems', or 'Spain tests fishing rights', etc. If nation-states view each other as individuals, it is a short step to characterize them as possessing the whole gamut of human foibles – that they will 'discuss', 'argue', 'agree', 'disagree', 'forge friendship', 'come to blows', 'seek each other's annihilation,' and so on. The personification of the state collectivizes millions of individuals into a single mentality: this is what statism implies. Consider: 'France demands peace in the Middle East'. How exactly does 'France' demand anything, except when we recognize that the subject implies a specific individual voicing an opinion. We can enquire who is that individual? On discovering that it is the president, we can conclude that one man out of 60 million demands peace, and if we are enjoyably pushing the logic we can assume that the other 60 million (less one) were not asked their opinion; yet the president speaks for them. Does that mean that modern leaders have usurped the epithet of Louis XIV, who allegedly said, '*L'état? C'est moi*', in what is generally accepted as an arrogant, if not, constitutionally speaking, truthful claim? The modern leader, with his eye on the ballot box, could not ascend to the feudal claims of a baroque monarch, yet we retain the language and thereby the political concepts of such absolutism. When a president asserts an opinion, he or she evokes what we take to be the measured tones of reflective judgement on affairs of state, but that is also what we are expected to believe. A closer look at the political affairs of any country at any time reveals a less than tidy or logically appealing mindset, and while domestic politics may suffer the brunt of myopic or lobby-driven policy, the effect on relationships between nations can be horrific.

The collective assumptions are interestingly invoked and dropped according to moral contexts, which should give us pause: war is declared on an enemy leader, not on the people of that country (on Saddam, not Iraq; on Hitler, not Germany), but attacks upon 'our own individuals' constitute an attack against all. Such interesting asymmetrical morality pervades statist thinking, for what the statist looks out upon over the borders are other states, and if they do not behave as such, then they are 'rogue' entities: political entities not quite deserving the full status of statehood.

This prompts a fruitful query: what justification is there for borders in the first place? Geopolitical scientists attempt to find natural borders to define indelible limits to a state's jurisdiction, but such vivid examples are rare. The history of humanity has, from the beginning, been one of constant migration and integration with neighbouring peoples; recognized borders of even the oldest of states have a fluidity to them when looked at closely. Realist-oriented thinkers prefer to recognize those borders that have been ably produced and defended against neighbours, but the libertarian, environmentalist and anarchist sees nothing natural or justifiable in a particular border: humans have until recently been free to move around the planet voluntarily – now they require passports and visas, and their visits, purposes and even details of transactions are to be recorded by the host state. In a world in which new generations are growing up accepting such policies, a world without them must seem strange – perhaps less secure, especially when considering the global reach and effects of terrorism. Yet the critic is ready to ask why the world has become politically insecure and points to the rise of the state as the main culprit.

War abroad is just one facet, some would say an inevitable facet, of the state's intervention and regulation of life at home. Modern commentators on the state from Herbert Spencer to Ayn Rand have noted the connection between regulation and resulting 'domestic slavery' and the impetus to infringe upon others' rights across the borders. In the nationalistic phase of statism, when states embodied a range of jingoistic caricatures of national character, this was readily visible; today, when states have shifted towards a democratic socialist or American 'liberal' philosophy, the obviousness of bellicosity is hidden by appeals to a 'liberal' and 'free' order. The true liberal (now called a libertarian) could not condone interfering in others' political affairs, but since the early twentieth century, following on British evangelical imperialism to civilize the barbaric masses of the world, 'liberal' (i.e., Rawlsian or President Wilson's liberalism) Americans have sought to 'make the world safe for democracy', a cry which asserts the righteousness of the democratic, 'liberal' state and the concurrent rights of individuals to seek their own destiny the Western way. The indignant reaction to poverty or oppression riles the statist into demands for action, and if the target nation is sufficiently soft, troops and 'liberalizing' missionaries will be ordered to intervene. Reaction in the target state is rarely as amenable or as gracious as 'liberals' would desire, and arguably recent global insecurity is tempered only by the present relative strengths of the Western powers (notably the USA and Britain) to further their interests around the world. When a nation of dependencies is created by Western intervention and aid, long-term problems (such as recurring famines or the persistence of war) are introduced, but a review of how thinkers and activists on the receiving end portray things is much more shocking to the statist 'liberal' who believes he is acting for the good of the world.

Moreover, reaction against Western intervention has often had a Western intellectual underpinning: many guerrillas and leaders of the postwar independence movements were educated in European and American universities and took Marxist revolutionary thought back home to incite their peoples to revolt. The unfolding history was less clear than such revolutionaries expected – many were puppets to the convoluted interests of the Soviet Union (which once bragged it had an agent in every organization in the world); or their Western-trained voices were ephemerally powerful in fomenting rebellion against occupying forces, but in the aftermath left their countries torn by factional and civil wars. The briefly successful ones set up governments (and were sometimes trained to do so by the departing colonial administration) which were then used to pilfer and exploit their national, civil and ethnic divides on an unexpected scale, especially in sub-Saharan Africa. The critic readily points to the failure of statism to secure peace around the world, but is the criticism justifiable? Surely, statists reply, politicians are vulnerable to corruption and the power of the state can be used for evil ends, but what other model is there? The state, properly used, can foster peace and exchange, the rule of law and order both domestically and internationally. Its failure only reflects the fact that the wrong people have seized the helm; better captains may be drawn, for example, from democratic processes, and democracy – the rule of the majority – is peace-loving.

The shift towards 'liberal statism' in recent years reflects the belief (emanating from nineteenth-century optimists) that the people would not desire war. War is the product of elites feuding and squabbling over territory and dynastic claims, so once the ballot box extends out to the people, the desire for war diminishes. That optimism was forcibly shattered by the First World War (1914–18) and the later election of Hitler. Critics note the correlation between the expansion of the franchise and the expansion of the state and warfare, which should make us pause and rethink the connection posited between the franchise and war and more importantly between the state and war. If we date the rise of the modern nation-state to the 1490s, when Columbus's voyage opened up the Western mind and when Charles VIII invaded Italy, over 150 million people have died violently through state-sponsored warfare: the number is mind-numbingly huge, but the fact should always remind us to think carefully, especially when considering the tacitly dominant political culture of our time.

CHAPTER 3

REALISM

Political philosophy is concerned with man and his relations with others, and while the other theories seek to provide a political–ethical framework to guide both the actions of man and his social relations, *realism* rejects any such notion and claims that all human motivations, both personal and social, are driven by power and the desire to secure mastery over others or at least to ensure personal independence from the will of others.

Realism can primarily be described as an attitude to political philosophy that may be shared by conservatives, libertarians, socialists, anarcho-libertarians, and even environmentalists, alike – each arguing that political structures and guiding laws or rules reflect the disposition in men to seek mastery over others, either because of man's natural inclinations or because of culturally induced expectations. Although realist analysis is complicated by various schools of thought (some seeking the quantification of human affairs) and by various methodologies, the philosopher can draw upon the essential ingredient of political realism: the recognition that human relations are governed by power.

Generally speaking, *power* connotes an ability to do something, suggesting a causal leverage between work done and a resulting consequence. Applying power produces results, which is what all 'realists' seek, but whether those results are desired or not depends on the initial justification of power and its desired outcome. We can distinguish between power used in the natural sciences and power used in the human world to effect a change of affairs: its causal nature in the scientific world is readily quantified as Power = Work Done ÷ Time Taken, and despite various attempts to extend scientific analysis to human relations (*scientism*), the analogy breaks down. Add two powerful leaders together and you are more likely to cause a complex division of loyalty or fractious civil war than an arithmetical increase in power available! In the human world, power usually implies the ability of an individual or a political institution to muster resources into a common cause. Hence power is through the state's organs of coercion – notably the courts, army and police – whose mandate to tax, arrest, detain, punish, penalize, and even kill, is the foundation of state rule, regardless of the kind of government instituted.

We should also note that the term *realism* is often deployed as if it defined an embracing of the truth or of how matters *really* stand, compared to opponents' *idealistic* suggestions otherwise. (Realism proper is actually a metaphysical and epistemological theory concerning the independent existence of physical objects, or in scholastic philosophy, the independent existence of universal concepts.) But in political realism, supporters like to oppose their realistic or factual descriptions of human nature with the pejoratively labelled *idealist* visions of their opponents, which are implicitly ethereal, otherworldly or downright mistaken. This makes for poor philosophy – for the dualism between 'realism' and 'idealism' becomes too vague to be of use and falls into being popularly abused to invoke a generalistic approbation: 'Our position is realistic' means 'our position is true', which is surely what all philosophers strive for in the first place – a mere label will not secure veracity.

The innocuous-sounding label of *realism* may thereby act to cloak the implication of its policy prescriptions, which, so long as they point to a future state of affairs, immediately and logically join the chorus of so-called idealists' visions of what the future should be like. Arguably, there is no need for a philosopher to adhere to or subscribe to a name if it does not adequately capture its implied references: the term *realism* is patently inadequate – it does not do what it says on the packet, and it would be better and more honestly described as powerism. *Powerism* is a relatively underused term and certainly provides a more efficient comprehension of the general vision implied. Nonetheless, two important reasons arise for keeping *realism*: it is the generally employed and recognized term and it also reflects the claim that the theory deals with humans *as they are*, not as how we would wish them to be – realistic not idealistic. Realism accordingly purports to view nations and international affairs according to the cold facts and not wishful thinking. Advocates describe the world according to the use of power and the relations it engenders, and thus realism supposes that ethics, either domestic or international, ought to be driven by considerations of power. For the libertarian and anarchist, power is demonstrated only when one man, a committee or a parliament forces subjects or citizens into forms of behaviour they would not normally choose; for the environmentalist, power comes into play when man raises a tool against his natural world; for the socialist, power is embedded in the ethos and collective will of the group to be channelled by the state for the good of all; for the conservative, power is a reflection of the social hierarchy that naturally evolves in society. But while there are several variations on realism, power in the human realm ultimately depends on the successful application of force and violence by one set of people against another, and typically it is to be wielded by a political body of some form. Realists thus distinguish between legitimate power and the illegal use of violence by the criminal, and at this juncture, political realism becomes an identifiable theory that attempts to explain, model and prescribe political relations by taking power to be the primary end of political action, whether in the filial, cultural, domestic or international arena.

Realism has two major characteristics. Firstly, realists are keen to distance their theorizing from the what-if scenarios that involve a radically different human nature or world; they thus impress upon us the need to see humanity as it is and not how we would wish it to be. Realism emphasizes an essentially *descriptive* theory of human affairs, sketching them as they are and accordingly analysing them in the light of *facts*; thus the realist simultaneously and necessarily presents a *theoretical structure*. This is because the researcher filters and prioritizes information according to an a priori belief in what are pertinent data and what are not. Facts and theories cannot be separated: the mind strives to organize and categorize information and does so by virtue of theories learned implicitly or explicitly either before the data are examined or during the examination as dynamically generated conjectures. Priorities may change as new information comes to light, but given that the totality of all facts is inaccessible to mortal creatures, the realist is guilty of constantly invoking a theoretical framework to guide research, and it could not be any other way.

The resulting realistic framework is thus pragmatic – that is, it concentrates on and emphasizes *action* and *ends*, rather than allegedly being a thoroughly deductive procedure stemming from a few axioms describing human nature. Pragmatism and realism are intellectual soul-mates and have merged into a powerful philosophy underpinning Western foreign policy since the seventeenth century. I say 'allegedly', for the realist must of necessity also be selective in her or his choice of subject matter, and realists tend to emphasize the power institutions possessed by societies or construe apparently non-powerful relationships as exuding and implying power.

The second characteristic of political realism is its alleged *prescriptive* amoralism in which ethics should be rejected as being useless either in all human relations (or, in a weaker version, just in international relations), or it proposes that ethics should embrace power as the proper goal for man or for state. Since realists emphasize the descriptive nature of their thesis, they also claim that moral ideals are all but useless: we should witness what agents do instead of what they profess they *should* do. Action is thus more important than lofty moralizing; moreover, when pressed into action, the agent (individual or nation) will always pursue his own interests, and, most importantly for this theory, those interests can only be pursued at the costs of others' – that is, human life is inherently conflictual despite the refined drapery with which we may cover our true motivations.

Accordingly, if we are to draw an ethical theory, political realism in essence reduces to the principle that *might is right*, and whoever holds power does so by virtue of their ability to wield it intelligently against all competitors (as Machiavelli encouraged his rulers to do) and is thereby the legitimate moral primate.

MAN

If we rip away all institutions, all laws and all governments, what is man supposed to be like in his naked state? In what is called the 'state of nature', realists depict man in a somewhat brutal light: hardly cooperative and barely sociable, man for the realist is characterized as predisposed to violence and predation in his struggle to preserve himself against the predations of others. Generally speaking, man is deemed inherently self-seeking, self-regarding and driven by base passions such as the seeking of pleasure and the avoidance of pain. As Machiavelli argued, man lives for the now; he is persuaded by appearances and results; he is inherently corruptible (i.e., he is always open to abuse any power that he may possess); and if he is not clever enough to secure a monopoly or impregnable position, he must be carefully watched (a view of man which is also held by conservatives). His values may be bought and he is necessarily covetous of the wealth and power of others. Unlike the libertarian, the realist does not readily discriminate between wealth and power, and answers those who do discriminate between the highly market-dependent power of wealth and that of military might by arguing that wealth can purchase arms.

In this respect, the thoroughgoing realist is a calculating cynical pragmatist whose intermediary or secondary values and ethics must always adapt and give way to the primary goal of self-preservation and/or aggrandisement. We can also consider the realist support of *psychological egoism*: a theory of human nature and motivation which entails that the individual cannot but act in his own self-interest. Logically this would tighten the realist position that men act for their preservation, but would also render pointless the need for criticism of so-called idealist visions of man: after all, if individuals are *necessarily* self-interested, then the realist description of their behaviour cannot be invalidated or validated – egoism prevails regardless of any illusions to the contrary. Nonetheless, if we are unable to verify or falsify realism's assumptions, psychological egoism reduces to a mere logical assumption concerning human nature, which also acts as a warning to supporters of realism: if the evidence is so mustered as to warrant no exception to self-seeking behaviour, then realism itself collapses into a closed theory that cannot be refuted.

Man seeks to preserve himself, but in the realist's eyes, he is similarly covetous, for the realist believes that he cannot gain except at someone else's cost. This view is paraded in Plato, Aristotle, Aquinas, Montaigne and also in the mercantilist literature of the eighteenth century, whose many authors conceived the world's wealth to be fixed and hence the problem of resource distribution to be solved by seizure and control. Hence conflict becomes inevitable when agents seek the same interest or resource; agents may ally and cooperate so long as they share a similar goal and their policies may be adapted to include each other.

Initially though, realist man is an individualist who is driven by self-preservation and the fear of death, and thereby into competition with others. While the realist may permit the legitimacy of self-ownership, the individual's realm of sovereignty is constantly benighted or threatened by others fighting to secure their own realms.

For some, this means that man's precarious existence will prompt him into cooperation with others, or as Hobbes argued, to give up his rights in favour of security and peace to a policing government. For others, this inherent and necessary clash between individuals implies that the self can only come about through being powerful in relation to others: personal identity emerges from implicit or explicit conflict and is sustained by possessing enough weaponry or money to secure that independence. Man must thus always be on his toes, worried that his neighbour will take away his property or life. Hobbes prompts us to consider the depth of our trust when we lock our doors and chests at night and arm ourselves on journeys.

Yet does the realist present a truly pessimistic vision of human nature? The realist may logically reject such an epithet and prefer to claim that he is describing life as it is, not as we would like it to be. It would be pleasant if all could join in a mutually loving brotherhood and renounce aggression and conflict, but that is not going to happen, the realist contends, so long as man is constituted in the form he is. It would be encouraging to permit the free market to reign and to witness unprecedented economic expansion under small, self-determining republics, but the realist fears that they would become prey to those who would wield arms against trade, who will always exist where legitimate power structures fail to stretch. Pacifism is most certainly a pipedream that can never be realized in this world, for as soon as man lays down his weapons and 'turns the other cheek', his neighbour will prey upon him.

The 'dog-eat-dog' world of the realist is not necessarily an *amoral* existence: most realists, as we have seen above, do offer a moral vision of the future – one in which peace is secured, for example, by powerful states; or they comment upon common codes of ethics that retain a place in human conduct despite pragmatic powermongering. Again, if we re-evaluate the realist's image of a purely positive description of human affairs, as one that necessarily focuses on certain aspects of life and of history, virtuous action becomes apparent. Heroism is the chief virtue that the realist approves – the man who is able to sustain his independence or who is able to command the service of others; diplomatic ingenuity is similarly commendable, as is a pragmatic ruthlessness. The individualist warrior who defends his patch against predatory neighbours, or who expands his territory through stratagem and force, is the archetypal realist hero. Heroism in turn demolishes any possibility of an egalitarian society, either that envisaged by socialists or by libertarians: the hero seeks power and that brings fame and glory – he is Hegel's 'Great Man' of history who bends common morality to suit his own destiny.

SOCIETY

What does realism have to say about how men should relate to one another? It is arguably redundant for realists to retort that what are deemed to be men's interests cannot be drawn from how they *ought* to relate but how they do; for, as we have seen above, what is drawn from the complex intricacies of human society is necessarily filtered by theory, and realism's driving theory is to show how violent those relationships can be and how individuals or states ought to act to defend themselves against life's vagaries. Nonetheless, when we examine human society, the realist has much to say – that relationships can only be, or should only be, about power.

Firstly, a distinction ought to be made between the power wielded by wealth and the power wielded by arms. To proceed thus is to draw the fire of capitalism's critics who prefer not to make the distinction. 'The greatest bulwark of capitalism is militarism', wrote anarchist Emma Goldman, confusing workers, who are free to remove their labour from companies, with conscripts marshalled into armies by the state whose penalty for disobedience was often brutal imprisonment or death. The two uses of power – one resting on voluntary agency, the other on coercion – must be separated.

A large company may be said to wield a lot of power, and it does so in that it controls the deployment of people and resources according to managerial agendas and commercial criteria; however, so long as it exists as a free company and not supported, subsidized, or controlled by government privileges and law, its power is daily and continually dependent on the *voluntary* transactions accorded its products by both its consumers and the people who work for it. That is, a private company operating purely in the free market with no government subsidies to protect its existence can only be sustained so long as it provides a product or service demanded by the consumer. All production is aimed at consumption, and as soon as their custom dries up, producers must adapt either by enticing customers back at a lower price or through an altered marketing strategy. In the present climate, economic understanding of how profits and price signals work is certainly at a low ebb, so such explanations must be made, which is as unfortunate a situation as a chemist having to explain molecular theory each time he wished to mention compounds. Every commercial endeavour is dependent on the customer purchasing its product at the end of the day: no customers means no 'power' in the market-place. Similarly, labourers and owners of capital, resources or entrepreneurial services that a company depends upon are, in a properly free market, free to leave or to withdraw their services for better remuneration or working conditions, and the greater the breadth of the market-place, the greater the possibilities available for a resource-owner or labourer to sell elsewhere. Such power being dependent on voluntary contracts is not the kind of power that realism deals with. Although historically companies have often connived with governments to develop protection rackets which hamper or even extinguish free competition and trade, and the resulting political cartels are guilty of horrendous acts against other traders and consumers.

It is important to note and to understand power's potential breadth and limits. The extent to which a person will strive for self-betterment is governed by the ideas that they are brought up with and which they themselves generate. It is certainly an unavoidable fact of life that some people are less able or willing to stand up for themselves or raise their consciousness to focus on their situation, or to seek what from a third-party position can only be a material benefit to their well-being. Such people are likely to be relatively exploited for their cultural or psychological slavishness and hence to be bullied or cajoled into working under relatively harsher, demeaning, stricter or generally less pleasant conditions than if they were able or willing to stand up for themselves. But would it be right to call such situations *political?* In one sense it would – any relationship between individuals involves a modicum of guiding strictures and ideals that can be termed political in nature, and there are those thinkers who would describe *all* human relations in political terms; others, however, are inclined to note the voluntary nature of commercial (or sexual) relationships, which, in their eyes, necessarily depoliticizes the issue to one of mutual negotiation, and the fact that one of the parties is the stronger (and it does not necessarily have to be 'the boss' character – bosses can be just as weak and driven by unreal expectations of their own conduct or their workers' expectations) does not warrant a political exegesis or a Marxist–Hegelian analysis of master–slave dialectic.

Adherents to realism may stretch its boundaries to include all relationships – that between man and woman, parent and child, buyer and seller. For such realists, power emanates from all interpersonal relationships and cannot be avoided – such power can only be channelled or deflected by policy or by revolution. The connotations of power structure are implied in language, the body, clothing and other cultural effects, and while many of these structures are hidden in commonplace lexis and expectations, realists draw our attention to them, and what may be apparently an innocent exchange or discourse, is rendered violent and imposing.

Hegelians, for instance, are keen to politicize all human relationships: once two people meet, one of the parties strives to dominate the other to become 'master' and the other a 'slave'. This is a powerful conception of relationships, which has had a huge influence – direct and indirect – on a variety of political theories and philosophies. The struggle for power is endemic in all relationships, whether the relationship be voluntary or not: a salesman strives to master his customer; the customer in turn the salesman; a husband seeks to wield control over his wife; his wife similarly seeks to rebel against her enslavement. But is this philosophy liberating? Arguably not, for when two people come together, they will inevitably struggle for mastership, and there can only be one master, although in Hegel's rendition of what is a common theme in Western thought, the slave becomes just as much a master. Diogenes the Cynic, about to be sold as a slave, points out a potential buyer and says, 'Sell me to him, he needs a master.' Hence the master cannot survive without his slave – that is, neither party can be said to be independent. A realist thus has much in common with Hegelians, even if they do not explicitly derive their thinking or policies from Hegel's works.

The issue is even deeper: it is a matter of identity. Identity is born of struggle and cannot be otherwise. In a world absent of others, the solitary individual possesses no identity: that emerges in the presence of another and, as Sartre puts it, 'one must either transcend the Other or allow oneself to be transcended by him'. But why, at this level, should it be assumed that conflict presides? The Hegelian reading of power rejects equality and hence the realm of mutuality, and in doing so it rejects peaceful interaction: the individual strives to master his colleague, while at the national level, the nation strives to assure the world of its identity by conquering or fighting its neighbours. It is a peculiarly pessimistic vision of humanity, from which there is apparently no escape.

Except in Marx's version of Hegelian political philosophy. For Marx, the inevitable conflict between two people is driven by their class status, and on the ineluctable path that is our future history, the number of classes, and hence of conflicting faces to humanity, is destined to dwindle. In the industrial world, two classes remain: capitalists and labourers, but in the inevitable clash between the two, the workers shall eventually be victorious and the Hegelian dialectical clash between opposing interests shall be consigned to history. The future is thus rosy for Marx: one class emerges from history's class warfare and the slaves shall become the masters in 'the dictatorship of the proletariat', and peace and wealth will proceed.

For Hegelians and Marxists then, power and the struggle between opposing forces, whether they be people, nations, individuals or classes, is an inherent characteristic of human society and may readily be imported into the political realist tool-kit.

Theorists differ as to how and when power begins, or what shape it should take. For some, it begins as soon as two people encounter one another; for others, when one decides to impose his will upon another; and others still, when the state secures a monopoly of force on the citizenry of a land. Some (such as Rousseau) are content with ensuring the independence of the nation; others its expansion, and in this vein some worry or laugh at small nations (Treitschke). Some realists acknowledge humanity's natural gregariousness (Hobbes); others its innate individualism (Machiavelli). The vision presented of man's inherent sociability or otherwise impinges on the realist's description of society and hence to what extent the individual ought to be sacrificed to his society or the extent to which his society ought to respect his personal jurisdiction and sovereignty. Realists may thus divide on whether they consider the individual to be the essential agent of social life, the collective, or the state.

Collectivists look upon society as an entity deserving ontological or metaphysical status. The individual is merely a particle within the greater whole, and her life, purposes, dreams and desires are either fully dependent on the society that weans and provides her with a social life or are to be thoroughly relegated in favour of the values promoted and generated by her society. Consider Rousseau: 'Each of us puts his person and all his power in common under the supreme direction of the general will.'[1]

Society can either be defined as the totality of individuals living in a specified area, or as the more ethereal web that is constantly being altered from the complex matrices of interactions, relationships, breakdowns, ostracisms, births, deaths, etc. The collectivist may simply assert the primacy of the group; for the realist what becomes important relative to other groups is the population: a larger population implies greater power and hence standing in the international community. Or a more complex philosophy will seek to embrace the liminal bonds between people: bonds which produce a mystical collective spirit or soul with which all individuals can identify, even if they cannot enunciate the nature of that spirit, through a leap of faith or employment of a host of generalizations ('We British are warriors. We British are stalwart and vigilant . . .'). Either may be used by the realist who prefers to denigrate the sovereignty of the individual in preference to the group. Groups and neighbouring groups thereby enter the realist realm of power-seeking; nations, peoples, religions or cultures, whatever the defining collective, are thrown into the realist's equations that assess the balances of power or the strengths and threats surrounding each collective.

Population and economic power thereby enter realist calculations in the grand summarizing of each nation's position in the league-tables. Since power rests on numbers and might, the realist typically proposes securing a larger population and supports policies that will effect growth – historically these have included such invasions of privacy that would turn the libertarian's stomach (including, for example, the prohibition of *coitus interruptus* as a form of contraception, as well as the more usual and less invasive tax incentives to have more children). But a growing society will also show its divisions more readily than a stable one, which implies a need for the realist to ensure social cohesion driven by power. If the masses are to be united in their support of the nation-state, they should be accordingly herded physically and/or mentally into serving society; their selfish pursuits need a channelling into international competitiveness – domestic cooperation must thus be fostered for the more valuable goal of social or national greatness. Appropriately, realists support politicized education that encourages the young population to consider the importance of living in a powerful nation – patriotism and nationalism become the handmaidens of power politics. Gold medals at the Olympics become, in this reading, a peaceful reflection of national power-brokering (as they did in the Cold War era), whose true nature remains the struggle for mastery of one society over another.

STATE

Yet if man is driven by self-preservation and the desire to secure either his own independence or control over other, weaker neighbours, why should he form a government in the first place? For Thomas Hobbes, it was precisely because man cannot trust his neighbours (for after all when a man sleeps he is vulnerable to attacks from the weakest) that he seeks a contract in which he posits his natural rights in the institution of a state.

Thus it is his fear of his neighbour's desire to kill or plunder him that prompts man to create a government, which in turn will ensure that domestic society is pacific rather than belligerent. Apart from the right to self-preservation, men give up all other rights that they would have held in a state of nature to their government. The realist does not hold much faith in the ability of most men to reason: men are too myopic and self-seeking in their own thoughts. Accordingly, he believes that political (or religious or moral) pluralism is the cause of men's misery. The anarchy of plurality and the potential for discord and civil war are therefore something to be avoided practically at all costs by giving the state all the powers it needs to ensure and to enforce the peace.

The realist state is a necessary institution which emerges out of war or the threat thereof between people, and is justified to ensure the peace between civilians and between different peoples. It is not something man could live without: an argument the conservatives would acknowledge. Man's rapaciousness and innate belligerence, however optimistically construed, encourages him to seek peace in a troublesome world, and the realist declares that this is only possible if he shows strength. Thus the individualist-inclined realist will proclaim the need for a state to ensure the sovereignty of the individual and the inviolability of that sphere against predatory thieves, fraudsters, thugs and murderers. Yet the logic of realism withdraws from encouraging a libertarian framework of rights and inviolable spheres, for its thrust is to embrace power and that is best appreciated in the guise of rulers (e.g., in Machiavelli's *Prince*). The individuals of the polity thereby are viewed as pawns in political machinations, or as an immense, anonymous body against which the ruler throws his fortune and ability. That is, on this reasoning, the masses remain mass-like and a non-individuating power to be harnessed for the state; attention thus shifts from the hordes of humanity that remain historically anonymous toward the realist's heroes – those who seize power to force political or international change and thereby keep generations of historians and political thinkers penning books and articles. Such 'heroes' include Alexander, Cesare Borgia, Napoleon and Hitler. Machiavelli and Thucydides exhorted the effectiveness of the individual, but less heroically minded theorists prefer to emphasize the power of a committee, a state or set of institutions to effect change or defend status.

However, the people are not to be ignored: realists emphasize that power, so much as it rests in the majority's hands to accept or to deny the power of government and of men, must be played properly. Machiavelli advises that the people should not be roused to anger by arbitrary attacks on their property; they should not be disarmed unless they are newly conquered; they should be made dependent on government's largesse and redistribution policies; their loyalty should not be tested. Propaganda, welfare dependencies and amusements all assist the statesman to ensure his power; while generally leaving the people unmolested ensures their passivity and avoids their wrath.

When the heroism of rulers is condoned and cheered by realists who theorize upon and encourage 'Great Men' who seize power and bend it to their will, it is a small step to assert the *individuality* of the state and hence its political, legal and moral supremacy as an institution rather than the means for 'Great Men' to assert their dominance. The state may thus be the object of adulation and even worship, being accorded superhuman attributes that at once give it eternal apparel while simultaneously endowing it with life by means of myths of its birth and maturation and, in the case of the failed state, its death. Such statism breeds not just a belief in the moral and political primacy of the state over all other moral and political (or non-political) agents, but also a host of theories that seek to explain the nature of the life-cycles of states, as if the institution of government were a biological entity.

The state's ethic should be, beyond the value of preserving itself, completely amoral – or, better described, unprincipled. For Machiavelli, pragmatism should govern statesmen in their struggle for power: whatever is required in a certain situation must be adopted. Machiavelli advises that when a state's existence is at stake, 'there must be no consideration of just or unjust, of merciful or cruel, of praiseworthy or disgraceful; instead, setting aside every scruple, one must follow to the utmost any plan that will save her life and keep her liberty'.[2] From which we understand the realist's aim to secure the survival of the state, to which citizens owe their allegiance, time, resources and even lives, at all costs. Realism truly comes into its own when dealing with the affairs that could endanger the state – civil war and especially foreign invasion.

INTERNATIONAL RELATIONS

Prior to the French Revolution, in which nationalism as a political doctrine truly entered the world's stage, political realism involved the territorial and dynastic concerns of the political jurisdictions of the ruling families of Europe, whilst in the nineteenth century, national- ist sentiments focused realists' attention on the development of the nation-state: a policy that was later extended to include imperialist ambitions on the part of the major Western powers – Britain and France; even Belgium, Germany and the United States were influ- enced by imperialism. Nationalist political realism later extended into geopolitical theories, which perceived the world to be divided into supranational cultures, such as East and West, North and South, Old World and New World, or focused on the pan-national conti- nental aspirations of Africa, Asia, etc. Whilst the social-Darwinist branch of political realism may claim that some nations are born to rule over others (being 'fitter' for the purpose, and echoing Aristotle's ruminations on slavery), in general political realists focus on the need or ethic of ensuring that the relevant agent (politician, nation, culture) must ensure its own survival by securing its own needs and interests before it looks to the needs of others.

Generally, realists hold that in the absence of government, men distrust one another, and compete for resources, violently if neces- sary; but they contend that the formation of government, as an over- arching institution contracted into by self-seeking individualists who give up power to the regime, acts to enforce and guarantee peace between people within a territory. However, once the state's border is crossed, we return to the anarchic state of nature in which violence and predation are the expectation.

Descriptive realism commonly holds that the international community *is* characterized by anarchy, since there is no overriding world government that enforces a common code of rules. Whilst this anarchy need not be chaotic, for various member-states of the international community may engage in treaties or in trading patterns that generate an order of sorts, most theorists conclude that law or morality does not apply beyond the nation's boundaries, which takes the realist away from description and into the realm of prescription: a realm, as we have seen above, that thinking man cannot avoid. From describing the relations between self-seeking political entities as necessarily amoral, the realist implies that in acting abroad morality *should* not apply. Thinkers have often noted the duality in ethics between domestic and foreign affairs, between murdering a civilian and killing an enemy soldier; realism may either accept the duality and maintain the claim that morality is necessarily parochial and therefore ends at the border, or that international relations is, in the absence of a world government, merely an extension of the fearful anarchy that would rule were there no domestic government. Hobbes, for example, asserts that without a presiding government to legislate codes of conduct, no morality or justice can exist. Accordingly, without a supreme international power or tribunal standing over the individual nation-states, they will view each other with fear and hostility, and conflict (or the threat thereof) is endemic to the system.

From the realm in which the individual struggles to ensure his independence and perhaps his mastery over others, the realist contends that the jurisdiction of states and polities is similar and war is the inevitable form of conflict resolution: peace is the illusory calm before the storm of war. The ruler must always be prepared for war – he must acquire defences for the protection of his own state and engage in imperial adventures to gain prestige and reputation. Machiavelli writes that 'a ruler, then, should have no other objective and no other concern, nor occupy himself with anything else except war and its methods and practices, for this pertains only to those who rule'.[3]

War's origins and nature are then deemed reflections of state policy, and once initiated, war is deemed to be wholly subservient to political considerations and its direction, as the famous writer of *Vom Kriege* (*On War*), Carl von Clausewitz assumes: 'We see . . . that under all circumstances War is to be regarded not as an independent thing, but as a political instrument.'[4] If power is the end of war and power can mean survival as much as aggrandisement, war originates from balance of power strategies that rulers must, out of necessity, become embroiled in and seek to master. That is, by the interplay of kings and princes, each seeking power (territory, population, resources), which is a natural urge of rulers, each shall be *or should be*, according to realists, determined to improve his position in the international pecking order, and to insure against the rise of alliances or powers that would threaten his own status. 'Don't forget your great guns', wrote Frederick the Great to his brother, 'which are the most respectable arguments of the rights of kings.' The ruler should thus strive for hegemony or at least a secure independence.

Against the balance of power politics that realism's critics claim have led to more war than is necessary, realists tend to argue that attempts to create an overarching morality or to foster peace through international treaties are ultimately pointless. They may have their use in securing some values for the nation, but once those purposes are exhausted, the pretence that domestic guarantors of the peace can extend beyond national or colonial borders should be abandoned. The reality of the situation, realists argue, is that power rules the world's affairs – or should do, and the rules of this game are to ensure one's own nation is sufficiently powerful to avoid being taken over, and a world government would assuredly spell the end of the primary agent of politics – the state.

Another driving assumption behind realist analysis of international affairs is mercantilism. Mercantilists believe that a nation can only advance its interests at the cost of the interests of other nations, which implies that the international environment is inherently unstable. Whatever order may exist breaks down when nations compete for the same resources, for example, and war may follow or should be expected to follow. In such an environment, the realists argue, a nation has only itself to depend on and it should, so far as it is practical, strive for self-sufficiency in resources. Mercantilists explain that a nation grows rich by exporting commodities and poor by importing them; in so far as a nation depends on imports, it must indulge its traders and permit imports, but it must always struggle to produce a positive balance of trade in its favour. The economic theory is horrendously flawed, as trade is a mutually beneficial exchange (otherwise it would not occur), and to curtail imports necessarily curtails exports. Nonetheless, a bad economic theory does not stop people from believing it to be true or stop them from imposing relevant policies: it is interesting that the fact that the results are always counterproductive has never really prompted many to reconsider their theories! Economic incompetence ranks highly alongside political and military incompetence.

Regardless of the invalidity of mercantilism, some realists – and many philosophers who are not of the realist strain – argue for self-sufficiency. Autarchy, as it is technically called, was hailed by some of the Greeks as the ideal state: foreign trade, claimed Plato and Aristotle, was a lamentable necessity, but others disparaged the cultural effects of trade. Autarchy would remove a people from the disturbing influence of other cultures, but, as Plato recognized, it could only be secured by fighting for the requisite amount of land necessary to support the population. Accordingly, international relations may degenerate into discussions on border disputes or a Hobbesian 'war of all against all', as the nations of the earth struggle to secure the *ideal* state of autarchy. Cooperation becomes an intensely fragile occupation when the struggle for values is deemed to be inherently mutually exclusive; nonetheless, allegiances and treatises may be of use to competing nations in furtherance of their rationally defined self-interests. Accordingly, diplomacy is of paramount stature in the realm of independent nation-states. Realists worry, however, that crusades or jihads (unleashed by powers that transcend the state) will destabilize the nation-state system, and movements to secure an international body or global polity are similarly destabilizing.

Political realists are often characterized as amoralists accepting any means available to uphold the national interest, but a poignant criticism is that the definition of morality is being twisted to assume that acting in one's own or one's nation's interests is immoral or amoral at best. This is an unfair claim against serving one's national interest, just as claiming that any self-serving action is necessarily immoral on the personal level. The discussion invokes the ethics of impartiality; those who believe in a universal code of ethics argue that a self-serving action which cannot be universalized is immoral. However, universalism is not the only standard of ethical actions. Partiality, it can be claimed, should play a role in ethical decisions; partialists deem it absurd that state officials should not give their own nation greater moral weight over other nations, just as it would be absurd for parents to give equal consideration to their own children and the children of others. But if morality is employed in the sense of being altruistic, or at least universalistic, then political realists would rightly admit that attempting to be moral will be detrimental to the national interest or to the world as a whole, and therefore morality ought to be ignored. But, if morality accepts the validity of at least some self-serving actions, then *ipso facto* political realism is a moral political doctrine.

NOTES

1 Jean-Jacques Rousseau, 'The Social Contract' in *The Social Contract and Discourses*, trans. G. D. H. Cole (London: Everyman, 1993), p. 192.
2 Niccolò Machiavelli, 'Discourses on the first Decade of Titus Livius', in *Machiavelli: the Chief Works and Others*, trans. Allan Gilbert (Durham, NC: Duke University Press, 1968), p. 519.
3 Ibid., pp. 51–2.
4 Carl von Clausewitz, *On War*, Volume I, trans. J. J. Graham (London: Routledge & Kegan Paul, 1968), p. 24.

CHAPTER 4

CONSERVATISM

Conservatism presents an intriguing political theory: from some critical perspectives it barely presents a theory at all, and supporters emphasize that it should not strive to do so; yet it also provides an attractively mature vision of humanity and politics in contrast to what conservatives exclaim is the idealistic hot-headedness of reformist youth or megalomaniacs wedding themselves to abstractions that they wish to be imposed upon others regardless of cost to life and limb. This is because conservatives generally reject political theorizing as naïve or arrogant, preferring a vague, indefinable or holistic vision of life in all of its interconnectedness stretching around each of us in the present, emanating from the past and reaching out into the future. The essence of conservatism is allegedly inarticulate, finding its expression only in times of crisis, when traditions and customs are threatened by myopic plans for reform or revolution that threaten to destabilize society's natural development.

However, it would be wrong to dismiss the theoretical aspects of conservatism: adherents stress how it is simultaneously *a doctrine* demanding a maturity of thought in the recognition and acceptance of the great flows of human life as witnessed and experienced in and through societies over time, and that in itself presents a theoretical vision of what political philosophers ought to strive for. This may all sound rather vague, but we can at least initially outline conservatism as an *oppositional attitude* struck against those who would wish revolution and rationalist reform of society and its institutions, and from there present a theoretical description of what unites conservatives.

The conservative asks why we need a revolt or a reform of present institutions or norms of behaviour. Socialists, anarchists, environmentalists and libertarians all espouse the need for some kind of reform that will unleash their particular ideal of political life, but from the conservative perspective, change requires a justification that the other theories often take for granted as being necessary. This may seem strange: surely political study brings to the fore issues that demand our attention and the clarion call that 'something ought to be done' about poverty, inequality, lack of freedom, or destruction of the environment? To change the world is often what attracts people to politics in the first place, but it is against the clamorous cacophony to change a vast array of perceived problems that the conservative properly raises the need for justifying change: a scepticism that emerges partly from a deeply held suspicion of reform for reform's sake and partly from a historically based distrust of the effect of such programmes.

The conservative unquestionably opposes bloody or institutional revolution to overthrow incumbent regimes or to reform social, political, economic and legal practices. Lessons, he claims, should be learned from history, which, accordingly interpreted, sees revolutions and wholesale reorganizations of society as tending to unnecessary bloodshed and deeper problems than those that they replace. Revolution and reform are generally to be opposed on the grounds that they create more problems than they solve and lead to unnecessary upheavals, many unforeseen by the revolutionaries.

Hence conservatives tend not to present visionary utopias of what life might be like under their proposals, nor, contrary to ordinary preconceptions, do they necessarily seek to conserve the status quo. Accepting the status quo regardless of its values and expectations is not productive of a philosophical doctrine, although conservative *thinkers* do often verge on accepting the status quo as they find it. However, conservatism does not necessarily embrace nostalgia or atavism – the return to past conditions or values. Instead, conservatives generally argue that humanity should be freed from political, religious and scientific dogmas and abstract doctrines such as 'social justice', which they claim barely relate to human life as it is and which act to restrain the civil order and its potential developments down unforeseeable roads. Accordingly, conservatism may be judged as proclaiming the benefits of a passive political philosophy – accepting what is and what has been and what will come, so long as it is allowed to evolve without specific, politically motivated, human hindrance. Freedom from *abstract* philosophy thus becomes essential to the conservative programme.

The conservative is sceptical of 'new theories', which are seen as old policies that have been tried and tested, seen to have failed and are merely being remarketed to gain new support. The word 'new' is verging on anathema to the conservative, as Burke commented: 'We think that no discoveries are to be made, in morality; nor many in the great principles of government, nor in the ideas of liberty, which were understood long before we were born.'[1] Yet the conservative can also quite consistently approve of the intellectual and scientific revolution, which overthrew Aristotelian metaphysics in favour of empirical investigation, precisely because Aristotelianism had become an abstract *system* to be dogmatically accepted. It appears somewhat ironic to call the intellectual or artistic path-breakers 'conservative' rather than 'radicals'. The implications of the theory have it otherwise: conservative values flourish where there is no restraining dogma and corresponding legislative constraint on the natural flows to human life. To take an analogy: a conservative would approve of evolution and all of its pleasing and displeasing and unforeseeable offshoots, but would censure artificial genetic modification designed to secure 'better' produce.

Thus the conservative is not without a political reforming voice. Persuasion and reason, proponents declare, are vital for civil society, for civil society depends on a subtle recognition of freedom to exhort and exchange values and merchandise as necessary for peace. Freedom, though, is not an absolute, as it is for the libertarian or anarchist. It is defined by responsibilities and duties that can only emerge from a social context and is symbolized by the 'rule of law'. Freedom is thus contingent upon the rights and responsibilities accorded a people in their cultural context; it cannot be an absolute principle against which all actions and policies can be judged.

To a great extent then, the conservative focuses on 'how things are' rather than 'how things ought to be', which is similar to the realist's urge to recognize man for what he is rather than what he could be. The conservative may similarly emphasize the role and need for power structures in society that act to control and channel individual initiative and life, keeping destructive human tendencies under the control of powerful but intricate and invisible customs as well as explicated laws and codes of conduct. But conservatives do not consider power to be the essence of political life. They stress the persistence of overarching structures – the state and its institutions as an organic embodiment of cultural values which in turn evolve naturally in accordance with unhindered human social development. While many left-leaning critics of government and capitalism rail against alleged alienation of the individual from true cultural or collective norms, few would admit that they hold common ground with conservatives. Yet we can detect that conservatives share some collectivist elements with socialists and perhaps even at times recognize Marxist notions of the economic driving forces *behind* social evolution while rejecting the political economy of socialism and the abolition of private ownership. They also concur with environmentalism in stressing the particular role of a local landscape on man's development, and typically they espouse a conservationist love of the environment and animals, while avoiding the subservience to nature that certain forms of environmentalism require (e.g., the animal rights movement's moral inversion).

In its general encouragement of freedom, conservatism also has much in common with libertarianism, and some thinkers often subtly bridge the two philosophies. However, it rejects the individual realms of absolute sovereignty that libertarianism heralds as the mark of civil society: freedom can only be gained and sustained under the apparatus of state protection. Without the state, freedom shatters into the rule of violence and predation in which individual and social development would be constantly undermined by fear and the threats or actuality of violence. Under anarchy, therefore, freedom is thus a redundant phrase for the conservative.

Assuredly, the conservative rejects theoretical systems and hence 'men of system', as Adam Smith called them (we might call them 'box-tickers'), for whom life, policies, doctrines, individuals, choices and events should fit neatly into a prearranged format based on preconceived views of how our neighbours ought to live. The artificiality of all such schemes inevitably produces counterproductive results, as well as reducing the meanings implicit in human life and culture to petty schemes.

Indeed, because of its inherent scepticism and rejection of abstract political theorizing, conservatism attracts mainly ridicule from 'progressives', or is barely mentioned at all. The opposing attitude implies that the political philosopher ought to oppose the status quo, rise up in rebellion against tradition, question and demand justification for existing institutions and behaviour, and foster a rebellious manner driven by visions of how life could be if only his dreams could be impressed upon all, peacefully or otherwise. That is also why conservatism is a perennially but subtly attractive philosophy, which may not appeal to intelligent, rebellious youth, who often react against the material privileges of their family or nation, but which has a long pedigree including some of the world's greatest thinkers who demand that we stop and think a little more about justifying partial or wholesale revolt because we want 'something to change'. The impatient often reject conservative warnings, but its warnings are there precisely because of the effects of rejecting prudence and because conservatives bring our thoughts around to looking at the effects of the impetuosity and the impatience of rebels. In turn, conservatism thereby seeks a deeper vision of life and civilization, and while strenuously denying that the individual scholar can ever secure the ultimate truth of life to which all others should render obedience and awe, it underlines the superficiality and myopic attempts of social and political reformers who would abolish the vast array of present and often silent benefits for a few noisy and visible complaints.

MAN

For the conservative, man's status emanates from the cultural and historical time in which he is born – he can neither be a full-blown individualist nor a peripheral fleeting marginal entity in relation to his group. He is most emphatically a 'social animal' – or, as the preferred translation of Aristotle's famous epithet goes, he is a 'political animal' born enmeshed in a political situation with ruling elites, governing institutions and a host of locally defined rights and responsibilities that both support him and demand of him his allegiance.

Yet the conservative does not embrace collectivism, which reduces the individual to an anonymous indefinable entity. For the conservative, individual life is of wonderful importance, it generates the irreducible and miraculous subjective perspective that we each enjoy and must embrace. But both the physical and mental life of man is not unconnected to those around him: he is born into a family and hence a cultural context and flow of ideas and expectations that give form to his growth, thought and motivation; the family is part of a greater social nexus, whose apex is the state. Social structures flow through us, and as fleeting points of consciousness we reflect and interact with those around us. Hence, the conservative does not relegate the individual to a nothingness, but neither does he accept the libertarian view of man as an island devoid of social influence.

47

Action can only come from value and values can only be socially formed. Man is drawn to a 'third-person perspective' to find values and is 'nurtured', as Roger Scruton argues, 'and protected by forces the operation of which they could neither consent to nor intend'.[2]

Yet the conservative is deeply mistrustful of individuals' motives and desires, especially when they are removed from cultural structures that have grown up organically and adapted to economic and environmental changes over generations: remove those structures and, the conservative argues, the theorizing projects of the other political philosophies must fail, as they have always failed, for they seek to remodel man in allegedly new garments – garments that the conservative believes have been found ill-fitting time and again, and which belong more to the feral child or predacious barbarian than to civilized man.

Even within civilized society, man is naturally egotistical and untrustworthy, says the conservative, hence he needs morals and laws to secure his peaceful interaction with others. Conservatives follow Aristotle in declaring the lack of laws to be a barbarous, belligerent state: 'Man is the best of all animals when he has reached his full development, so is he worst of all when divorced from law and justice.'[3] History is replete with people abusing and killing others, for which conservatives blame the absence of authority and the rule of law (although the anarchist would counter that most killing has been done at the behest of the state or for the power that the state entices). In the absence of law, or in its ineffectuality, society crumbles: the lawless individual is riddled with desires to kill or to control, to take possession of others' values and sometimes to destroy them, or at least cannot be trusted in the absence of authority not to trespass against his neighbour. In this fear of man's motives, the conservative has much in common with the realist, but whereas realism's focus is the innate or ethical drive to power and mastery over others, conservatism emphasizes the darker side of human nature to highlight what works in controlling or channelling otherwise dangerous energies that would lead to the disruption of peace. Man needs laws to restrain him. Nature and cultural adaptation to nature, which can be read as both environmental and economic, inform him both explicitly and implicitly of right and wrong, and his society's deliberations and understanding of right and wrong are secured in judicial systems that reflect 'natural law': laws that have emerged over the centuries to embody, albeit imperfectly, the wisdom and censure of generations.

Despite the emphasis on the social world, the private world is also of great importance to the conservative, for although he places much importance on the interconnectedness of values, he recognizes the need for privacy and therefore of private property as natural and necessary for social peace. Privacy is, however, contingent on social structures and is a relativist term. What constitutes privacy (and hence its violation) in one society will differ in another – thus there can be no homogenous international policy of law and property. The libertarian thesis envisages cosmopolitan man, bereft of locality and denuded of prejudice, defining himself in a vacuum, contracting with whom he sees fit – but how, demands the conservative? Conservatives accuse libertarians of emphasizing man's freedom to define himself *too* much: freedom without government or culture does not amount to freedom at all. The assumption that man can form his own values, as some anarchists (Stirner, Nietzsche) claim, is ridiculed: a man without a culture is not a man, replies the conservative – he emerges within traditions that act to guide his development and maturation, that provide him with behavioural and attitudinal boundaries that he is free to cross, but at his own peril.

Within his society man finds social roles: his 'station' and all the responding duties and responsibilities that guide his actions and thoughts. Each individual is born into unequal circumstances, situations that vary from parent to parent, subculture to subculture, which generate inequality that only an horrific levelling war, with its ensuing bloodshed, could even attempt to assuage. But more importantly than recognizing the inequalities – which would be better read as differences – in cultural upbringing, the conservative emphasizes biological and intellectual differences that cannot be allayed by psychological retraining: neither therapy nor propaganda can remove the facts of difference and inequality in talent *and* application.

Although conservatives place much emphasis on the social nature of man's thinking, they do not reject his reason. They are certainly cynical of its powers, as reason is thoroughly embedded in the contextual prejudices and concerns of particular people living in a particular times and places; in rejecting the cosmopolitan man of the Cynics and Stoics, the conservative replaces an image of man in a web not of his making but certainly which gives him identity and hence the basis from which to think. Reason is thus parochial in its origins, and strive as it might to universality, man's restricted time and mind limit his abilities. In rejecting what Hayek[4] terms 'constructivist rationalism' – the idea that reason can be turned to making life and society better – the emphasis is placed on what is *reasonable*, which may or may not reflect purely rational conceptions, as they must originate from and reflect the thinking of man's particular station in life. The localized nature of knowledge implies that men should be left alone from state intervention to pursue their own lives, even if those lives are selfish by nature, for, as the father of economics, Adam Smith, noted, it is not from charity that we gain our bread, but from appealing to the profits of the bread-maker. Earlier, Bernard Mandeville noted that 'private vices' lead to 'publick benefits': an argument thoroughly characteristic of conservatism which approves of the unplanned direction of talent and effort which in turn produces social benefits, in the way that a well-kept garden does for passers-by.

Knowledge, which man draws upon in his work and life, is always beyond the ability of his mind to encapsulate in present conscious thinking. He necessarily relies on distributed knowledge in the society around him. He is thus replete with the prejudices of his social upbringing, which, unlike the reformer, the conservative does not absolutely reject, preferring instead to err on the side of cautious acceptance than logical rejection of forms and modes of behaviour and language. It is accordingly better for people, that is more efficacious for their lives, as Burke argued, to 'avail themselves of the general bank and capital of ages'.

The conservative is thereby sceptical of all attempts to remodel man in the light of cold logical 'rationalist' analysis – the kind of prescriptions in which the other schools of thought indulge, particularly those driven by carte-blanche utilitarian-based policies of 'ensuring the greatest good for the greatest number', or the armchair plans of philosophers and revolutionaries, or even the compromised plans of committees and parliaments far removed from their effects. What is therefore taken as an ill-founded scepticism of politics is grounded on an epistemological stance concerning human abilities: the individual man cannot know his neighbour's interest as much as his neighbour can; nor can he assume to know his neighbour's dreams, ambitions or skills. His intrusion would be as detrimental as it would be arrogant. Yet that does not mean that the conservative rejects change or development – man will change, mature, earn his wisdom through trial and error, and, all being well, will develop a sensible pattern of behaviour.

SOCIETY

Conservative society is an organic entity held together by the necessary bonds that naturally emerge between people, giving them a sense of identity and cohesion. This identity is in turn reflected in their voluntary institutions, societies and clubs, as well as their organs of government. It is more than a metaphorical entity: society is a living being, comprised of past, present and future members, whose values transcend the momentary beliefs and actions of the present moment.

Following Aristotle's exposition of the development of civil society, conservative philosophers have often begun their theoretical analyses with the natural procreative bond that generates a family. There is the natural and powerful sexual urge for men and women to associate with one another and produce children; from families, clans emerge, then villages and finally states. The emphasis on primary social bonding as found in the family has retained a grip on conservative thinking through the ages: it is from the family that the individual learns the basic rules and expectations to pursue the good and fulfilling life; the family is the primary social unit that empowers the individual and teaches values to the next.

Social life moulds the individual's identity, station and purpose, but this description is not sufficient. Society is an organism that can flourish or wither just as an individual entity may. Some conservatives certainly baulk at the personification of society, but others embrace it: the social entity is born, it lives a life, and it dies as its members die or move into other societies. While it lives, it gains its identity from intergenerational processes, so we can recognize it as 'English society': our ancestors impact on the present via their influence on landscape, architecture, morality and the economy; those living now look forward to the ongoing replenishing of society through their children and therefore act to preserve or provide for them.

However, in modern life the dominant welfare-state paradigm and corresponding institutions have, according to conservatives, actively undermined both the provisions of the past and those of the future, leaving the present generation increasingly demanding life for the now and producing, in turn, the dissolution of civil society's bonds that have sustained it imperceptibly for generations. The twentieth century's experiments in social engineering, the conservative explains, have left great gashes in Western societies, from which conservatives fear that they may not recover: participation and hence the social life has been systematically destroyed and undermined by statism, the empowerment of the state directly to rule life.

Civil man, born into a society, is also, as we have noted above, born into a station that he can also improve upon. It is natural for there to be a social hierarchy, for people to seek and to find a station in life in which they are most contented, which in turn reflects their outlook and occupation relative to the great aegis of law and order under which they receive protection. A station is not oppressive, for it provides a dignity for the individual which rewards him with the respect of position, whether he is working as a farm labourer or a professor. Hierarchies provide a natural ladder for the talented to rise and the not-so-talented to fall, and the status that diligent, prudent, intelligent and far-sighted members of the civil body can earn.

The conservative thus does not oppose social advancement; such advancement, which presupposes hierarchies, comes at the cost of learning the mores of the various strata that naturally emerge and teach the rising individual the etiquette of that class. Social advancement may thus be procured through education and political advancement to positions of trust and authority. However, given the emphasis on the family, it is unsurprising that conservatives look upon the family as the great vehicle for social advancement and maintenance of position rather than the individual in his or her own right. Conservatives see egalitarianism as denying the reality of success and failure. They commend social mobility against the hierarchical backdrop: a mobility which is driven by education and hard work.

Most conservatives argue that the free market (stemming from private property) is typically, although conditionally and hence pragmatically, the best mechanism to ensure the peaceful integration of otherwise different peoples, as well as ensuring that resources are distributed most efficiently and effectively. But ultimately even the market-place must bow to the more vital principle of maintaining political stability. Protectionism and import barriers may be deployed temporarily to protect a particularly important social stratum and its economic wealth: something the libertarian would deride as protecting an interest group (and usually a politically well-connected one at that) at the expense of the rest of society's right to exchange freely.

Similarly, while they accuse libertarians of upholding the market as the panacea for all humanity's ills, conservatives remain pragmatically sceptical, and worry about the potentially disturbing influences of poverty and/or huge inequity in wealth. Some conservatives may thus support a modicum of government welfare to reduce potential social friction between rich and poor, whereas others prefer to encourage private charity.

Social cohesion is of paramount importance to the conservative, for it is only against the backdrop of peace and cooperation that man can truly flourish as an individual, and peace can be best secured through the institution of private property (i.e., exclusive rights of individuals to particular domains). Private property is deemed the bastion of freedom and peace in that regard, although the conservative is not averse to state ownership in certain areas. Some anarchists, and all socialists and communists, disagree: for them, private property is the reason for social friction in the first place, but for the conservative it is both natural and efficient – it serves the purpose of securing the most effective distribution of resources through the free market, and prompts the owner to maintain and sustain the value of his property – private ownership entails the responsibility of care which is woefully lacking in collective ownership. The rejection of property is, from the conservative position, ill thought through, or is motivated to secure unearned gains from others' productivity (i.e., theft).

Property's origins lie in nature, not in artifice. Conservatives point to evidence in the animal kingdom and in early childhood. Children in communal groups that seek to remove any conception of 'mine and thine' nonetheless still exhibit a tendency to identify things as belonging to them individually, and what the conservative says is that this ought not to be abolished (for that will cause hugely disruptive and deleterious effects on human society) but that the instinct to own and to claim should be encouraged through proper moral channels of sharing and charitable giving to those in need. But for the conservative, property can only truly exist where there is power to support and uphold it. Unlike libertarianism, which, in its anarchist wings, tends to see private property as self-standing, perhaps backed only by the possessor's arms, the conservative sees property as requiring social support and political force. However, for the conservative, private ownership should not extend as far as the libertarian would encourage. Government is instituted to guard private ownership and its use, but the conservative permits intervention should the situation require it, particularly to ensure the survival of the polity. Government should own and control the court and police services; it should also set up services in instances where the market fails (something the libertarian refuses to accept) such as lighthouses and possibly schooling.

The open society of free exchange of produce and ideas is encouraged by the conservative, who seeks the elevation of the individual to the highest that his or her nature and inclination can provide. However, physical resources and human energies and abilities being unevenly distributed, the conservative sees the need to permit the natural social and economic tendency to produce a hierarchy. For the conservative, the existence of income and/or wealth disparities is not an issue so far as the adult population is concerned (they may engage in personal advancement through education and wealth-creation in a free society). However, it does pose a problem in respect of the nation's young, who may grow up without access to freedom of opportunity. Because of this, some conservatives, from Aristotle down to modern thinkers, tend to support universal and even compulsory education for a nation's young, asserting that each individual must be given the chance to improve her or his station in life through cultivating talents, learning skills and improving abilities.

The child symbolizes the future for the conservative and therefore must be prepared well to pursue ambitions; once an adult, however, the citizen must be assumed to know what lies in his or her own interests. Some conservatives, while encouraging education, denounce the state's right to interfere in family life. This is because the family is seen as the critical bulwark against state intervention as it forges its independence; such conservatives point out how dangerous it is when the state begins to interfere in the family and especially when it imposes on the child a politically motivated education. Other conservatives, however, chary of relinquishing the responsibility of ensuring social peace through a well-educated citizenry, argue for state-funded or compulsory education.

The appeasement of the masses that some conservatives believe vital for the life of society is derived from fears of the power of the mob and the violence that mob-rule engenders. The ignorance of the mob, the strategic ability of the elite and the violence of the strong all require proper channelling and deflecting from their injurious potential, but such channels can barely be invented a priori –

that is, deductively from premises – they must evolve over time and/or be given great consideration from deep studies of human nature and the experiences of history. 'Political slate-cleaning in the Leninist mode is no longer in fashion', writes O'Hear, 'but the progressivist cast of mind that inspired and underlay it is very much alive and well.'[5]

STATE

State and civil society are synonymous for conservatives. The state is said to embody the will or personality of the people it represents. However, 'representation' might not be the proper description for the conservative theory of the state, which considers the state an instrument of the people and the personification of their will. This does not, however, extend to adulation of the state. Such statism would view the political institutions of the state as providing the sole means to the good life, and, as we have seen, the conservative is very sceptical about this. However, the conservative position accords the state an aura of mystery, or at least implicit respect, for it is that drapery (if we may judiciously borrow Burke's useful term) that is required for the state to be a power that all citizens not only recognize but also obey, with their lives if necessary.

Aristotle impressed the principle upon conservative political theory that 'the state is both natural and prior to the individual'. That is, the state logically precedes the existence of the individual, which is slightly confusing since all conservatives, including Aristotle, tend to put their faith into the moral and logical primacy of the family. The conservative emphasizes that the individual is a mere animal without a state because civil order cannot be separated from the existence of government. Some thinkers write in terms of the organic nature of social and political life and the interdependent relationship between all the parts of the social body, which implies the subordination of the individual to the state, but not (as in socialism), the individual's complete subjugation and annihilation.

Although the conservative condemns autocracy as much as tyranny, what political institutions ought to be supported to promote peace and security cannot be answered deductively or apodictically. The state evolves a constitutional framework reflecting the contingencies and nature of the people whose will and voice it represents. That constitution will, of necessity, differ according to time and place and the particular beliefs of a people. A constitution cannot be established a priori: constitutions that have been produced (or reproduced) overnight typically do not work. Detractors, especially libertarians, point to the longevity of the American constitution, but the conservative replies that its strengths were garnered not from momentary human wisdom but from a long tradition of English cultural constitutionalism which the founding fathers distilled; its weaknesses have also been patently tragic – the persistence of slavery, a violent civil war and a messianic–imperialistic foreign policy.

The best form of state proves its worth by embodying the will of its people over generations. Against libertarian contractarians who argue that man's political status stems from his agreement, implicit or explicit, with his fellow men to live in a polity, the conservative laughs. There was no such contract, nor can there be one: the libertarian's retelling of contracted polities is a form of modern myth-making. The conservative rejects the reforming principles of libertarianism or socialism and the possibility that life can be made better through a rational organization of society and politics yet exist in an ever-changing complexity of relations, that can never be rationally described never mind rationally organized. Attempts to do so are pointless and can only end in misery: a conclusion that connects conservatism with anarchism in that respect!

Conservatives should either be very tolerant towards a variety of political forms (so long as they work) or remain non-judgemental in the sense that I remain non-judgemental of a family's values in another town: that is, my inherent lack of knowledge governing others' affairs should be recognized fully – who, the conservative asks, are we to judge others' affairs, as the libertarian or socialist would have us do? Not only do we not *know* about them intimately, but it would also imply that the other nation may suitably judge our affairs according to its own values, local prejudices and lack of knowledge of us! From such presumptuous impositions, conflict arises.

Thus, rather than upholding a universalist vision of government and people, the conservative retreats to insist that peoples should find out about such matters as they see fit, drawing on their legal and constitutional experiences to form and constantly reform the state in their particular and parochial image. The conservative is thus apprehensive of grand schemes of international federations and organizations designed by diplomats and theorists far removed from local issues. But also like the libertarian, the conservative is fearful of democracy proper – that is, the rule of the majority. As Burke warned, 'in a democracy, the majority of the citizens is capable of exercising the most cruel oppressions upon the minority'.[6] Universal franchise is not an absolute necessity for the secure political life, the conservative advises: it should, in most cases, be merely an act of judgement on the personnel of office rather than a fulcrum for power for the majority, whose tendency to seek immediate gains should be thoroughly curbed by constitutional checks.

By this reckoning, the state possesses a greater dignity than that accorded by statist, libertarian and even socialist instrumentalists, who see it merely as a tool for securing peace, distributing wealth, educating the masses, etc. To secure its full status as transcending the ephemeral interests of the present generation, the state must therefore cajole people into thinking that it has more power than it has, and through a self-fulfilling prophecy of monopolizing force in its jurisdiction it will gain that power. The purpose of the powerful state is to ensure peace from civil rebellion and from external aggression. Those are not its only purposes, however, for it must also exhibit frugality, liberality and fortitude to secure the awe and no doubt the appreciation of the people.

As the embodiment of power the state must be dignified and in its institutions and proclamations distant from the particular people who happen to be in office: that is, the office of monarchy, president, prime minister, etc., should be visually and hence aesthetically distinguishable from the person sitting temporarily in the chair: when she speaks, she speaks for the nation (or the office), not for herself. The stateswoman ought thus to transcend personality and seek to express the will of the people, and that will should represent the beliefs not just of the present generation but the force of reasoning and inheritance issuing from the past and reaching beyond the present into the future. Emphatically, that office should not be brought into disrepute or embarrassment, for the undermining of such required dignity would mark the dissolution of the state.

INTERNATIONAL RELATIONS

What of the conservative philosophy of international relations? given the suspicion conservatives have of domestic power and their justification of the state as necessary to calm the inherent belligerence or untrustworthiness of the citizenry, then we can see that conservatives will also look upon the world of international relations with similarly distrustful eyes. States, the personification of local attitudes and customs, must be considered as being in a Hobbesian state of nature relative to each other that individuals are assumed to inhabit in the absence of the state. Each state will look distrustfully upon its neighbour, but this is the cost of ensuring domestic peace. The solution of dispensing with nation-states in favour of an international government is unpalatable to the conservative, who sees in government the necessary embodiment of all that is local. Beyond the national borders, intervention would not only be counterproductive (in that it would encourage rebellion amongst people not desirous of imperial rule) but also culturally implausible.

The conservative would thus primarily accept a mosaic of states relating peacefully to one another, whose leaders would understand the unreasonableness of waging war to secure an unsympathetic population within its boundaries. However, this apparent pacifism does not necessarily imply the rejection of all war to secure *land* rather than people, for that land could then be occupied and its landscape and resources culturally appropriated. Genocidal wars or ethnic cleansing could be justified by conservative philosophy, especially when the philosophy is tied to the vision of peoples falling into their racial or national hierarchy. Conservatives could argue that there are some societies destined to push others out of the way, and force weaker groups into migration to secure valued lands. In which case conservative political boundaries are certainly not to be held as sacrosanct but rather guarded against a potential push from ever-present external threats.

Conservatism possesses a strong streak of realism in its preparedness for war, but in contrast to realism, it does not enter quantitative methodologies that seek to play number-games with nations and peoples. Instead, the conservative calls upon the nation's elite to enter negotiations and relations with other countries using commercial and personal ties to smooth out international diplomacy: such relations depend upon the interplay of human talent and personality and not preconceived theories of the balance of power.

NOTES

1 Edmund Burke, *Reflections on the Revolution in France* (London: Penguin, 1986), p. 182.

2 Roger Scruton, *The Meaning of Conservatism* (Basingstoke: Palgrave, 2001), p. 192.
3 Aristotle, *Politics* (London: Penguin, trans. T. A. Sinclair, 1986), I, ii, 1253.
4 Friedrich von Hayek, *Law, Legislation and Liberty. Vol 1: Rules and Order* (London: Routledge & Kegan Paul, 1973), *passim*.
5 Anthony O'Hear, *After Progress: Finding the Old Way Forward* (London: Bloomsbury, 1999).
6 Burke, *Reflections on the Revolution in France*, p. 229.

CHAPTER 5

SOCIALISM

For more than a century, socialism rose to political prominence out-pacing libertarianism and conservatism; its language and rhetoric altered political thinking and expectations, and the extensive pro-grammes of reform, redistribution and nationalization proposed under its banner remain embedded in much of the generally statist manifestos of the West and the culture of the people.

The socialist, or communist, cause is broad; it appeals to many who seek redress for the ills that plague human life who call them-selves socialists or for whom the label is synonymous with having a 'social conscience', or who seek a radical overhaul of society along 'socialist' lines. But the political philosophy of *socialism* is quite dis-tinguishable from the genuine as well as the passing laments for poverty, inequality and injustice: concerns which adherents to other theories may also legitimately and logically possess and on which socialism cannot therefore be said to possess a monopoly. We must therefore detach socialism from a concern with social causes, issues and moral or political problems: all political theories attempt pro-posals designed to make life better for others and to remove 'injus-tices' – they just disagree on the political–ethical framework and means to be used.

Socialism also needs to be detached from the *philosophy* of Marxism, which sees socialism as a particular historical stage in man's unfolding and inevitable history towards the final revolution that will overthrow the class system. Marxism presents a compli-cated philosophy of history and theory of economics whose breadth and intricate analysis cannot be adequately dealt with here; nonethe-less, Marx's writings, and those of Marxist philosophers, may justly be used in outlining the socialist programme.

Socialism has old roots (Thomas More's *Utopia* speaks of class warfare and abolishing property), but much of modern socialism grew, like conservatism, out of a reaction to the doleful conditions of the industrial revolution in which thousands of people migrated from the countryside to the cities and became a new, urban working class. Whereas conservatism also reacted against the scientific and rational culture developing in the eighteenth century's 'Age of Reason' and what they saw as man's audacity to control nature and disrupt age-old traditions, most socialists eventually embraced rationalism and science as necessary for improving the working man's lot. In the early nineteenth century, it thus parted company from mystical, romanticist reactions with which it was entwined, against science, machine and industrial man (which now resurface in the political philosophy of environmentalism). Socialism's embracing of the scientific revolution is important – some thinkers within the very broad socialist camp may decry the modern world with its electronic gadgets that they believe alienate man from man (criticism that is usually given a postmodern twist); but, sentiment apart, socialism seeks to improve the human condition and recognizes the power of the 'white heat of technology' as a 1960s British Labour Party slogan put it, echoing the earlier vision of the socialist pioneers such as Saint-Simon and Robert Owen. They sought to use the wealth-producing capacity of mass production and its technology to help improve the livelihood of the workers and families at the factories: that is, to divert wealth creation into the alleviation of obvious poverty. Capitalism was to be harnessed for the greater good – and while some socialist thinkers were attracted to small-scale socialist operations (where cooperatives or guilds produced and catered for local markets in which the price mechanism may or may not be appropriate or allegedly required), most began to turn their heads to what the nation-state could do if government took control over ownership of the incredible forces released by industrial society.

Early socialist reformers were horrified at the degradation and dangerous working conditions of early industrial society. The reasons for the growth of a sudden interest in the lot of their fellow man need not detain us here, except to note that in periods of economic expansion, when the gaps between classes of people widen, the disparity in wealth and living conditions becomes more pronounced, and the wealthier may feel guilty about their luxurious lifestyle, especially when the dominant culture or religion invokes wealth-guilt. Such a feeling is not unusual and is reflected in many of the great thinkers' works – especially those thinkers who came from privileged backgrounds. While motivation for choosing a political theory is incidental to the task of fleshing out that theory and checking its premises and logical consistency, the socialist reaction against early capitalist modes of production (usually synonymous in socialist writings with *mass* production rather than capitalist production *per se*) provides the form and temper of much of its analysis. Mass production tempted people away from their traditional social structures of working collectively on farms or in small village production units in cottages; villages were denuded of labourers, who had left to live in the burgeoning cities. The rapid growth of cities meant that the infrastructure was barely capable of dealing with the population influx. The obvious degradation in which some found themselves, together with the anonymity of urban life, prompted the concerned to call for reforms. Socialists – those whose political goals are defined by a desire to nationalize production and distribution – were not the only thinkers and writers affected by the emergence of an 'urban proletariat' and the corresponding social, economic and moral costs. Conservatives and romanticists blamed the loss of tradition and moral structure that urban growth seemed to foster, and the cartoons of Hogarth well reflect the nascent immorality perceived by commentators in the early days of urban growth. Classical liberals, on the other hand, emphasized the advantages of urban growth. Mass production, they pointed out, increased productivity per labourer, which in turn enabled him to earn more, and the fact that voluntary migration continued to the cities showed that people chose to seek the possibility of higher standards of life despite the risk of slum-life and its moral degradation.

City life offered choice and hope to the impoverished population of the countryside, for whom life was rarely as idyllic as urban or university-educated elites believed it to be. The masses voted with their feet to leave poverty and lack of opportunity for the promise of greater choice and a better standard of living. That cannot be denied, as less nostalgic socialists realized; however, the expected opportunities for the migrants were not always fulfilled (as portrayed for example in the novels of Dickens and Zola). Those who were less able to adapt to the multiplicity and flexibility of skills required in the more dynamic and open-ended society of a large city fell through cracks in communal assistance into desperate poverty, drink, drugs and prostitution – issues that became (and remain) part of the socialist's critical repertoire. In the villages, adequate social nets existed to support the indigent, although the reality should not be confused with the often idealized visions critics of the industrial revolution presented of 'the good old days': a vision shared by some conservatives, romanticists and socialists alike with scant knowledge of history. The simplistic life of the idyllic past was ruined by the advance of capitalism – a term which is rarely defined well but may be understood as an advancement in 'roundabout' production: that is, instead of individuals producing to consume, they produced goods which went into the production process (i.e., machinery, tools), and thus, in the eyes of critics (including, long before Marx, the economist Adam Smith) they become removed or *alienated* from the final act of consumption. Images of fruit-pickers and harvesters abound in socialist thought, and while some thinkers were nostalgic for the pre-capitalist days of simplicity and low and stable expectations of life, others, such as Marx, embraced the urbanization of the working poor as heralding the future.

The nineteenth-century writers and commentators tell their stories well, and the shock and embarrassment we feel for the plight of the poor has not left the Western conscience. Much of that shock was channelled into calls for social justice – a loosely bound set of ideas that included votes for all, a redistribution of income and levelling of wealth, land reform to permit the poorest the chance to own land, basic welfare provisions for the poor, mass education of the youth, infrastructure for the cities, reform of prisons, and so on. In the ideological confusion – which still reigns – political programmes overlapped and politicians drew upon those policies they thought could get them elected. As the vote was extended to increasing numbers, unsurprisingly, the majority began to call for socialist policies that they believed would benefit themselves as against the interests and wealth of the minority. It is against this backdrop that the socialist envisions the individual attaining a higher or better status and sense of self than in any other political system.

So what is socialism?

Some definitions of socialism express it as opposing competition and profit-seeking and upholding cooperation and service to society. However, this would be a weak and non-exclusive characteristic: anarchism, conservatism and free-market classical liberalism express the importance of cooperation, without which no society could exist, and the differing schools of thought may argue that cooperation is better fulfilled without political structures or within the realm of private property. Similarly, expressing the importance of dutiful service to one's fellow man is not exclusive to socialism – it is, after all, an ethical proposition common to many political and religious persuasions. Such notes have to be made, for often socialists argue as if socialism had a monopoly on morality or a concern for others – a position theologians would contest! – that its doctrine is the most noble of all causes, because it is essentially other-centred and it appeals for a universal brotherhood, as does Christianity. That socialism is other-centred is true – the individual must live for as well as within society. But the morality of altruism is itself challengeable on many grounds; moreover, the incidental appeal to morality has to be put aside, and while it would be wrong to ignore the moral teachings of any political doctrine, especially those that aim for internal consistency between morality and politics, it is wrong to assume that a specific political doctrine possesses moral primacy. That has to be established, and language either of revolution or of social justice does not constitute an argument for morality.

Socialism, succinctly defined, seeks to put *control* of political, economic and legal institutions in the hands of society, which typically means the state. Socialism is 100 per cent statism. Most commentators and supporters acknowledge the breadth of definitions of socialism but converge on the collective ownership or *control* of resources as the key element. It is foremost an economic doctrine, but the primacy of *political* control over the means and distribution of resources gives the doctrine a momentum to deal with all aspects of life, both to ensure equality in production as well as in access to resources. Lenin's proclamation is useful to note: 'Socialists demand the *strictest* control, *by Society and by the State*, of the quantity of labour and the quantity of consumption . . .'[1] Some socialists distance themselves from the actual nationalization of companies, but favour *control* and direction of the economic life of the community: a position which ironically barely distinguishes them from their traditional totalitarian enemies of the twentieth century – fascists and National Socialists. The distinction is, however, academic. Control over a resource entails ownership: ownership is an economic concept, while control is a legal one defining who has access and rights to a resource which can only be recognized socially. Ownership implies the power to exclude some from its use or distribution according to certain criteria. In the market-place, privately controlled resources are subject to the great nexus of the market – the millions of decisions that are subsumed in the price mechanism when people purchase (or fail to purchase) resources for production and consumption – but when resources are removed from private exchange and put into the hands of political deliberation, production, distribution and consumption are decided upon other criteria – ideally, according to rationally explicable means and ends, but more often according to interest groups and political factions. The socialist welcomes such other criteria, either totally in the full abolition of private markets, or partially through social or political intervention in private exchange which in effect forces a third-party wedge between traders.

Socialism is thus logically anti-market, which means it seeks to replace the anarchic nexus of market coordination with commands. Marx was clear in his desire to eliminate market relations (as being necessary for the rise of socialism); he wanted money abolished and distribution of all produce to be entirely planned by officials – for Marx there could be no statist 'mixed' economy, nor any 'market socialism'.

Socialists also emphasize their revolutionary nature, for in contrast to the other political philosophies, socialism does not seek to conserve traditions (with the possible exception of those that embrace its own ideas or institutions), socialism does not promote glorification or love of the environment, nor does it uphold power or individual spheres of sovereignty as primary political values. Society's will or voice is to be heard in all aspects of political life, and that life extends beyond the libertarian's and conservative's domains of law, order and defence to include economic arrangements of resources and distribution of income. Socialism proposes a radical overhaul of morality and traditional institutions, removing what it sees as 'bourgeois morality' (which literally entails the morality of the city but more generally speaking the morality of the middle classes). While some note this to be one of the defining elements of socialism, it is not exclusive to it – anarchists, free market libertarians and environmentalists also seek an overthrow of restrictive practices that they believe act against the quality of life.

All other aspects of socialist thought – the debate on *whose* voices should be elevated to command the direction of socially owned resources, for instance – are secondary to the thrusting call for state control of property. The socialist state should thereby, it is also argued, embody the will of the people and act as the ultimate arbiter in deciding who should produce what, at what price and in what quantity and quality. That is, the market economy should be replaced by the command economy. Although socialist reformers have targeted other areas of life for change (promising a better morality for all as a result of socialism), the driving philosophy is to seek social control over the means of production and distribution.

MAN

Socialism – as its name suggests – opposes individualism and the 'atomization' of society into individualists who, it is feared, will not be concerned about the well-being of their fellow men and women. Furthermore, political life ought to strive towards the equality of all people, in a life that is communally oriented with shared resources. Socialists thus opposed the culture of individualization that modern civilization has unleashed since the Renaissance. But more than this: man's nature is to be found in his social roots – he is defined and formed by the society in which he lives. Unlike the conservative, the socialist rejects hierarchies and their resulting prejudices and artificial privileges as being unnatural – they should be rejected and removed.

According to socialism, the individual is born and dies in equality with all the members of the rest of his race. What distinguishes individuals from each other are artificial barriers to learning or employment that correspond to traditional political and economic cultures. Some, but not all, socialists envisage men born into mutually antagonistic classes whose interests are diametrically opposed – a ruling class (often synonymous with the propertied class) and a working or ruled class. The clash will only be destroyed with the abolition of the ruling class and/or their property. Even if life is not characterized by class antagonism, socialism seeks the radical overhaul of all that stands in the way of the equalization of men and women. For some, the driving egalitarianism of socialism defines its creed – it seeks to abolish the visible distinctions that class and privilege provide and to rend hierarchy asunder in the name of equality. But egalitarianism can take many forms, while socialism can be distinctively defined as social control over economic resources.

Aristotle argued that man is a social animal – and in the socialist tradition we find an alternative political expression (and expansion) of that view compared to conservatism; just as Aristotle argued that the individual requires solid and effective social conditions for improving himself and for living the good life, so too does the socialist; but whereas conservatives explain that those conditions are better met through a gradually evolving and developing society based on the sanctity of private property, privileged classes and small government, the socialist claims man will be freer if all the resources and their distribution are removed from private ownership and put into state ownership or communal control. Socialism demands collective control, but it barely matters from an economic view (except for particular political programmes and rhetoric) whether a firm is owned by the government (i.e., the government buys its shares) or controlled (i.e., the government directs a company's decisions), the result is the same: someone, somewhere, at some time must make decisions on what to produce, the resources to be used (including labour resources) and whom to sell the product to, etc.

Yet despite their rhetoric, few socialists explicitly seek to abolish the individual into the anonymity of the herd. Despite the high appraisal of society in their reasoning, socialists envision a better life for the individual within a socialist context. This seems paradoxical, and there are serious logical issues for socialists *qua* socialists to deal with once they begin applauding individualism and extolling how socialism will bring forth greater individuality while subjecting the individual's economic life to social (i.e., governmental) control. We can note that socialists in the West have generally drawn upon the individualistic ethic of Western society, borrowing libertarian and romanticist notions of the aesthetic and moral primacy of the individual – after all, it has had to make itself appealing to the relatively individualist Western culture!

In more liberal moments, the socialist waxes about how the freed man will then be more of an individual, for he will be able *to become* whatever he wishes, and choose any employment from day to day, untrammelled by past or social expectation. The individual worker employed in the market, socialists bemoan, is subject to external forces over which he has no control: a reduction in demand for his factory's product leaves him without work; price rises in the staples of life force him to alter his expenditure. While such causes were visible to small-scale societies that did not engage in foreign trade, they were assumed to be comprehensible and therefore more palatable. Now that such causes are 'global' and spread over millions of people making millions of decisions daily, the socialist reacts: earlier socialists and utopians may have sought refuge in small-scale communes that closed the doors to trade abroad, but the rationalist socialists that emerged from the mid-nineteenth century preferred to give the state the powers to control and hence direct such causes accordingly. Old protectionist schemes may thus be redefined as protecting socialist causes – i.e. the particular working classes of particular cities in particular countries. However, such a ploy clashes with the international drive of much socialist thought which perceives national boundaries as oppressive contrivances that restrict the movement of the poor, and which in turn are used by ruling elites and big businesses to thwart competition. One sees how confused socialist ideology may become in practice!

Marx, for instance, railed against the division of labour, which he believed to be so destructive of individuality, which the socialist state would relieve him of and permit the worker to choose how he should spend his productive time. This, however, can only come about if all labour were homogeneous and hence all skills readily exchangeable for each other: a principle that socialists untainted by libertarianism's (or conservatism's) emphasis on plurality and difference necessarily espouse. Distinctions in earnings and contemporary skill levels as witnessed by the socialist are viewed as the result of the inequitable capitalist system of market arrangements, which exploit labourers for their work-time and have a tendency to keep the labouring classes oppressed, poor and restrained in developing their particular selves. If the institutional restrictions on the classes' freedoms were lifted, the argument goes, then each would be as equal as his neighbour, and being freed from the strangling effect of the division and specialization of labour, would be able to pursue whichever occupation or trade he wishes – changing at whim. At this point, the socialist is dreaming, appealing to the world of Cockaigne and a utopian society in which economic wealth that is currently enjoyed will be maintained by freeing individuals from the need to specialize. Any rhetoric appealing to individualism reduces to a mere marketing ploy that does not reflect the core drive of socialism to reduce all individuals to a homogeneous mass – that cannot be avoided in the logic of *socialism*.

Other, more realistic, socialists have rejected the illusory and ill-defined future that Marxist visionaries portrayed, in favour of an egalitarian society in which each shall produce according to his abilities, which are apparently heterogeneous after all. The resulting goods and services that the able and hardworking produce return to the hands of the state or similarly construed political authorities possessing the power to direct and control economic arrangements: the individual finds himself nationalized and again disappears, as he must, in socialist policy.

We may ask if in fact the centralization of control might improve the lot of the individual. Freedom from the market-place, the socialist programme proposes, will ensure that each individual is provided with the necessities of life without distinction: that seems fair. The individual is to be freed from the degradation of having to sell his labour, which Marxists call 'wage-slavery'. Otherwise, socialists have striven for reforms to improve the lot of the working class, which, it is implied, will not suddenly disappear in a glorious communist revolution but must therefore be looked after by the state: a sentiment close to the conservative's emphasis on *noblesse oblige*. Such an outcome is even acceptable if the resulting economic product is less than that produced by the inequitable market society: for the socialist (and especially the Christian socialist) equality in poverty is to be preferred to inequality, *even if the poorest in the market society are made worse off*. The equalizing of income or access to resources is held to be a better situation for all individuals in that it also removes the temptation to steal or pernicious envy. Bukharin (1888–1938: executed under Stalin) enthused in a quotation worth repeating in full:

The communist method of production will signify an enormous development of productive forces. As a result, no worker in communist society will have to do as much work as of old. The working day will continually grow shorter, and people will be to an increasing extent freed from the chains imposed on them by nature. As soon as man is enabled to spend less time upon feeding and clothing himself, we will be able to devote more time to the work of mental development. Human culture will climb to heights never attained before. It will no longer be a class culture, but will become a genuinely human culture. Concurrently with the disappearance of man's tyranny over man, the tyranny of nature over man will vanish.[2]

Who except the logically and empirally minded would not fall for such a vision? A life without hardship, without toil, a return to Eden and to a life of pleasure? The sceptic demands how will food be produced in practice and how will it be distributed? The assumed plasticity of man in this utopian realm of freedom reflects the socialist conception of man's innate equality both in mental and physical potential. There is thus an intriguing accolade of individualism in such socialist dreaming in which the individual attains *authenticity* through shedding capitalist or bourgeois (i.e., urban middle-class) sentiments and structures: in the context of Western philosophical and cultural traditions, it is doubtful whether socialism would be so appealing if it sought the annihilation of the individual in the crowd. Yet that is what it logically calls for, as Marx explicitly states: the individual 'must, indeed, be swept out of the way, and made impossible',[3] and in ridding the world of the middle-class or classical liberal notion of individuality, 'we shall have an association in which the free development of each is the condition for the free development of all'.[4]

Individualistic man – eccentric, hedonist, innovator, thinker – must therefore disappear. The glorious vision of communal society is only glorious to the socialist because in it all artificial distinctions between men and between men and women disappear and we shall look upon each other as equals – expendably so, one could add. A relationship with this woman is as equal to me as a relationship with that woman – all are equal: partiality will fade away. As a consequence, the family will disappear – or if no revolution is forthcoming, it too should be nationalized to ensure the proper socialization of children from an early age – that is, the removal of any individualistic tendencies to seek private property or egotistical patterns of life. This attack on the individual has an ancient history (reaching back to Plato), for socialists have recognized the countereffective power and independence of family life and the individualism it tends to foster. While many socialists recognize the logic of socializing resources to include the control of the individual and his life, others, especially American socialist 'liberals' (firmly entrenched in the statist camp) prefer to seek selective intervention designed to remove contemporary prejudices and barriers (child abuse, racism) to individual improvement. Such advocates retain one foot in the libertarian and one foot in the socialist camp, preferring a 'third way' or compromising alternative between what they see as the extremes presented by classical liberalism and socialism.

Yet in so far as any philosopher upholds the innate value of the individual, he is not a socialist – logically he is an interventionist in the statist camp.

SOCIETY

Socialism denounces individualism both ethically and economically in favour of raising the collective to moral and political primacy. The group is to be viewed as the agent of change and therefore it is the will of the group that is to decide policy, the production and distribution of resources, and accordingly the allocation of work. 'Each of us puts his person and all his power in common under the supreme direction of the general will', wrote Rousseau[5] in a phrase sufficiently vague to be turned into several philosophies; yet it also distils conveniently the socialist view of society. The individual subordinates his self – and therefore his property and liberty – to his society: the ruling vision is that the will of the people *is* the will of all. Detractors may be defined as misguided or as retaining traditional, egotistical prejudicial views that require either ignoring, re-educating, or silencing. The logic cannot have it any other way if the 'general will' is to be the will of all – only the incompetent or deluded may reject it.

The will of the people implies the existence of a collective mind, which some socialists may reject in favour of different methods of ascertaining the content of people's beliefs through referenda or elections. Depending on one's perspective, socialism's vision of the will of the people ruling political affairs is marred or confused by notions of class warfare (which predate Marx) – that society is necessarily divided into two or more classes whose interests are necessarily opposed. The conservative recognizes classes but accepts them as each individual's due station, a position that modern conservatives defend as having adequately adapted (in a free society) to social change and innovation, which earlier feudal systems and their legally defined castes could not permit. Conservatives relish class distinction as being a necessary part of the social fabric, but socialists fully condemn such distinctions as being oppressive and restrictive on individuals and hence communal flourishing.

Much rhetoric has been, and is still, spent on class warfare (a quick web search on headlines in newspapers and magazines reveals how complacently the assumption is bandied around, more for rhetoric than meaning), which assumes that barely defined classes are at war with one another and that one class, the 'working class' ought to, or will, overthrow the other oppressive class or classes, typically styled as the bourgeoisie or capitalist classes. In early activism, socialists sought to fight aristocrats; now they fight the capitalist class, which in pamphlet-land is synonymous with global corporations and the people who work for them, and any bourgeois institutions that, to bring Marx in, have 'resolved personal worth into exchange value . . . [and] substituted naked, shameless, direct brutal exploitation'.[6] Yet big corporations employ 'working people', so to attack them is to attack the means of enrichment for those employees: a description socialists will not recognize, preferring instead to define it as 'exploitation'.

Although socialism does not have to accept class warfare, it has been such a critical element in its history and its language remains powerfully politically evocative that its reasons must be addressed, for even if socialists discard their attachment to class, a core political–economic theory will remain that will continue to attract followers and prompt explanations of economic inequality and injustice. That theory is the labour theory of value, also known as the 'exploitation theory'.

Exploitation of one class by another derives from classical political economy's division of society into separate catallactic (market) classes, and while these held some use for a theoretical exposition of the creation and distribution of wealth, politically the class analysis was used to assume the existence of easily definable social classes, whose economic interests were thus defined by class membership. Behind class interests lies the labour theory of value, the cornerstone for much socialist thought.

Economics explains the nature of value, and the political philosopher who trades in the product of such theories (such as extolling the benefits of 'fair trade') cannot afford to ignore the logic behind them. Throughout most of the history of economic thought, writers turning their attention to economics believed that value was somehow inherent in the product being sold: it was held to be 'objective'. Therefore if a particular seller was deemed by a third party to have sold his produce for more or less than the 'just value', he would be fined or punished. The theoretical justification of the present 'fair trade' movement stems from the notion of a 'just price', a price that is usually deemed by others to be different from that which prevails in market exchanges. When labourers are paid a rate below what is deemed 'just' or 'fair' according to a third-party perspective, it is said by socialists to constitute exploitation.

A product, according to the labour theory of value, gets its value from the amount of labour that goes into it. The more time, effort and skill involved in making a product and bringing it to market, the greater its value ought to be relative to goods and services that require less time, effort and skill. Marx and Engels both drew heavily on the labour theory of value as outlined earlier by Adam Smith and David Ricardo, who had unfortunately resuscitated the objective theory of value of goods from logical oblivion – for over a century, economic thinkers had been slowly moving towards the subjective theory of value, which states that production, consumption, use of time, etc., is as valuable as the individual agent perceives it to be, and hence there is no value set in stone by nature, God, parliament, or man's labour. Smith's and Ricardo's influential rescue of the labour theory of value became very useful for Continental, and especially German thinkers, and notably Karl Marx in his exposition of why he believed labourers were necessarily exploited in the capitalist or market system.

Briefly explained, the theory may be put like this: if a labourer works ten hours and puts X amount of value into a product, based on his skills and tools used (these tools in turn possessing inherent labour value from the people who made them), and his employer, by virtue of his rights to the property, sells the product for Y, then the discrepancy between the two $(Y-X=Z)$ is the amount of profit drawn from the labour (i.e., exploited from the worker and usurped by one who, according to the theory, did very little to produce the product). More sophisticated analysis may accept the employer having some labour input (say, entrepreneurial talent), but the gist is that an *unproductive* class draws an unearned income from a *productive* class: hence exploitation. Profit (or interest) is thereby acquired by exploiting a situation in which a worker is coerced into giving up his rightful share.

Critics observing the advance of mass production and the increasing disparity in wealth deployed the labour theory of value to explain why factory workers were paid less than their bosses. Exploitation was in the air and the theory was subsequently developed by Sismondi, Proudhon, Rodbertus and Marx and Engels. That labour is the source of *all* value became the premise of the exploitation theory *and* hence of class-based socialism. The 'theft' of labour value from the worker stems from the private ownership of the land (or capital), which the labourer does not possess: he has to sell himself into wage slavery to subsist, and according to Ricardo and others who followed his thinking, the poor will remain on the subsistence level of income; but since labour is the cause of all value, the labourer has a natural claim to the product of his work.

However, explaining what constitutes *fair value* becomes, in the theoretical analysis of the labour theory of value, as increasingly complex and convoluted as did the Ptolemaic explanation of the heavens. Here is Engels in his *Anti-Dühring*: 'Society can easily reckon how many hours of labour inhere in a steam engine . . . Of course, society will have to find how much work is required for the manufacture of every article of consumption . . . The people will decide everything quite easily . . .'[7] The supposed ease of calculation runs into immediate methodological and logistic problems of reducing complex and varied tasks and products into a common denominator *without* any valuation on the part of the consumer of the product. All attempts to explain value on the basis of the quantity or even more elusive quality of labour imbued in them have failed. Yet today they retain a powerful influence on political slogans: a fact which would be risible if such slogans championed an earth-centric conception of the universe!

Theoretically, socialism could dispense with the labour theory of value and instead examine the 'fairness' of outcomes regardless of any alleged underlying eternal values to goods and services; it can reject the complex alchemy attempted by Marx and others to deduce a common denominator to all prices, in favour of accepting the subjective theory of value (value is what a trader perceives something to be worth at a certain time and in a certain place), or by ignoring fully the debate and embracing the full nationalization of society regardless of how values are to be prioritized in the new scheme of production and distribution. It can also be noted that socialism may retain a class-based politics while rejecting the labour theory of value; as such it will reject its catholicity in favour of division and plurality. But where the conservative perceives mutuality in division, the socialist may see strife and antagonism between the defined classes – looking ahead, such socialists typically envisage the overthrow of the ruling or propertied classes by the proletariat, and hence the theory will return to embracing a vision of a single collective regardless of how economic products are valued.

This argument demands attention as to what aspects of individual and social life are thereby defined as belonging to a class: something that is not easily drawn from socialist thought or from life. Defining who constitutes the group becomes a slippery task once the rhetoric of working for the 'people' or 'the working class' is translated into policy, for some will apparently always be in charge and some will have to obey the wisdom of those who speak for the people (even if it is merely the fact that children will have to listen to the wisdom of their elders). The general definition most socialists have in mind is that people are divided between 'those who have' and 'those who have not', or between the propertied and propertyless, which requires elucidation as to what people are supposed to have and not have, and who has what rights to what things. If the division is assumed to be defined by the possession of property, then sociologically – empirically – such divisions are more complex than can be accepted: people who work predominantly with their brawn may possess land or shares or have rights to tools or access to property.

Critics will counter that it is too thoughtlessly accepted that people divide into social classes. But if we accept the claim, it follows for socialists that these classes tend to be antagonistic to one another. At the bottom of society are the propertyless, those who have only their labour to sell to the classes above them (the owners of land and factories). The division reeks of a feudal description in which the lower echelons are serfs – free to sell their labour, but not much else, and while this may be true of early industrial society, it cannot be so simply held today in economies that are multifaceted in their divisions and specializations and which, despite groans to the contrary, have become increasingly atomized – or individualized, with property more *widely* distributed.

If, on the other hand, the vitriolic rhetoric of class warfare is wholly abandoned in favour of an egalitarianism supported by social ownership of all resources, which reflects the direction that Western twenty-first century socialist thinking is taking, the socialist must either contend that all people are equal and ought to possess equal access to equally valuable resources or accept that one or all of these conditions is invalid. Since the equality of man is a strongly held premise, the socialist must then devise explanations but, more importantly, methods of ensuring equality of outcome.

However, in calling for the nationalization of all resources and their distribution the socialist effectively seeks the abolition of markets and hence potential income and wealth differentials: all resources are to be distributed centrally and theoretically evenly. But some people's needs may be deemed greater than others' – here recognition of individual differences creeps in when the socialist champions the causes of the traditionally ignored or impoverished, or groups within society who are unable to live on the equal distribution that sustains others. But generally speaking, all should live on the same amount of resources decreed by the central state.

Once the state has taken control over the production and distribution of resources, and ignoring for a moment *how* that is to be effected, society will be at peace. There should be no more competition for resources, for all resources will be owned by all; there should be no more income inequalities and hence need for envy; 'there will vanish all need for force, for the *subjection* of one man to another' (Lenin)[8]; all will be alike in outcome, regardless of input; sameness shall prevail. Money, the medium of exchange, will disappear because there will be no exchange except, perhaps, rudimentary barter for services. The socialist seeks the ultimate abandonment of money as being unnecessary in a society in which production, transaction and consumption are governed by decree and not by voluntary exchange. But once we turn to how that must be effected, the socialist has to own up to an all-powerful state removing all possibility of freedom.

The romanticist rhetoric that still underpins much socialist thinking ignores the pressing need for control. If money and trade were abandoned, some socialists have believed that all the world's problems would disappear, without explaining how; otherwise socialists recognize that when the state takes over all resources it effectively annihilates freedom. Thus theorists divide between Marxists who believe that the state will one day no longer be necessary and socialists who assert the need for continued state control.

THE STATE

On the one hand, for the socialist who sees the world as inherently divided into classes, the state is the tool of the ruling classes, who use its tools of force and coercion to oppress the underclass of proletarians or workers. All legislation and policies, domestic and foreign, are thereby portrayed as serving the interests of the ruling classes. Accordingly, the revolution will bring forth a new world order in which the workers, the dispossessed, the disfranchised will be the new rulers. But once the underclass takes power, the state will be overthrown and disbanded in order to effect a socialist political order that will not require any governmental apparatus. The rhetoric is palpably utopian: 'The state', Lenin wrote, 'is withering away in so far as there are no longer any capitalists, any classes, and, consequently, any *class* whatever to suppress.'[9] In effect, the vision presented is that following the revolution there will be an anarchic paradise in which all notions of class, and therefore endemic prejudices, will disappear; and at that point we must turn to the theory of anarchism and its philosophy.

On the other hand, for socialists who transcend class-warfare issues and avoid what they consider to be the utopian dreams of the socialist-anarchists the state provides the power and resources to effect social justice programmes of removing contrived inequalities in wealth and resource ownership. We have seen that socialists tend to emphasize political control over the distribution of resources as being a critical element, not only to understanding life but also for providing the means to better human existence in which the individual attains a freedom to be (whatever you are when you have no freedom to get other things). This emphasis on any kind of individual freedom empowered by redistribution schemes is secondary to socialism's primary focus for the state (or society) to take over ownership and hence control of the means of production and distribution.

Whether the socialist pushes for complete control or full nationalization (i.e., ownership), the state's apparatus of force and coercion is certainly required. The state is to control the means of production, which for early socialists may have been understood as the equipment and buildings privately owned and deployed in production but which logically entails the ownership of all individuals in the community. Each capable individual is thus to be a productive unit (Marx is emphatic on that point): if the state is to own the means of production, it accordingly owns all the individuals within its remit. This may not be the desired implication that some socialists prefer to accept, as state ownership of individuals hardly differs from private slavery but dwells in the logic of 'social ownership of the means of production'.

We have noted that a socialist government should reflect the will of the people – and not, in the usual rhetoric, the will of the few. This raises enormous problems that the other political philosophies tend to avoid: if all are to rule and the will of the people is the will of all, how is that will to be known or assumed? Conservatives relish the thought of the elite few ruling, while realists acknowledge that the strongest will always rule; anarchists reject government; libertarians seek to restrain whoever is in power from exacting any more than the minimum required to ensure the maintenance and defence of property; only environmentalists may share with socialists the desire to control all resources. So whose voices should be heard? While socialists have often allied themselves with *democracy* (and hence term themselves social democrats), it is less the aspect of universal enfranchisement that they cheer than the rule of the majority which attracts them. (Historically, socialists and libertarians both allied their policies with an expansion of the franchise in the nineteenth century.) In the Marxist elements of socialist thinking, it makes sense that the majority, who are oppressed by a self-serving ruling elite, should rise to have their voices heard; but even here, as in non-class analyses, there ought to be mechanisms that channel the will of the people – which brings socialism back round to the Ancient Greek problem of how best to run the polity. Representative government, referenda, parliaments or dictatorships: all have been tried and socialists find fault with them all, leaving the socialist either content to work with whatever form of government he finds in his nation or dreaming of the state's abolition in the anarchic paradise.

INTERNATIONAL SOCIALISM

Socialists divide on the issue of what international relations ought to be. Initially and still in Marxist thinking, political boundaries that restrain the movement of labour will be abolished and all workers of the world will be united in their creation of a new world under the 'dictatorship of the proletariat', which will then disappear as anarcho-communism evolves: 'the working men have no country', as Marx and Engels stated in their *Communist Manifesto*.[10] And just as crime will disappear when property is abolished, so too will wars, which Marxists argue are the necessary product of capitalist society. The utopian and messianic drive of the Marxist dream, while originally gripping many in the late nineteenth century, adjusted into practical socialist doctrines dealing with the world as it was with its boundaries and controls. Accordingly, in the early part of the twentieth century, socialists turned their attention to securing socialism *within* the nation-state and effected national socialist policies.

One of the most powerful drives in socialist thought has been the desire to return to a simpler economy, one that is self-sufficient in resources. Autarchy has an ancient history – Plato and Aristotle thought of it as the ideal which only practicality hindered the polity from securing. Foreign trade was thus rejected for bringing super-fluous commodities, ideas and pressures on local customs – that is, it was politically dangerous. The socialist utopians did not give much thought to the size of their planned autarchies, although Plato had noted in *The Laws* that a limited polity would need to wage war on surrounding polities to gain resources when it was lacking. Thus arose a dilemma for socialists: could it exist within limited areas or should the whole world be converted to socialism for it to work?

For Marx, socialism can only be an international phenomenon: just as capitalism is international in its extent so must socialism take over its global reach. But others argued for a partial socialization of the world, nation by nation, which meant that socialist nations would live side-by-side with capitalist nations, which would put strains both on the theory and practice of socialism. Lenin main-tained: 'socialism cannot triumph simultaneously *in all* coun-tries . . . This will create not only conflict, but direct attempts on the part of the bourgeoisie of other countries to destroy the victorious proletarian socialist state.'[11]

In his *Socialism and War*, Lenin presented his version of justifi-able socialist wars – those that liberate nations from imperial powers in their drive to self-determination ('wars of liberation') and those that sought to instil socialism in the nation ('revolutionary wars'). Such wars that are 'progressive', or 'good' (i.e., tending towards the fulfilment of socialism), are legitimate and justifiable; liberation wars are to be supported and encouraged, not because they will produce a system of small independent states, but because, Lenin argues, they will assist the ultimate removal of all boundaries by ridding the lands of their oppressors; nonetheless, wars will not dis-appear until the class system disappears. Accordingly, socialists have tended to support any liberation movement as being crucial for the global development of socialism.

The history of socialism, and hence the reaction of its thinkers, has been that it has had to deal with a mixed global economy. Pure Marxists tend to espouse global capitalism as being necessary for the eventual overthrow of the system in favour of global socialism; any attempt to effect national or regional socialism is thus seen as doomed to failure and even as an impediment to socialist evolution. World government will be inevitable – so long as socialism requires any propping up through violent and coercive methods, but ultimately it too will wither away to leave peace and unity on the planet.

However, in this vision what will stop workers from one area seeking the resources of another? Trade – mutually beneficial voluntary exchanges – will have been abolished, and should one area's need not be rectified by its local resources, the people will clamour for the wealth produced by another area – after all, under socialism there are no private property distinctions, so there will be nothing to stop workers from moving around to take control of other areas. But if the present occupiers refused entrance or access, global socialism would collapse into independent communities seeking autarchy – that is, syndicalism. This need not be rejected by the socialist who, baulking at the intractability of local pressures for more wealth, may gladly accept the early utopian view of small self-sustaining communities.

But acceptance of that would necessitate a reduction in the population – capitalism has unleashed wealth-producing capacity never hitherto seen before on the planet, as Marx was all too ready to accept, but if that capacity is reduced, the population must fall. Our mind thus turns to question the alleged nobility of socialism.

NOTES

1 V. I. Lenin, *The State and Revolution: Marxist Teaching on the State and the Task of the Proletariat in the Revolution* (London: British Socialist Party, 1919), p. 100.
2 Nikolai Bukharin and E. Preobrazhensky, *The ABC of Communism*, trans. Eden and Cedar Paul (Harmondsworth: Penguin, 1969).
3 Karl Marx and Friedrich Engels, 'The Communist Manifesto' in *A Handbook of Marxism* (London: Victor Gollancz, 1935), p. 40.
4 Ibid., p. 47.
5 Jean-Jacques Rousseau, 'The Social Contract' in *The Social Contract and Discourses*, trans. G. D. H. Cole (London: Everyman, 1993), p. 192.
6 Marx and Engels, 'The Communist Manifesto', p. 25.
7 Friedrich Engels, 'Anti-Dühring', quoted in Ludwig von Mises, *Socialism*, trans. J. Kahane (Indianapolis, IN: Liberty Classics, 1981), p. 114.

8 V. I. Lenin, *The State and Revolution*, p. 85.
9 Ibid., p. 97.
10 Marx and Engels, 'The Communist Manifesto', p. 43.
11 V. I. Lenin, quoted in R. Craig Nation, *War on War: Lenin, the Zimmerwald Left, and the Origins of Communist Internationalism.* (Durham, NC: Duke University Press, 1989), p. 158.

CHAPTER 6

LIBERTARIANISM

Standing on the edge of anarchy with its full expression of freedom but not desiring to give up government entirely is libertarianism. The libertarian ideal of maximal individual freedom with a minimal state has long been part of political philosophy, although rarely has it been a dominant ideology either in mainstream thinking or in popular culture. We hear liberalism's echoes concerning the inherent dignity of the individual or the freedom to live life as the individual chooses, and certainly libertarianism is most intimately connected to the moral and political primacy of the individual. But it distinguishes itself from modern liberalism (sometimes calling itself classical liberalism), which it criticizes for being too statist and interventionist in presumption and prescription.

Libertarianism emerged as a modern doctrine with the Leveller movement under John Lilburne in the seventeenth century, but its most influential time in history was in the late eighteenth to mid-nineteenth century. For many libertarians the American Constitution and the Bill of Rights stand as the political epitome of the libertarian ideal. The second half of the nineteenth century saw the classical liberal ideal give way to the emerging socialist and statist philosophies; two world wars promoted a resurgence of liberalism's general ideals of freedom, especially in the human rights movements and the free trade doctrine of the postwar global institutions. Elements of it certainly rise to the fore every now and again in domestic politics, when voters believe that government is overstepping its legitimate boundaries in enforcing statist policies or prohibiting or curtailing individual rights.

The driving force behind political libertarianism is self-ownership, from which all other rights are deduced. 'Every man has Property in his own Person', wrote John Locke[1] in what is the most useful start-ing-point for understanding libertarianism and a most constructive argument by which to compare it to other doctrines. It is, needless to say, an intriguing and deeply contentious position from which to begin a discussion of political philosophy. Libertarians oppose equality of outcome – that is, they oppose the use of the state to mould people into an homogeneous mass. In their criticism of feudal or hierarchical stations and corresponding privileges, early libertar-ians emphasized the moral and legal equality of man and the need to reform privileged institutions to permit equality of opportunity. However, libertarianism proper, as defined by self-ownership and the freedoms that may be appropriately deduced from this axiom, can only uphold a weak view of equality; it rejects, for instance, liberal-ism's notion that all men are born equal as patently false, but main-tains that all should be equal before the law; it rejects socialism's equality of outcomes (such as income or capital) while emphasizing the right of all to strive for their own goals as they see fit.

For man to be free, he must be described as owning himself and thence as being entitled to exchange his labour and command of resources with others as he wishes. Property – self-ownership and ownership of resources – is thus critical for libertarianism. Yet the word property often causes apoplexy in some political and philo-sophical circles; it is a particularly misunderstood concept and too often dismissed out of personal or envious prejudice against owners of resources or out of its alleged obstacle to true human happiness or progress. 'Property is theft', cried Proudhon, in his overused lam-basting of contemporary institutions, and many thinkers throughout history saw the abolition of property as bringing happiness to all of humanity. Yet the libertarian doctrine of self-ownership presents a powerful criticism not just of slavery but over any kind of control exerted by some over others. Strictly speaking, libertarianism rejects all forms of taxation and government regulation of mind, life and limb as being inimical to a free existence, or at least sees them as necessary evils only under certain very strict conditions.

Coercing others, as we shall see with respect to the libertarian theory of government, is to be thoroughly rejected as a means of living for the individual. Yet libertarianism does not make the leap into anarchism. Libertarians fear that the absence of government would lead to moral and social breakdown and they agree with con-servatives and realists that humanity is not to be trusted – people will break contracts, destroy others' property and infringe their rights to freedom, and such violations will require an impartial institution ready to lay down the law and to back it up with violence against offenders if necessary. Nonetheless, some libertarians (Machan) argue that government need not be coercive in its relations to innocent others: they reject involuntary taxation in favour of voluntary insurance payments, for instance. Government is thus to be formed in case one person breaks a contract or is aggressive towards another or her property – it should be the sole institution capable of punishing offenders, arresting them, or ensuring that civil fines are paid.

Unlike the anarchist doctrine of no government, the libertarian accedes to a minimal state, but its jurisdiction is to be severely limited to a background role of police, law courts and military defence. If anarchism is considered too idealistic, perhaps libertarianism offers a credible alternative of retaining the power and protection of the state?

A key problem is ensuring that the state does not extend its influence beyond the minimum, for when it does, the libertarian argues, it commits an offence against the people it was designed to protect – in effect, it becomes a criminal organization, serving its own ends (i.e., the interests of those working for it), and being aggressive towards individuals. The legitimacy of states may be severely questioned by libertarians: not only do they condemn invasions of other states' territories, but they begin with condemning any interference in the lives of its own citizens.

For those who believe that the state and its organs are necessary to manufacture the conditions and culture of the good life through regulation, redistribution and proscription, the libertarian viewpoint may seem outrageous – surely, it means giving the people a freedom that they cannot adequately or maturely use? Libertarians would give freedom to drug use and prostitution – what does that say about the moral application of its philosophy? They would permit the market economy free rein, regardless of standards and prices. Who would protect the weak and vulnerable from exploitation? To which the realist may add, if the libertarian fears the abuse of power, what would stop companies and governments colluding to extend their remit, subtly at first, until we have increasing statism? A chorus of other questions and concerns challenges the libertarian, but she remains steadfast in her belief in the minimal state and the right of the individual to pursue happiness: either a social contract or strictly limiting constitutional law should ensure that government does not interfere in peoples' personal and moral choices, even if the majority of people believe those choices to be wrong (immoral or irreligious). Similarly, government should not intervene in the people's right to exchange their labour and property as they see fit – and this is not just because such intervention is often counter-productive (e.g., a minimum wage rule makes it harder for poor and low-skilled people to find work), but because such intervention constitutes a violent intervention in a voluntary exchange between two people. Regarding the poor, the libertarian argues that they only exist as an immobile class when there is heavy regulation and restrictions in labour markets, which are often designed to protect ruling or wealthier classes: remove those impediments to social mobility and the individual becomes free to work and study as hard as he desires (or not, as the case may be). That there will always be a class of relatively poor people is of little political concern for the libertarian, so long as people are free to move out of relative poverty as well as fall into it should their actions warrant it. Poverty may, however, be a burning issue for the libertarian – she simply argues that its reduction and elimination cannot be had from state intervention or the redistribution of income from rich to poor: if economies are free and governments do not interfere in voluntary transactions, then the conditions are provided for people of all backgrounds to improve their lot. Whether they do or not depends on them.

MAN

The libertarian looks upon man as an individual who owns himself.

To own oneself sounds oxymoronic: given a self, it must belong to the possessor, but does it mean anything at all to 'own oneself'? For the libertarian, it certainly does, for it may be retorted who else owns you? If you do not own yourself, then there must be someone who controls and thereby owns you. A critic may reject any form of ownership including self-ownership as contrived, but she cannot reject the need to control actions, unless life and action are thoroughly rejected as meaningless and the ethical individual is encouraged to seek a vegetative existence. Once it is accepted that humans must act to live, it follows that action, involving plans and goals, implies a need for control over those actions and ends, and either that control comes from within or from without – that is, from the individual agent or from an external authority.

Although liberals derive much from humanists (cf. Erasmus) emphasis on the dignity of man in seeking moral perfection and autonomy through independent thinking and learning, libertarians generally remain thoroughly value-neutral as to men's pursuits. Along those lines, Jeremy Bentham proposed that 'Prejudice apart, the game of push-pin is of equal value with the arts and sciences of music and poetry. If the game of push-pin furnish more pleasure, it is more valuable than either.' How a man lives his life, what pleasures he seeks and what ambitions he has, what gods he worships and what pursuits he engages in, so far as they do not obstruct his neighbour's life, are of no concern to libertarians who emphasize value neutrality. Such thought rejects the Aristotelian pursuit of the good life and does not present a utopian or millenarian goal accessible to all should they struggle harder or sacrifice others or their current material goods; it offers a present freedom and *an open-ended future*. What the future holds in store depends on the driving ideas that people possess as individuals freely interacting with friends, family and traders. What the end-processes of freedom should be (either for the individual or for society) is not up for discussion – we would not wish ourselves beholden to the decisions and judgements of our ancestors, so we should not interfere with our present view of the future and impose upon our future selves (and future generations) ethical judgements as to how we should live.

Some libertarians disagree: Objectivists, who follow the writings of Ayn Rand, emphasize the ethical nature of freedom and the moral values of certain kinds of activity (rational as opposed to irrational, for instance). Ethics is an intrinsic part of life, they counter, and cannot be avoided. As Rand writes: 'ethics provides a code of values to guide man's choices and actions.'[2] For what end should man live? asks the Objectivist, replying that man should live for himself and that he should live rationally. Objectivists deny that ethics should be cast aside or that its content is relative, arbitrary or mystical in nature; they emphatically deny that man ought to sacrifice his time or life for others (he may choose to put another, such as a loved one, above his own life, but that is an act of rationality rather than sacrifice). What the good is flows from what man is, and Rand and her supporters stress the rational nature of man and the concomitant political need for freedom. Just as morally a man must strive for independence from others (i.e., cooperating with them as he sees fit instead of living off them parasitically), politically he must be protected from those who would impose their violence or theft upon his life.

The claim for self-ownership, we can note, is an explicit rejection of collectivist thinking and an avowal of man's unique and individual nature. For the libertarian, only the individual exists autonomously, for ultimately it is the individual who chooses to act in a particular manner. While modern liberalism may seek to validate the existence of the self through various forms of analysis – historical, dialectical, introspective, deductive, etc., libertarianism posits the self as an immediate known: the seeker is a self, the acting agent is a self, the ponderer of self's nature is a self – the self cannot be ignored or logically dismissed: it is integral to human life. But that can be defined in terms of ownership, which is where libertarianism proposes a radical conception of the self that disallows any metaphysical theory of the transcendental or annihilated self of collectivist theories that claim, 'we are all one', or 'the individual is nothing'. In this they find an ally in the writings of some existentialists, who on the whole were not well disposed to private property but who have some pithy sayings about individualism, such as Sartre's 'you're free, you choose'. While much philosophy rises to extinguish that inescapable fact and to posit the self into a grander scheme of higher entities such as Universal Spirit or Mind, the libertarian can reject these as either pointless or unnecessary: instead, the libertarian stresses the nature of secular life and the obvious fact that people use resources in order to live.

Critics often maintain that libertarianism upholds an unrealistic, atomistic vision of man in which the individual is removed from all social influences: a fact that can hardly be rejected by any political philosophy since the language, ethics and etiquette people use are social and man is born thoroughly dependent on others. However, to call libertarianism atomistic or solipsistic constitutes an unwarranted attack, for the libertarian understands the relations that exist between people but maintains the claim that the acting individual always acts of his own volition – even when running with the crowd. Few libertarians espouse the kind of anchorite egoism of Max Stirner, but what the libertarian does claim is that the individual is the ultimate given beyond whom it is impossible to seek for further causes: when a person utters the word 'I', no further clarification is required as to whom they are referring, but when a person says 'we', then clarification is needed as to whom is indicated. The first person perspective is an ineluctable fact of the universe which cannot be rejected, although it can be ignored or displaced in convoluted reasoning, which is how libertarians perceive the other political philosophies.

Historically, most of humanity has been enslaved to others who have wielded violence, intimidation and fear to sustain an abject dependence, and appropriately such political forms promote privileges for certain individuals but not all. By upholding the unique sentience of each individual, the libertarian rejects any feudal hierarchy of status as much as any division between master and slave – and not merely on consequentialist grounds that slavery and feudalism are not as productive as free markets, but because no man can own another – each person can only own himself.

The libertarian's view of man is thus proprietary, with some thinkers adding that self-ownership is also moral. Being more interested in what follows from this premise, the libertarian avoids engaging in philosophical disputation as to what constitutes a self – while accepting the role science has to play in unravelling the workings of the brain and body, it insists that ultimately why an individual acted in the manner he did cannot be pushed further than 'because that is what he did' (Mises).

When we return to consider the libertarian's view of man's nature we find a surprisingly unprejudiced attempt to leave his nature very much in the hands of his own self and action. The general vision of man is that of a man set free from men, developing his talents and exchanging freely with others voluntarily. Critics underline the costs such freedom can entail for those who are not good at self-development and exchange – some people are too irrational, conservatives may argue. Mises's libertarianism prefers a vision of man acting within a mutually interdependent and dynamic system in which irrationality is constantly penalized as being of a (relatively) higher cost to follow – people will learn from their mistakes, if you let them.

Some philosophies are concerned about where man is taking himself (i.e., on what path he may be walking), but libertarians deliberately refrain from speaking about what they consider historicist reasoning. Man's freedom is open-ended and its consequences unpredictable: attempts to model the future according to a present plan, or to insist that hidden forces are driving man in a certain direction are rejected as useless.

SOCIETY

Despite its insistence on the primacy of individuality and self-ownership, libertarianism does not reject society: it rejects any conception of 'society' possessing a self, a mind or an intention, for only individuals can possess volition and sentience. A social life is not only appropriate to man from the libertarian perspective, it is necessary for his advancement.

The reason is that advantages of cooperating and exchanging far outweigh the autarchic life, which for a child is barely possible and for an adult highly dangerous. Some libertarians may view society as an ethically neutral entity – the backdrop against which individual action takes place; whereas others argue that societies may possess differing moral values depending on how well they cultivate political and cultural freedom. Thus, even if politically two societies permitted freedom of exchange and contract, that which fostered an innovative and encouraging culture would be preferable.

Libertarianism's analysis of society stresses that ability and resources are unevenly distributed across the population and the planet; it then proceeds to enquire what social system ought to be supported that will enable men to derive the best from this inevitable and irremovable inequality. Two methods of resource distribution are available to humanity – coercive or peaceful. Invoking the principle of self-ownership, the libertarian asserts the mutual benefits to be derived from peaceful exchange based on the right to private property, although libertarians disagree on what justifies the private ownership of things beyond the self.

Commonly, Locke's defence of property is used. Property arises when a man mixes his labour with a previously unowned resource: by working a specific plot of land, by picking fruit from specific trees, or by mining a mineral from a specific location, the one who mixes his labour with the resource is said to own it. Against criticism that would have a man owning a continent or a planet if he were the first to land there, the libertarian replies that he can only own that which he actually works on.

Mixing one's labour with the resources of the land is a necessary condition for gaining ownership over them, but it is not a sufficient condition for Locke, since he asserts that initial ownership must not be to the detriment of society as a whole – at this point, liberalism takes a different reading of traditional libertarian thinking. Nozick calls this 'Locke's proviso', and it plays a crucial role in limiting the extent of property ownership – ownership rights are conditional on them being useful – they cannot be absolutely held. For example, I would not be justified in assuming ownership over the only food-producing valley in an entire region, or by encircling another with my property thus allowing no exit for the hapless individual. The provisos restrict the extension of property rights on a consequentialist argument that the formation of property rights beyond those of the individual's rights over the self do not harm the rest of society. The notion, however, that a single person could monopolize a planet's-worth of resources is ludicrous – only states can do that.

Other libertarians are not interested in being drawn on justifying the origins of property but focus instead on the benefits of possessing private boundaries to resource use and consumption. This is a consequentialist justification of property, and libertarians are divided as to whether the consequences are to be described in terms of the general welfare benefits private ownership brings or, as Mises argues, for the constant overturning of resource managers through the market system which avoids any need to justify or prove original ownership. The latter is worth considering: if a plot of land were stolen from a person or people in the mists of time, its present owner must daily prove his ability to manage the land properly. If he neglects it, for instance, the income derived from it will fall and hence its value in the eyes of others (as substantiated in the prices they are willing to offer for it) also falls. So long as he can subsidize his mismanagement of the resource from other funds, he may not be untowardly worried; however, the more he mismanages his land, the greater the fall in its income and value will be, and there often comes a point (so long as people are free to exchange their resources) when another may offer an attractive price, and so the land may pass to one who will manage it better.

When people face each other in the libertarian world, they face each other as potential traders for whom an exchange may bring about mutual satisfaction and improvement – a betterment of their state of affairs. (That is not to say that all human interaction is to be a form of exchange, although some economists do try to model friendship and love according to such criteria.) Earlier libertarians deployed a 'state of nature' argument to show how men may relate to one another, but the scenario is not necessary although it is a useful abstraction from any particular historical context to elucidate how two men may deal with one another. Again, the libertarian emphasizes that two choices are available: either they resort to violence, or they resort to trade. Only the latter provides for a constant readjustment of exchange for mutual benefit. (In recent decades, some economists have attempted to model exchange mathematically, and in so doing have whitewashed out the fallible human element that is necessarily a part of trade: parties to an exchange may err, but they are also free to learn from their mistakes, and as mistakes are costly they have an incentive to improve.)

Secondly, the libertarian emphasizes that traders do not have to care for each other and may view each other through bigoted or ignorant eyes; but again in the market-place such prejudice is costly to uphold and to maintain if it involves avoiding some traders because of their cultural, racial or religious beliefs. Libertarians emphasize how the market-place tends to smooth out irrationality: war and violence tend to diminish, as Kant predicted, where the market-place is dominant. Similarly, the conservative's acknowledgement and even embracing of human context, prejudice and irrationality is of little concern to the libertarian who exhorts freedom of exchange and contract. Therefore, forcible integration and proposals to unite the world into brotherly love are impermissible to libertarianism, which asserts that prejudicial attitudes are so relatively costly that people, while free to follow their ignorance and prejudice, will be cajoled into more mutually respecting relationships.

Similarly, despite uneven talents the Ricardian principle of comparative advantages explains why all may mutually benefit from exchange. So long as interaction is freely chosen and voluntary, people will trade, or not trade, as they see fit from their own particular contexts – not as they are told to deal, work and spend their money and energy from an authority's point of view.

Libertarians are champions of the 'open society' – they do not advocate liberalism's economic growth for its own sake or any kind of end-state but the free interplay of individuals seeking mutually beneficial trades, which may or may not produce economic growth. The 'open society' connotes a freely operating complex matrix of interpersonal relationships that are forever in flux, as compared to a closed society in which the position of each *vis à vis* any one else's is frozen by law or other forms of social control. Popper's and Hayek's works provide widely ranging explications of how the free society should operate, which is summarized by the individual's unassailable position to *know* his own affairs and interests better than anyone else. Mistakes will arise, but again only the individual is in a position to learn from those mistakes, either first-hand or through the exhortation of his friends.

Libertarianism thus seeks to ensure a morally and politically neutral social framework which begins with the individual's right to self-ownership and the corollary right to trade and to associate with whomever he pleases and to try different kinds of lifestyles and communities, so long as people are free to leave. In turn this helps to explain the libertarian's conception of government which ranges from an anarchic abolition of government to a minimal or night-watchman state.

GOVERNMENT

Libertarians differ in their views on the legitimate extent of government, from those who would reject any need either practical or moral for a state (e.g., Rothbard, Hoppe) to those who would have the state maintain a rigid minimalism ensuring the rule of law (Jefferson, Machan, Rand), to those who, more contentiously, would permit a modicum of state education or social services to ensure peace (Hayek).

Statism – the expectation of the central state to control society and its resources – is thoroughly rejected by libertarians. The libertarian disdains arbitrary power – and has this in common with the political realists: people will abuse power and be abused by it. Jonathan Swift quipped: 'Arbitrary power is the natural object of temptation to a prince, as wine or women to a young fellow, or a bribe to a judge, or vanity to a woman.'[3] The libertarian seeks to remove that temptation.

Critics of libertarianism often refer to Robert Nozick as proffering the standard libertarian defence of minimal government; however, other libertarians present much more radical and consistent options. Whereas Nozick accepts that at some point a central state is necessary to ensure an impartiality between competing property or legal claims and that it would emerge naturally as competing protection agencies converge on to an overarching, impartial framework,

Rothbard and Hoppe argue that the market is well situated to provide its own mechanism of conflict resolution. They reject the need for a monopoly institution to resolve claims, which they argue can be dealt with through a plurality of options offered as services on the market. Such libertarians therefore reject the need for any state at all, and are fervent proponents of liberalizing police and legal services, which they declare can only be inefficiently run by the state-owned monopoly. Similarly, the armed forces should be disbanded and any defence organization required by a community may be provided through private subscription and initiation. They readily indicate the violence and war that standing armies have produced. Locke commented that they can only produce mischief, which, when one considers the past two centuries, is difficult to disagree with.

Inverting Proudhon's maxim that property is theft, the libertarian retorts that taxation is theft. This follows from the principle of self-ownership which leads, for the libertarian, immediately to private ownership boundaries over resources; any forced exaction of the product of a person's time and energy constitutes a violation of the right to non-interference, and as taxation is a violent form of interference, it is immoral. Should a community seek to raise funds for a project from which all or the majority would benefit, libertarianism requires that fund-raising must be voluntary.

Correspondingly, the welfare state is rejected *in toto* by libertarians as being an immoral and/or an inefficient mechanism that reduces free citizens to subjects of the state, and just as earlier libertarians sought to free men from the strictures of feudalism and the presumed entitlement of the monarch over his or her subjects – often seeing them as children to be directed and nursed, so later libertarians castigate the modern state for usurping a monarch's or prince's presumptuous ownership of people as being just as demeaning and for violating the principle of self-ownership. The welfare state, libertarians argue, subsidizes irrational or irresponsible behaviour by setting the cost of risky activities too low, and then requires that more taxes be raised to fund the growing pool of subsidized illnesses and irresponsible behaviour. While some theoreticians in the libertarian camp are morally conservative and would privately castigate irresponsibility, they cannot support the state's interference in what they view as private affairs. They are thus tolerant of irresponsibility to the degree that a man is free to act as he sees fit – and to learn from his mistakes; but when the cost of those mistakes is removed from the individual by distributing them across the community, people are not likely to learn from detrimental behaviour and responsibly acting individuals are forced to subsidize less prudent neighbours.

At this point critics will claim that people do not always know what is in their own interests and should be cared for by the impartial agency of the state. Libertarians firstly attack the notion that the state can be impartial between competing interests, for programmes and policies are driven by political processes not by impartial analysis, which would anyhow be redundant once funds had been coerced from a population for a particular project. Secondly, they criticize the assumption of the ignorant masses requiring an enlightened elite to direct their behaviour or spending: Thomas Jefferson asked if people cannot be trusted to run their own affairs, how can they be trusted to govern others' affairs? The early libertarians rejected the title of the monarch as patriarch over a nation of people, and so they reject the modern incarnation of the managed state.

At one end of the libertarian spectrum are 'anarcho-libertarians', who seek the dissolution of the state in favour of permitting private agencies to serve people's needs, whereas at the other end are libertarians who recognize that the state may have a legitimate, albeit tightly controlled, role.

INTERNATIONAL AFFAIRS

Borders for the libertarian are artificial constructions whose existence demarcates political boundaries; however, since libertarianism entails a reduction of politics to a bare minimum, borders should be of little use or consequence. That is, the state should not interfere with freedom of trade and movement of people: it may design a flag or similar object representing the people under its jurisdiction and survey the application of its laws, but it should not interfere with any kind of international commerce between people.

Free trade, argues the libertarian, is not only mutually beneficial but it also reduces mutual animosities and prejudices, which can never be removed if people are forced to integrate or to subsidize foreigners' lives through government aid programmes. Therefore, all subsidies to exporters, quotas and tariffs on imports, are immoral and unjustifiable interventions, which amount to a forced expropriation of resources (money) from one group of people to support another, usually politically well-connected group. That they tend to privilege specific producers, as explained by economic theory, is of secondary concern to recent libertarians as the morally unacceptable intrusion in commercial activity.

Yet are there any justifiable interventions for the libertarian? What if there is a war – would it not be right then to secure borders to hold back domestic produce for domestic rather than foreign consumption? In such situations, libertarians differ on policy – the situation is after all horrendously complex. Some argue that export controls on arms would then be excusable, while committed free traders note that such controls would decrease the amount of imports a country could purchase (and thereby leave it more economically vulnerable) as well as set a dangerous precedent for further encroachments. War, libertarians observe, increases the vastness of government intervention and regulation of life and the ensuing peace rarely returns a nation back to the freedoms it enjoyed beforehand. While aggressive war, or wars of intervention in other lands, is prohibited by libertarian politics, wars of self-defence are justifiable, but again the concern is that government will expand its remit and not relinquish it in peacetime. Accordingly, libertarians present a range of arguments as to how the state should deal with external aggression against its citizenry: temporary militia; insurance company-led or paid-for defence; voluntary purchasing of mercenary armies and soldiers. Once the libertarian removes discussion away from a state-supported and controlled army, he enters an improbably idealistic realm for most critics, especially realists and conservatives, who would ridicule the possibility of fighting a defensive war without a professional army. The libertarian response that wars are state-sponsored does not adequately silence philosophers of war. Much war exists below the political horizon as endemic to cultures – states certainly amplify bellicose tendencies but they cannot be held to be the sole producers of war: many peoples around the world fight (and have fought) each other in the absence of state apparatus.

Similar difficulties arise for immigration. The libertarian would ideally support free migration around the world, yet a strong realist vein in many proponents' writings underlines the problems that may follow unrestricted immigration of peoples from illiberal cultures – peoples from nations or parts of the world where the notions of freedom and concurrent personal responsibility have yet to take hold. Such thinkers emphasize the importance of ideological cultures in sustaining political freedom; others argue that so long as the state does not bend its minimalist principles to the growing demands of immigrants seeking economic protection, welfare or other subsidies, then the new migrants should fit well into their new culture, understanding the principles of voluntarism and political freedom – such is the history of the American melting-pot, they claim.

The obvious tensions that cultural clashes create are not to be quickly dismissed; libertarians may blame such tensions on the disparities in incentives that statist policies engender, but they are there nonetheless. Inner-city riots and racial tensions are a growing part of Western culture that the libertarian has to confront: the realist and conservative are perhaps on stronger ground in demanding the full powers of the state to ensure the peace, but lose ground to the libertarian who indicates how state interference typically exacerbates social problems.

NOTES

1 John Locke, 'Second Treatise' in *Two Treatises of Government*. (Cambridge: Cambridge University Press, 1997), §27.
2 Ayn Rand, quoted in Leonard Peikoff, *Objectivism: The Philosophy of Ayn Rand* (New York, NY: Meridian, 1993), p. 206.
3 Jonathan Swift, *Selections*, ed. Hardin Craig (New York, Scribner's, 1924), p. 129.

CHAPTER 7

LIBERALISM

What is liberalism? Despite being one of the most prolific political words bandied about in the past century and seemingly the most befitting description of the post-Second World War order, it is the hardest political philosophy to define – not only has it become a term of abuse but its coverage is apparently so vast as to defy exposition. Nonetheless, in seeking the best of what a philosophy implies and offers, we can reject the more abusive descriptions of liberalism as implying 'wishy-washy' or 'Western and white middle-class' or 'unable to make up one's mind' and instead elaborate on what its key elements are as expressed by notable liberals.

Firstly, a note on the history of 'liberalism' is worth considering, as this can help us clarify where the confusion and potential for misunderstanding and unwarranted criticism have arisen. Up until the twentieth century, 'liberal' had a perfectly respectable pedigree and a readily understandable political meaning: it was used to describe the belief in the freedom of the individual to live life without political interference. 'Liberal' derives from the Latin *liber*, meaning free, unrestricted and independent, which implied and still implies *freedom from coercion*. But during the interwar period (1919–39) the term liberalism was uprooted from its natural etymology to imply a social democratic vision of state intervention in the economy, income redistribution and a welfare state. The decline of 'liberalism' *qua* freedom has been readily noted in history: statists, those desirous of expanding the institutions and reach of the state, openly pilfered the attractive and common language of liberalism. Notably, the emerging new liberals lifted the word 'freedom' and its implication of 'freedom from' to produce a host of 'freedoms to' policies – freedoms to education, happiness, love even – and similar 'rights to':

shelter, education, health, etc. They also grabbed socialist ideals of government ownership of the means of production to forge a new intellectual power, whose central justification connotes that it defends the people from the extremes implied in the other theories.

After a century's misuse and abuse of the word, there is little foreseeable chance of resuscitating its proper meaning. North Americans use the word 'liberal' to describe democratic socialist and generally pro-statist policies, and Europeans too are slowly moving in that direction. 'Liberalism' nowadays embraces a host of policies and beliefs that are patently inconsistent, contradictory and illiberal, so today, writers on liberalism through history distinguish between 'classical' and 'modern' variants. In the past few decades 'libertarianism' has gradually gained currency to express the philosophy of what others call 'classical liberalism.'

Gripes, prejudices, laments, characterizations and caricatures aside, we return to what modern liberalism can mean. The liberal raises the standard of rights and freedoms: of freedoms to certain activities, as well as freedoms from harmful activities such as aggression; rights to particular values and rights from particular acts. Philosophically, this is an uneasy alliance, but one that remains highly appealing to many, even if they disagree on the balance or reach of the various freedoms proposed, or even if they reject a clearer logical analysis of principles. What does this mean? A liberal typically claims that a person has a right to life and a right *not* to be attacked, but unlike the libertarian sees this as an insufficient condition for life, so he adds that man has a right to enjoy particular things, such as a decent or basic standard of living; or a man has a right to express his opinion so long as it does not offend in some meaningful and understandable manner; or a man has a right to seek material success so long as he recognizes his broader responsibilities to his community (or planet). The liberal apparently enjoys seeking the mean between political visions and avoiding binary visions of 'if this, then not that' – perhaps therein lies its general appeal: it recognizes life's complexities as driving into the heart of political thinking and, like the conservative, baulks at the apodictic certainty implied in other political visions.

Pushing through liberalism's somewhat ambiguous proposals there can be seen a more robust core: neutrality. Not all thinkers may agree, preferring to identify liberalism for its individualism or its programme of rights or its conception of justice, but arguably these can only be drawn from posterior principles, and most consistently in their explicit and implicit prescriptions, liberals uphold a neutral political framework: the state ought not to privilege any one group or individual over any other. Critics may retort that this is political tosh – that there can be no such thing as a neutral framework for the state as taxing some to pay for others necessarily redistributes wealth according to political rather than neutral principles; or that liberalism in all of its aspects is in itself contentiously value-laden and inherently serves variously defined interest groups or classes. To understand better liberalism's notion of neutrality, we might see from whence it came.

The liberal tradition emerged from humanist Renaissance thinking in the sixteenth century and its emerging principles were exposited by those seeking a political solution to the religious reformation in which states sought to impose one form of Christianity upon all their people. The concept of religious freedom and toleration were gradually shaped in the seventeenth century, notably by the pens of Locke and Milton, and the principle of toleration, which presumes a permitting authority, gradually evolved into a principle of neutrality. Rhode Island was the first state in the world to issue a declaration of religious freedom – its elders baulked at some of the folk that they attracted but adhered to the principle nonetheless.

The principle of neutrality gained impetus in the eighteenth century: liberalism's proponents actively sought to reform institutions and customs that were inimical to the implied neutrality demanded of the state. In many fields we can say that the liberals were highly effective: political corruption was targeted and institutional reforms based on checks and balances became the guiding standard; slavery was attacked and gradually abolished throughout the West; economically privileged government monopolies and practices were curtailed and freedom of trade championed; political inclusion was gradually expanded from a restricted male franchise to universal adult enfranchisement; toleration towards others' beliefs was encouraged; freedoms of expression and association were promoted, leading to the key liberal principle of the nineteenth century – self-determination of the peoples of the world. By the mid-nineteenth century, liberalism's momentum was infectious and a new world of freedom, toleration and peace looked to be within humanity's grasp. But Civil War in the USA (1861–65) and the Franco-Prussian War (1870–71) in Europe were followed by a century of world wars, revolutions and political violence enacted on a hitherto unprecedented scale. Liberalism was swamped by the fierier ideologies of aggressive nationalism, militarism, imperialism and revolutionary socialism. Its hallmark individualism was undermined by a barrage of collectivist ideologies that sought to replace liberalism's alleged atomistic individuals with the alluring power of numberless masses identified by race, class or nation who could be channelled into aggressive adventures against other groups. Liberal assumptions of ineluctable progress and development were crippled by reactionary romanticists of many hues who criticized the Age of Reason and the industrial revolution for destroying the traditional mysteries and rites of culture. The emphasis on rights was damned by those who believed that rights were often necessarily asymmetrical and privileging only the middle class. Finally, the liberal vision of democratic world peace was shattered by the reality of democratic imperialism – the masses in Europe and America cheering on colonial adventures and battles and the imposition of Western cultural mores and political models on unsuspecting peoples.

Under such strains liberalism split into its two major variants – modern liberalism (what is generally termed liberalism) and classical liberalism or libertarianism. The libertarian tradition sought to remain true to the principles of individuality and freedom, of restricted government, free trade and pacifism; the modern variant effected compromises with socialist ideas and attracted a host of thinkers who believed that the power of state, which was waxing with war, could be harnessed to impose neutrality on citizens through legislation and welfare policies – and the exportation of the liberal dream to the world's oppressed and poor. Of course at that point the libertarian cousin cries treachery – that is not what the state is for; but the impulse to harness the swelling jurisdiction of the state to bring about, in varying degrees, liberty, equality and justice was too great. From a critical perspective, a new ruling class of highly educated administrators attained the power to direct people's lives and to manufacture the Platonic dream of the well-tempered and just society. From the liberal perspective, against the commanding competition vying for people's minds and especially their bodies, what else could have been done but to shift on some principles to secure a stronger defence of freedom broadly written?

After being sidelined by the horrific events of the first half of the twentieth century, liberalism can claim ultimate victory – the postwar peace, split indeed by the Cold War, was nonetheless highly liberal in spirit and intention, and despite inevitable party-political colouring, it remains so. Following the collapse of the Soviet empire, socialists have had to find alternative avenues of criticism, notably on the environmental impact of the liberal order, or the factual disparity of incomes around the world; others simply attack liberalism for its political inconsistencies, while deeper attacks are laid on liberalism's individualism and concepts of man and society.

MAN

'All men are born morally equal' says the liberal. The principle is naturally shared by socialism, but what flows from the liberal premise differs. Socialists believe that all are born equal – especially in latent talent – and that they should remain homogeneous throughout their lives; the fact that cultures or individual initiative promote some to further their talents more than others implies that they should work to help those worse off: 'From each according to his abilities, to each according to his needs' was the Marxist rallying cry for massive redistribution of wealth. The liberal, we can say, proposes a more forgiving vision of humanity's chances – even if we are not literally all born with equal potential, that equality can be cultivated by institutional reform and perhaps a dynamically adapting welfare or educational system. The able should be free to pursue their talents, but most emphatically all should be given an equal opportunity to become as able as they reach adulthood.

Children's potential is arguably the driving principle in modern liberalism, and distinguishes it from the other political philosophies. Socialism's egalitarian emphasis is placed on both children and adults, whereas liberals tend to believe that adults should be free to stretch their earnings or talents as they see fit. However, as a result of its emphasis on children's entitlements to equal opportunities, the modern liberal quietly opens up the prospect for wider interventions in the adult realm – and it is at this juncture that liberals begin to divide into those who disdain to interfere in adults' lives beyond the bare minimum necessary to help children, and those who claim a greater breadth of intervention to secure the rightful moral and economic inheritance of the newly born, and who, therefore, begin to sound more like socialists (hence Social and Liberal Democratic parties).

Initially, the child-centred ethic was straightforward and was first proposed by the great nineteenth-century liberal, John Stuart Mill: Mill held that the ideal of equality must be maintained for children, while adults can be left to fend for themselves in the voluntaristic spheres that they will inhabit. Children cannot make voluntaristic agreements in the sense that adults can, so they need protection from demeaning and stultifying traditions. They need the right or the opportunity to begin life on a level playing-field. If we imagine that children can be raised equally, then subsequent inequalities in outcome (e.g., wealth) that emerge in adulthood are thus nominally acceptable to the liberal mindset. 'Nominally', in the sense that so long as such inequalities do not in turn endanger the equalizing of children's prospects. This raises a problem: if a talented couple enrich themselves through their work, why should their children be relatively penalized by a policy designed to equalize the opportunity for all (i.e., give more to the children of those parents who do not advance themselves materially)? The conservative and libertarian baulk at such interference in family decisions, which implies that liberalism requires a constant flattening-out of children's life prospects in favour of those less well-off.

Liberals argue that childhood is a critical period morally and politically: if the conditions are not propitious for an equal and confident education and upbringing, then society will never cast off the prejudices and contrived injustices that concern the liberal mind. Some children in each generation will be thwarted by residual bigotry and demeaning attitudes until new generations surface who are not abounding in their parents' chauvinism. Proposals vary on how best to achieve an equal childhood: insisting and even forcing parents to educate their children in a certain manner; demanding that all children are pushed through an equal curriculum; intervening in schools' examinations or intake to give greater help to those from poorer or more illiterate backgrounds; prohibiting or taxing heavily parental inheritances; enforcing employment quotas on companies to ensure school-leavers are employed or apprenticed without discrimination; broadening schools' curricula to encourage children of ill-educated backgrounds to remain active in school (although proposals along those lines differ from teaching more of the classics from a young age to teaching more non-academic subjects, both of which stir liberal sentiments). The more libertarian-oriented liberals shy away from creating too much interference either in the market-place or in families' lives, preferring to insist on a parental duty to educate their children but leaving the particulars to the family. More socialist-leaning liberals believe such intrusions need only be temporarily necessary, lasting only several generations, but critics may point out that such interventions are rarely called off and seldom work in the first place.

Libertarians and conservatives complain that modern liberalism implies that children are owned by the state. Since they are not morally self-sufficient, children are either to be under the jurisdiction of the state or their parents, and it is only right, according to these critics, that they are the responsibility of the people who decide to bring them into existence. However, Mill emphatically argued for the dissolution of traditional parental rights over children: if the just state is to be produced, all impediments must be removed – and that primarily means the parents' claim to own their children. Mill notably does not support the statist thesis that their education should thus become the state's duty, for state-run education is likely to produce uniform minds and extinguish the beautiful and useful differences that flourish across people; however, he believes it consistent with his thinking that the state may prohibit some people from having children if they are deemed to be potentially inappropriate parents. To ensure children's advance is secured, they should take annual examinations in a core curriculum, as long as the state, in remaining pedagogically neutral, does not seek to impose value-laden topics or beliefs in the examinations; instead children should be tested on facts and positive science. Failure in the public examinations warrants a fine or forced labour from the parent, Mill argues. Why? Because the parents are undermining their children's prospects and should be suitably punished.

Critics immediately rush to the growing range of intervention in adult life that modern liberalism begins to imply. (Dickens for instance had fun with Mr Gradgrind's factual pedagogy in *Hard Times*.) To secure the rosier future of flourishing adults existing in a liberal world, much interference is now apparently required: the conservative rejects the assault on family life, for the child belongs to the family not the state in his eyes; the libertarian and anarchist are horrified at the growing requirements of the liberal order; the socialist, however, does not believe that they go far enough of course, for their target for intervention necessarily includes all of humanity, not just the children.

Children are thus the natural focus of the liberal – adults are generally accepted to be capable of living their own lives, so long as they do not harm others: once children become adults, the liberal ostensibly returns to the libertarian ideal of self-determination and inviolable rights. But the nature of those rights has become twisted from what libertarians could condone and when considered closely they are logically difficult to couple together. Taking our cue from Mill again, modern liberalism began with extolling the potential brilliance of individuality – of a life unfettered by privileges or chains which in turn will produce a better society. But securing that life has meant that the same proposals for providing for the best in our children have been extended to securing a level playing-field for adults – and despite liberalism's rhetoric to favour freedom, intervention and interference abound and statism is on the cards once again.

SOCIETY

A liberal society should be as free as possible while ensuring that no one is excluded from the benefits that a free society can bring – that is, it is to be just and fair without privileging any one individual over another and without obstacles to prevent some from ascending social and economic hierarchies.

Philosophically, defining what is meant by justice and fairness has been a recurrent political problem since the Ancient Greeks. Realists define them as what the stronger may enforce; socialists by ensuring that each owns exactly the same as anybody else; conservatives by recognizing the people's stations in society and their corresponding duties and rights; environmentalists by what are the planet's long-term biological requirements (ecological sustainability and climatic stability); libertarians and anarchists by the recognition of individual self-determination and inviolable spheres of freedom. Liberalism – as it has evolved over the past century – has come to define justice and fairness in terms of securing equality of opportunity, as distinct from equality of outcome – we have seen how this relates to children, but those on the more egalitarian or socialist-inspired wing desire to reform present and up-and-coming adult generations.

Society provides the individual with the means of fulfilling her life's aspirations, and the liberal maintains a keen eye for what may hinder that fulfilment. For the liberal, society is a collection of individuals, and while they may act in concert they cannot be grouped into a moral and political aggregate possessing independent consciousness or will: there is no such thing as society in the sense of a self-determining person – only individuals can be so called. Liberalism thus rejects the collective consciousness notions of socialism and its variations but it retains a pragmatic grasp of how people acting in concert may damage the life prospects of any individual. The individual should possess an inviolable sphere of action, namely that which pertains purely to his life and which does not impinge upon the lives of anyone else. Liberalism's guiding social principle is that none shall use force against any other individual, except to prevent harm done against others. When the individual's behaviour begins to, or intentionally is designed to, affect others' rights, the state is justified in preventing the offence (or punishing the perpetrator). Thus, for the liberal, the individual has a perfect and inviolable right to an opinion but not necessarily to express that opinion, for in acting upon his thoughts he may endanger the lives of others. For example, believing that terrorism is justifiable against an enemy is an opinion, and opinions should not be forbidden; but to propagate or to call for terrorist action in front of a mob seething for violence against their enemy constitutes no right for the liberal. As soon as the general welfare of others is at risk, argues Mill, then the individual loses his right of action, but so long as his action pertains only to his own self, then he should be at complete liberty.

Society is viewed somewhat sceptically by the liberal, who is only too aware of the general tendency to conformity and fear of the unknown beliefs of others, or the eccentricity or innovation of the individual genius. Civilization fails when the greatness of the few is curtailed, repressed or even extinguished, notes the liberal. For example, the last flower of the Greco-Roman civilization, a beautiful woman mathematician and lecturer, Hypatia, was brutally murdered by a mob of Christian monks in 415, symbolically representing the barbaric extinction of philosophy in the ancient world. Today, liberals are only too aware of the effective prejudice against nonconformists, especially in the school systems where intelligence and academic ambition are easy targets for mockery and repression: their criticisms do not stop with the vindictive bullying of vulnerable children but extend to the adult realm in which sexism, racism, ageism and other forms of voluntary discrimination are practised. Modern liberals are thus not unconditional supporters of the free market – although the price mechanism and the interplay of the market is seen as the most effective means of producing and distributing resources, the freedom of the market-place is not sacrosanct: should other values be considered to be more important then its reach may be restricted or controlled, or even prices and wages may be tampered with.

Throughout the history of economic thought, free-market thinkers have often held back a pet project that they believe ought not to be subject to market exchanges; such projects typically tend to be what are presently lumped as 'public goods', services and products that the market either does not produce enough of or does so at a price that not all can afford. Adam Smith favoured public support of lighthouses, for instance, while most liberals have accepted the need for the public provision of security and judicial services. Originally, liberals such as Mill rejected state control of schools, but that has now generally been dropped as state-controlled schools have monopolized education in the West. Contentiously, we could claim that the power that presently rests within the grasp of liberally minded reformers is too much to reject: millions of school-children can be brought up according to philosophical notions of the good life and citizenship. The reality is of course far removed from the liberal ideal, as the apparently monolithic structures are pulled and stretched by pressure groups and political interference. Platonists long for the day when such a system could be brought under rational control by experts, but critics react sharply to such dreams either because the rational control of society could never be effected or because the nature of power attracts those who most likely would abuse it for their own ends.

The pressure rises to reduce further the alleged inviolable rights of individuals to live their own lives as they see fit, if their acts effectively diminish other people's welfare. Here an uneasy alliance is made with socialist critics who have complained about the self-serving nature of liberalism's rights (and potent but economically vacant phrases such as 'profits before people'): liberals who are swayed by considerations of social justice and fairness in outcomes are prepared to propose more complicated defences of liberalism that seek to blend its defence of individual rights with conceptions of positive or community rights. On the left wing of liberalism, as it were, we find proposals for 'rights to' resources and values that are not found in the original liberalism of John Stuart Mill but which are defended by modern liberals such as Kymlicka and Dworkin, and this substantially alters the liberal conception of society from a vehicle for individual flourishing and progression to a vehicle for redistribution of resources and equalizing of opportunities effected by a government increasingly looking statist.

GOVERNMENT

Neutrality is the primary political concern for liberalism. Its political programme minimally seeks to remove all forms of bias, prejudice and privilege in political institutions, but then for other liberals neutrality can be expanded to include non-political human interaction such as commercial arrangements. That commercial arrangements are discriminatory by nature (not all people may produce or consume a product, as the price signal informs both sides to ration their choices) presents an intractable problem for the liberals and may weaken substantially the general presumption that they tend to hold regarding the sanctity of property rights.

Superficially, liberalism's conception of government has much in common with libertarianism, which shares a common philosophical root. Government is designed to protect the rights of individuals to those aspects of their lives that may be pursued without harming others. Such rights are known, following Isaiah Berlin's popular terminology, as 'negative rights' as they imply a right not to be subjected to aggressive interference: each person possesses an inviolable right to freedom of conscience and to opinion, for example, for such rights do not intrude upon anybody else's choices or rights. Liberalism usually produces the following popular list: the right to life, free speech, free assembly and freedom of movement. Immediately, critics point out the deeper problems involved in defending any one of the above either because the definitions are weak and open to ambiguity or because they involve contradicting one or more of the other rights.

Elsewhere I note that defining non-contradictory rights (or core rights) is a difficult exercise. For example, the right to life necessitates defining what is meant by life. When does life begin? When does it end? Should we consider the rights of the dead (which conservatives generally believe we do by means of wills)? Should we distinguish between those enjoying living a normal human life and those incapable of doing so, and should the rights of the latter be diminished somehow? Should we consider the rights of future generations (something environmentalists are keen for us to remember in our present actions)? Liberals reply that what is meant is that each living being possesses an inviolable right to pursue his or her life in the absence of violence from others. However, pursuing a value, even one as apparently as basic as 'one's life' is a complicated and generally social affair. We need others to assist our movements, even if all of those acts are completely voluntary; we rely on social institutions and customs to help foster our values and goals as well as to provide the vehicles (institutions, morals, customs) for our advancement. More critically, what is deemed a right is nothing but a legislative recognition of a particular political culture. Jeremy Bentham quipped that a right independent of legislation is a 'nonsense upon stilts', and the cultural relativity emphasized by critics is used to undermine the liberal ideal of universal human rights, or what have been called natural or self-evident rights. (Calling anything self-evident always raises philosophical eyebrows!)

Freedom of association is to be severely curtailed on Mill's thinking, if such an assembly exists to intimidate or to oppress another person or people, for then the state would be justified in breaking up such an assembly. Similarly, with the right to freedom of movement, which demands answering what is meant by movement – on foot, by plane, or by car – and in what direction? Can such a freedom be consistent with the freedom to possess property and exclude others from it? Once we move beyond the ideal of non-contradictory core rights, complications necessarily arise.

Liberal government is thus loaded with an unenviable task of defining what in actuality may constitute a particular right. Conservatives merely nod to the evolved customs and laws of the land, which of course will be highly culturally specific and which negate the concept of universality; libertarians assert the primacy of self-ownership, from which, they argue, all other consistent rights follow (e.g., the right to property ownership). But not all liberal theorists rest their defence of inviolability on rights – Mill also presented a utilitarian case for liberty, but utilitarianism, which extols maximizing the greatest good for the greatest number, can quickly gallop away from liberal notions, as any ethics primer explores. If the greatest good is to be achieved, what is to stop the logical implication of causing suffering to minorities or individuals in such a pursuit? Liberals have their replies of course, arguing that other rules have to be introduced to stop illiberal acts being justified by utilitarianism, but we need to examine the other side of liberal rights theory – the claim that people should enjoy positive rights to values or resources.

In a sense, it was the argument for positive rights that produced the great liberal schism, splitting liberals between those who defended a minimal state, inviolable private property and negative rights (i.e., libertarians) and those who argued that liberals had to become 'progressive' and adapt to the socialist cause of protecting the poor and meek, who were not going to inherit the earth without someone giving them a handicap. It was useless for an individual to enjoy the freedom of movement or association, the new liberal preached, if he was too poor, too ill-educated, or even too weak to pursue his goals. During the twentieth century, we heard again and again the call for 'freedom from poverty' which equates to a 'right to' others' resources (blandly disguised by the epithet 'the haves' and 'the have-nots' and consequent policy calls 'to do something about the poor'). The philosophical roots are ancient and have never left Western thinking – Aristotle proclaimed that a man must enjoy his health and a degree of wealth before he can truly act as a good citizen and pursue his own happiness; and of course, Jewish and later Christian teaching emphasized the duty of charity to the poor. 'Freedoms to' personal or social advancement are particularly vacuous in the eyes of critics, yet tremendously powerful in attracting adherents and supporters willing to fight for them. The fight for freedom from intervention and persecution certainly has altered political destinies and awoken people from slavish slumbers, but the fight for rights or freedoms to certain things – claims – unleashes open-ended demands. So long as there are some who are without, there will be claims that they should be provided for: justice is not served unless they are.

Yet we can again detect that the more redistributive justice is attempted, the further liberals remove themselves from their principle of state neutrality. Consider the logic of claims: if a person has a 'right to' a minimal amount of welfare that implies that someone ought to provide it – that others have a duty to ensure that they cough up the required amount. In simpleton logic, the 'government' has a duty to pay the welfare rolls, but a second thought elucidates that government is merely an instrument for exacting wealth from other people (by force as the anarchists remind us) for redistribution. The libertarian smells a statist rat at this point and argues that if we adhere consistently to the inviolability of self-ownership and the corollary right to private property, then thieves or governments do not possess any right to our produce regardless of any moral intention to help the poor. A claim to property, land, a certain lifestyle or education, is contradictory and implies that others who are productive or who own certain resources should in effect work for and provide for target groups such as the poor or disabled: thus liberalism dangerously collapses into a modern slavery.

To allow such people to suffer reeks of injustice the modern liberal cries, hence we must accept apparent inconsistencies in our thinking for the greater good of a just and fair world. Nonetheless, various defences of such thinking have been proposed, and again critics bemoan that they stretch the credulity of the cherished liberal policy of political neutrality: some are being forced to pay for the misfortune or indolence of others. In liberalism's defence, many thinkers conjure up imaginary scenarios – modern versions of the state of nature – to assess how society may justly proceed. Rawls imagines an 'original position' in which a new contract produced by people choosing the entitlements and rights of a society without knowledge of each other's abilities or disabilities: they would choose to make sure that the worse-off were taken care of, he argues, as any person may find themselves in such a situation. Dworkin uses a construction that requires the subsequent solution to satisfy an 'envy principle', that in the beginning when resources are to be purchased through an auction, none would be envious of any other's purchases for they would have all begun with the same resources. This can be adjusted to give those with greater needs (the unable or the disabled) more purchasing resources to start with.

Such ideas are to act as guides for the liberal in enacting social policies. They are criticized and counter-defended in the secondary literature, but we can raise a couple of pertinent points: how are needs to be measured and assessed? A look at any policy requiring needs assessment (e.g., in health-care) quickly collapses into subjective posturing on what defines need and how needs are to be categorized. And attempting to produce a fair and just world based on not offending or making anyone envious is dangerously expansionist and utopian: if needs are subjective, then they can be invented at will and expand with imagination, and the principle of neutrality is annihilated. Critics reply that justice and fairness could never be secured on such vague and open-ended criteria, and it is thus unsurprising that modern liberalism suffers such broadsides as it does in the critical literature. When it advances such imaginary explorations of how to assess needs, no matter how appealing is their internal logic, the libertarian is quick to rejoin that the state grows correspondingly large and intrusive, much to the glee of statists, whom libertarians unmask as wearing the garb and language of old liberalism. Cast such implausible ideals upon the world arena and critics warn that the outcome can only be instability and war.

INTERNATIONAL RELATIONS

World peace and prosperity are the principal goals for the liberal, who seeks to see the end of war and of poverty. Liberalism does not possess a monopoly on such a grand vision for the future: all the political philosophies consider themselves to present such tempting prescriptions for humanity, but of course they disagree on the means by which such a future is to be accomplished. In its origins, liberalism placed much emphasis on the role of commercial interaction, even claiming that as long as people are free to trade, mutual animosities and prejudices will gradually fall away and be replaced by a world peace (as argued by Kant in his *Perpetual Peace*). Accordingly, the liberal looks upon the peoples of the world not as distinct collectives but as being one people, whose adherence to reason would lead them into mutually beneficial free trade and mutual respect of individuality as well as cultural customs. Prejudices and the institutions hostile to life, limb and mind would be reformed or would simply disappear as voluntary exchange expanded.

The free new world of liberalism moved many thinkers from the free-trade economists to the romantic poets as to the wonderful opportunities and creativity that would be released. But the growth of nationalist sentiment drowned the cosmopolitan ideal – liberals defended national self-determination as a corollary of individual freedom, which makes sense: a people should have a right to rule their own local affairs rather than be ruled by a foreign power, which had often been the case for many smaller communities around the world. But cooperation with nationalists led to a confusion of what exactly was meant to be the driving goal – whether the nation's right to determine its own political affairs extended to a right to control the action and especially the commercial ventures of its citizens (a review of, say, Italy's history brings these political issues to the fore).

By the late nineteenth century, self-determination of political destiny had been quietly supplanted by national control over economic and educational resources – socialist ideals were on the ascent and a heady statist concoction of nationalism and socialism shattered the liberal dream and unleashed upon the world unprecedented violence through revolution and war. When trade and migration borders are closed, the classical liberal warns, wars are soon to follow as the economic and social pressures and frustrations building up in poorer zones tip past critical points: the disparity between the world's rich and poor becomes all too obvious and the intervention at the border effectively halts what would otherwise be a relatively peaceful, continuously fluid, migration of peoples, mixing and merging voluntarily.

As the West has returned to peaceful relations between the major economies, dreams of a new liberal order have resurfaced prompted by the immediacy of poverty and war in other parts of the world as witnessed by the modern media. In the aftermath of the Second World War, the major powers sought to cultivate a new world order in which the contributions of the superpowers would be invested into the poorer countries of the world. If we put aside the political machinations and overarching power play between the Soviet Union and the West, which at times threatened the very existence of the planet in a nuclear exchange, codes of conduct and rights were agreed upon by the United Nations as guiding international standards. Enshrined in the human rights codes were the classical liberal ideals of the freedom of conscience, movement, association and religion, but so too were the modern liberal ideals of rights to healthcare, water, education, etc. Wars in defence of member-states against aggressors were to be subjected to UN approval, and rebellious regimes and the actions of their military personnel subject to UN scrutiny. In a sense, the UN sought to replicate liberalism's domestic blueprint of providing a central government charged with securing people's rights and acting as the court of adjudication in international disputes.

Yet the cosmopolitan liberal order does not necessitate the formation of a world government – government beyond local borders becomes inevitably problematic and superficial in its power and hence its reach. Liberals divide on the appropriateness of international agencies or political institutions such as the European Union, some preferring to foster the advancement of locally based democratic institutions around the world in conjunction with relatively free market conditions. In the great political upheavals of the nineteenth century, democracy – as understood by the inclusion of all the citizens in the political process – acted as an important common principle that brought together various political parties and it has retained a powerful grip on political consciousness despite the interwar dalliance with totalitarianism in much of the world. Liberals thus tend to support democracy.

Here we again detect a shift away from the principle of neutrality earlier mentioned. The modern liberal now wishes to see not just the removal of all debilitating institutions but also the formation of democratic governments throughout the world. President Woodrow Wilson of the USA rhetorically brandished a phrase that has come to mean a lot in the past century: he wished to 'make the world safe for democracy', which has several connotations, but the guiding principle has been the introduction and even imposition of democratic government as the standard against which all governments are to be judged. With judgement also comes the effective moral, political and economic weight of international agencies, and especially American power, to impose sanctions or even take military action in situations where there is democratic failure. Critics complain that an international liberal order is in fact a blatant contradiction of liberalism. Egalitarian liberals such as Kymlicka and Walzer prefer to consider the world in terms of communities of peoples whose rights and particular manner of looking at themselves and the world should be recognized as morally self-sufficient and not in need of Westernizing adjustments. This may be not palatable to other liberals who argue that the world will not be safe so long as ignorance and prejudice remain. For when individuals are repressed by their local cultural traditions, they cannot be free; when their governments restrict their rights to religious freedom, association, or expression, dissidents and critics cannot be free; when their traders are subject to a multiplicity of arbitrary decrees, there cannot be freedom of exchange. In such situations, internal rebellion or external war becomes all the more likely. What is needed is democratic reform of the political institutions to ensure that all the peoples of a nation have an equal right of access to political processes (from voting to standing for election) and that the institutions are guided by impartiality.

In Wilsonian thinking, more 'advanced' or liberal nations have a duty to reorganize the politics of countries that fall short of liberal principles – for the sake of the new generations emerging there. Children of the Congo have as much right to a liberal life as do children of Ohio, say; but does that justify armed intervention into another country's way of life? The classical liberal would have demurred (and was derided for being parochial), but the modern liberal, unwittingly or not, entertains such principles as a matter of course. Liberals disagree on what constitutes a justified intervention, and they adjust accordingly the conventions of just war to suit: some claim that the target nation must also be a threat to others (the so-called 'rogue nation' status of recent American foreign policy); others that the people are suffering economic and political hardship because of their government and need rescuing; pragmatically, most look to the chances of success versus the cost of the operation. In the absence of threats to other nations, an intervention appears patronizing to some critics and potentially destabilizing to others, but more importantly, do all countries need recognizable liberal credentials and do they need central governments at all?

Most human cultures possess guiding rules and conventions of conduct backed by procedures of communal discipline – in fact, when either the rules or forms of punishment are absent, a group cannot last. Anarchists are the first to admit that communal living necessitates rules, but they believe such rules do not necessitate the formation of a central state and/or the use of physical punishments. If human groups can be left alone to form their own systems of discipline, should they be left to do so? Liberals can readily trace much of their modern thinking back to John Locke, but also to Thomas Hobbes, who declared that the want of a central state leaves people vulnerable to aggression: a state is assumed necessary to the liberal mind, and those peoples around the world who are without a state are deemed to be correspondingly benighted and impoverished for their lack – it behoves the advanced countries of the world to help such unfortunates form liberal governments.

Here we must note a strong liberal implication that some forms of government (democratic, impartial) are better than other forms of government (non-democratic, privileging) or none at all. It is a principle that dates back to Aristotle's assertion that a man without a polity (a state) is an outlaw and effectively a non-human. Yet Aristotle's thesis does not have to be translated as requiring a central government but can be weakly translated as people require laws, and law, the anarchists and libertarians explain, emerges quite satisfactorily and spontaneously without a monopolizing governmental body. A powerful criticism of liberalism is thus to ask why it must be assumed that a stateless people are in need of a state? In Somalia, for example, clans (*jili*) act as judicial bodies governing members' behaviour: civilians are free to remove themselves to other clans, and judges that give poor decisions are not likely to be chosen again to adjudicate – unlike liberal western judges.

Western attempts, from British imperialism to American and UN foreign policy, to impose a state upon such apparently lawless communities have typically produced rebellions and civil war resulting from the contrived political distortions. A further pointed question can then be asked: if such peoples are able to proceed with their own affairs without a recognizable central government, do the Western peoples themselves require an overarching state? This naturally leads us into anarchist thinking, which complains of liberalism that it seeks to impose a particular vision of political philosophy upon peoples who may be far removed from liberal thinking. It also reminds us of the pragmatic advice of realists to leave other populations alone as interventions tend to produce dissenting and rebellious citizens. And the libertarian adds that if the liberal disdains the illiberal practices of others, he should, referring to his political roots, respect their ways even if they offend, or would debilitate the life-chances of, a liberal Westerner. Indeed, the liberal who sustains a belief in the power of reason must retreat to encouraging and educating others on the error of their ways: if liberalism's ideals of neutrality and the equalization of children's chances are sufficiently appealing, then other nations will gradually take up liberal reforms, but if they do not, it is remarkably illiberal to impose a putative liberal regime on the recalcitrant.

CHAPTER 8

ANARCHISM

Anarchism is the rejection of all forms of control over the individual and society in the belief that the absence of the state and its corresponding legal system will improve humanity's lot. Violence, war and the exploitation of classes, races and individuals, and even crime, all stem from what the anarchist sees as the artificial mechanism of coercion forged for no other reason than the control of others by the few; accordingly, once the fetters of control are removed man will truly be free to develop naturally and peacefully. All forms of authority – beyond the wisdom of reasoned advice and voluntary codes of conduct – act to distort humanity and its culture and are thus to be opposed and overthrown. 'We are Anarchists', proclaimed Kropotkin, 'disbelievers in the government of man by man in any shape and under any pretext.'[1]

The theory of anarchism prompts severe and often unjust knee-jerk responses – the name itself conjures up chaos and violence, the unleashing of all that is evil in a perpetual revolution upholding disorder and predation. Against anarchism, a leader of the moderates in the French Revolution, Jacques Pierre Brissot once wrote, that it entails: 'Laws that are not carried into effect, authorities without force and despised, crime unpunished, property attacked, the safety of the individual violated, the morality of the people corrupted, no constitution, no government, no justice, these are the features of anarchy.'[2] His description usefully captures the common fear of anarchism and hence its popular meaning, but proponents of anarchism complain that its critics confuse the political ideology of a stateless society with *descriptive anarchy*, which is commonly held as a chaotic and dangerous disorder, when in fact the political philosophy relates to an orderly society that is merely envisaged *without* government.

The breadth of Brissot's attack, although a common characterization of anarchy, is neither fair nor sufficient. Firstly, the political philosophy of anarchism should not be confused with the moral doctrine of nihilism. Nihilism is the rejection of all moral and political values; although particular anarchists may espouse nihilism, the two theories should be distinguished. Anarchism rejects government and privileged institutions, but it does not necessarily reject the need for rules and a moral order; whereas moral nihilists, on the other hand, reject all forms of guidelines, moral precepts, orthodox living, rules, catechisms and even parental or peer-group expectations of just conduct. The nihilist rejects rules as being arbitrary or unjustifiable incursions into the individual's right to pursue his life as he wishes *regardless of the impact on either his own life or that of his neighbours.* This is not the same as rejecting the creation of a privileged group of officials and the requisite institutions to form a coercing government that then codifies expected conduct.

The nihilist can hardly be said to enjoy society: his very ethic seeks its annihilation or at least his distant removal from it. But codes of conduct can emerge spontaneously through human interaction: when men want to interact to better life through trade, exchange, or even just friendship and company, they tend to produce codes of conduct that are the result of human action even though they may not have been deliberated. They thereby form anarchistic rules without any need for a presiding figurehead, politician, committee or parliament. The nihilist's rejection of such rules is the rejection of social life, which is not what the anarchist seeks; he should not be confused with that of the anchorite, even if the latter parades anarchist phrases. Much political philosophy is invested in confusing the logic and implications of competing theories, and anarchism particularly feels the brunt of misrepresenting descriptions and deployment of its term as a description of nihilism and chaos.

Anarchism does not reject moral rules, or, it follows, the safety of the individual, which, others have claimed, requires a state to ensure his freedom and property. Thomas Carlyle intoned: 'Without sovereigns, true sovereigns, temporal and spiritual, I see nothing possible but an anarchy; the hatefullest of things.'[3] But that is to be proved – and the anarchist is emphatic that the burden of proof should rest with the statists (of all hues) than with the anarchist trying to prove that the stateless life will be peaceful and convivial. (Innocent until proven guilty comes to mind.)

Detractors cannot assume the political and moral high-ground because of their characterization of anarchy as constituting tumult and disorder. Just as anarchism has to present its arguments and own the consequences of its logic, so too must its critics accept their own arguments, for they often assume, rather than argue for, the brutal and violent Hobbesian characterization of life and society in the state of nature which are in desperate need of an overarching, monopolistic state to control those aspects of life they deem to be conducive to disorder. They assume that men need leaders, heroes even, to exhort them to great things (i.e., the demagogue's visions); they assume that the majority of humanity are incapable of either leading their own lives without the direction and planning of a supra-authority (assumed to be an 'expert'), or cannot be trusted to resolve their differences and conflicts without a mystical or all-powerful state embodying law and justice (see Chapter 2). Anarchism does not embrace disorder – it merely asserts that men would be better off if there were no state.

The anarchist rebuttal to statists of all persuasions is twofold: why should I obey the state and why should the state be the sole organization of my protection? It is a powerful question and one, in effect, that underpins much of Western political philosophy, although other schools of thought weigh the question differently or invert it. The conservative cannot conceive of the individual *without* a state, so the question of why I ought to obey the state is not one of pragmatics or conferred benefits but fundamental to man's nature: without a state, man is a barbarian – a savage or animal. For the socialist and statist, the lack of the state would lead to detrimental consequences of reduced welfare or equality or justice without which a man could not attain the social status that he is morally due, for the state is required to effect an expropriation of wealth from some to distribute to others. The libertarian rejects the anarchist's vision as being impractical, sharing with the realist a pessimistic view of humanity that some will seek be aggressive towards others. The libertarian conceives the minimal state as being necessary for security and the protection of private property. The realist believes that the state is a necessary outcome of humanity's innate disposition to seek and to wield power, and no utopian wishful thinking will remove the human need to rule or to be ruled. Yet when pushed, all these theorists implicitly recognize the anarchist's thrust that the state requires philosophical legitimization and that its power to protect needs outlining. Against all such attempts offered by their opponents though, the anarchist remains unmoved.

In a sense, the anarchist rejects politics *in toto*, for politics concerns the legitimization of, and the debates and policies regarding, the rules and expectations governing the use of authorities possessing accepted monopolies or near monopolies of force. Politics assumes the justification of power and its use, and anarchism begins by rejecting the need or even the possibility of its justification. Society, anarchism argues, does not require institutions of force and coercion to ensure the peaceful interaction and cooperation of its members: the very existence of coercive structures forces a division between people, subjecting them to the dictates of the governing or bureaucratic classes, or encouraging citizens to use the laws and its agents against their neighbours, thereby disseminating distrust. Government is by definition an institution of force and the anarchist cannot see that it will be used for anything good. It is well worth considering Proudhon's famous (but today underused) evaluation of government from his *General Idea of Revolution*. It is delightfully provocative, but against the mystic visions of the state drawn from Hegel, it presents the Emperor without his clothes:

> To be governed is to be watched over, inspected, spied on, directed, legislated, regimented, closed in, indoctrinated, preached at, controlled, assessed, evaluated, censored, commanded . . . To be governed means that at every move, operation, or transaction one is noted, registered, entered in a census, taxed, stamped, priced, assessed, patented, licensed, authorized, recommended, admonished, prevented, reformed, set right, corrected. Government means to be subject to tribute, trained, ransomed, exploited, monopolized, extorted, pressured, mystified, robbed; all in the name of public utility and the general good. Then, at the first sign of resistance or word of complaint, one is repressed, fined, despised, vexed, pursued, hustled, beaten up, garrotted, imprisoned, shot, machine-gunned, judged, sentenced, deported, sacrificed, sold, betrayed, and to cap it all, ridiculed, mocked, outraged, and dishonoured. *That* is government, *that* is its justice and its morality![4]

But all those are necessary, reply the realists, conservatives, statists and socialists; not so, replies the anarchist.

Anarchists differ, however, on the moral order that society will take. Here we need to note some very important splits that emerge in anarchist thinking. Some are champions of particular political or religious doctrines that others would claim to be restrictive and illiberal – early anarchists were often very religious and were striving to succeed in separating the Church from the state's encroachments. While such sectarian ideologies may be identified as 'Christian' or 'Jewish anarchism', religious communities need to pursue a political philosophy as advised by clerics, hence their particular doctrines can be subsumed under one of the following splits.

Firstly, anarcho-communists extol the group – society – as being the end to which all will direct and live their lives in a communal idyll. All property will be held in common, and therefore all acquisitive or egotistical drives will disappear. The removal of the state will allow people to follow their natural inclination to be mutually cooperative and sociable, enjoying the benefits of what Kropotkin called 'mutual aid'.

Secondly, anarcho-libertarians proclaim that private property and the resulting market order will provide all that is necessary in both rule-formation and the security of the individual. Although individualist in temperament, the anarcho-libertarian does not reject the sociability of man but asserts primarily that private property and market exchange are inevitable under freedom and, secondly, that for them to be abolished would require a persistent level of coercion and violence that the anarchist must logically reject: that is, anarcho-communists could not practically reject private property as it will inevitably evolve, even if society were forced through revolution to begin again without private ownership.

Some may wish to add *militant anarchism*, but if the intention is merely to wreak havoc on present society, we can safely shuffle it off into nihilism; however, if the militant anarchist's goal is the destruction of the state and statism in order to bring forth the anarchic state, then its goals can be deposited either with the anarcho-communist or anarcho-libertarian cause. Most anarchic militants have been of the communist wing, although libertarians may point to the fictitious war of self-defence waged by the talented in Ayn Rand's *Atlas Shrugged*,[5] or the right to life and liberty that the Americans fought for in their War of Independence.

Since both major schools agree on the need for the absence of a coercive government, but differ on the means and the results, they will be examined in tandem, pointing out important differences where appropriate.

The absence of a state presents an appealing, romanticist image of the truly free man, free, that is, in the sense of not being beholden to any other person or institution; only then will man have the proper chance to develop untrammelled, uncoerced and, therefore, *naturally*. As Kropotkin maintained: 'The human freedom to which our eyes are raised is no negative abstraction of licence for individual egotism, whether it be massed collectively as majority rule or isolated as personal tyranny.'[6] Anarchists criticize present statist and bureaucratic conditions as being detrimental to the welfare and hence psychological and moral development of the individual man, for everywhere man is in chains – the chains of state control and the fetters of contrived legislation, most of it motivated by the interests of lobbying groups, a managerial class or ruling elite, or the chains of oppression forged by unnatural and detrimental cultures, or ideologies of class or racial segregation. In turn, anarchists complain that companies (protected by privileging legislation, the anarcho-libertarians add) can also produce a culture that is inimical to the true life of man – to his mental, physical and social development, which can only ascend to its natural heights in an atmosphere and polity of freedom.

We must acknowledge that in the history of anarchist thought, some have sought the spiritual salvation of man in anarchist communities, and while, in the West at least, such dreams have been replaced by more secular versions of individual freedom and growth, all anarchists believe that removing government and its institutions of coercion will create the proper conditions for people to thrive. Man is corrupted by the expanse of power surrounding, controlling and modelling him according to another's will if he is the subject of legislation, or becoming a mindless automaton if he works within the bureaucratic machine. Creativity requires freedom rather than rules and impositions, regulations defining what kind of person one ought to be: creativity and intellect are stifled under statism of any sort. The only apparent freedom to be gained in the state is one that the realist recognizes but which the anarchist absolutely rejects: the freedom to deploy power against others. But those who possess power, runs an ancient critique, are there by virtue of the acquies-cence of the multitude who passively or actively support them: they are thus puppets to the mob and are not free at all. If the leader cannot be free, then neither can the bureaucrat be free; and certainly not the controlled citizen – all such strictures on movement and mental development must be rejected to permit the unfettered freedom and potential growth of the individual.

The modern communalist vision of man, which originates in the literature of Gerrard Winstanley (1609–76) and his intellectual descendants such as William Godwin (1756–1836), considers private property to be a contrivance of the ruling class: its abolition will free man from the constraints of ownership. Unsurprisingly, this anar-chist vision is what Karl Marx turns to in his exposition of the future communist society following the (historically necessary) demise of socialism and its dictatorship of the proletariat. The communist-inclined anarchist follows Marx and Kropotkin in damning the divi-sion of labour that Adam Smith had hailed as the cause of the increase in the wealth of nations. Such resulting material prosperity comes at too high a price: 'The division of labour means labelling and stamping men for life – . . . And thereby they destroy the love of work and the capacity for invention . . .'[7] Dividing labour under-mines the individual's capacity for innovation it is conjectured. But innovation also distinctly comes from specialization: a great many inventions are the product of huge numbers of unknown people who have tinkered and messed around with their work, their tools and their methods – knowledge which then gets passed down into the vast pool of human capital. Presently, the world has never been so specialized and skilled, and it would not just be impractical to unravel people's specializations but hugely detrimental to social welfare. This is something the communist or communo-anarchist does not grapple well with: whence the skill to stop power plants from blowing up, or cars from seizing up, or roads to be repaired, if no one specializes? Or in the humorous words of Joyce Grenfell, who will sort out the drains?

The libertarian version, which in its modern form stems from (but is not unconditionally found in) the writings of John Locke, postulates the need for private property as necessary for the peace-ful society. Self-ownership is recognized by most anarchists, but only the anarcho-libertarians follow the Lockean argument to claim the natural right to private property for that person who mixes his labour with a resource. Therefore, if society were to begin again without property, private property would necessarily re-emerge both as a reflection of the natural right to ownership that Locke explains and as a result of people converging on efficient methods of production and exchange. With the development of private property, the division of labour will develop and flourish, if people perceive the benefits of specialization. That is, in a small community, A is better at fishing than B, who is better at gathering; by specializing in their labour the two of them dividing their labour can produce *more* than if they worked together on the same job. And the anarcho-libertarian does not see anything psychologically or sociologically unnatural in individuals using their innate or cultivated talents in successful production.

It should also be noted that much theoretical political attention is given to imaginary rudimentary societies and not much to the vast complexity of modern civilization: Hayek pointed out in the *Fatal Conceit* that socialization programmes are a cultural throwback to earlier times and that they do not rise to explaining the level of intricacy characteristic of the modern market economy.[8] Today, millions derive pleasure and/or income from occupations that cannot be even considered in the simple economies of hunting and gathering; some even prefer to work in mundane jobs because it provides them with a remuneration to pursue leisure activities, while others work at something for a relatively low income because it provides them with so much pleasure. The anarcho-libertarian rejects the communist version as thus simplistic and for not understanding either the complexity of markets or the subjective nature of value, relying instead on simplistic economy of barter and the labour theory of value (see Chapter 5 on socialism); extolling the virtues of individuality is pointless and mere rhetoric, the anarcho-libertarian retorts, unless it is backed up by a philosophy that supports a man's right to pursue life as he sees fit. Progress is defined by Ayn Rand as setting man free from men.[9]

We can see that both positions come together in their emphasis on the freedom from state control that is required for *authentic* living. A man cannot live the morally authentic life if he is registered, licensed and controlled; he cannot form free and (morally) equal relationships with people if others draw upon his income to fund their lifestyles, and if behind their back they wield the full panoply of guns and courts to enforce their morality.

Authentic living means being true to oneself: here the anarcho-communist enters a logistical minefield for he stresses the communal nature of humans and, perceiving them as members of a group, thereby denounces any egoistic flourishing that the anarcho-libertarian desires. Communal or individual life should become authentic in the sense that it will be removed from the oppressive regulation and coercion that emanates from the state. But it would be wrong to argue that anarcho-libertarianism necessarily leads to the solipsistic universe of independent egos that the conservative criticizes: as man is set free from men, he can choose his associations, and the very instinct to seek company and conservation, love and family, need not be overridden by the removal of legislation: the anchorite's existence is short and brutish, for he has renounced cooperation with his fellow men; but the anarchist is freed from the violence and depredation that princes and laws have wrought. Anarchists certainly tap into the romanticist idyll of the 'noble savage' living anarchically close to nature or into the Golden Age myths such as the Genesis story of Eden – it is their detractors who pose the alternative face of man as the face of deception, violence and war: a metaphysics that sees man as born in original sin.

Yet we enter problematic logical territory: if the success of anarchism depends on an assumption concerning human nature, then its critics may reject the assumption in favour of an opposing pessimistic or more complex one.

However, the anarchist need not rely on a priori conceptions of human nature – empirically, anarchic societies have existed and usually have survived very well, until impeded by interfering states. The early Jewish community is held to be anarchic, and unsurprisingly, given their emphasis on the Old Testament, seventeenth-century Puritans sought to rekindle the Jewish 'federation'. In the 1660s, Pennsylvanian Quakers enjoyed an anarchic experience which was thoroughly peaceful both within the community and with its external relations with Delaware Indians. The anarcho-communist emphasizes that evil and idleness stem from man's warped nature under state rule and the institution of private property. Remove both and man's need to secretly connive against his fellow privileged man disappears, and if then an individual prefers to act antisocially, there are many peaceful mechanisms to encourage a change of behaviour that do not necessitate the imposition of violent means. Historically, anarchists remind us that the state is relatively new, and other societies recorded by anthropologists exhibit forms of discipline against the unruly that do not require physical punishment.

The problem is that historically anarchic societies often possessed illiberal cultures that stifled individual creativity in other ways, either through the grip of religious and mystical fears or through other powerful moral restraints. The modern anarchists' broad acceptance and toleration of, say, sexual permissiveness, will not be found in most primitive societies that are upheld as peaceful rulerless communes: the modern anarchist seeks the moral plurality corresponding to modern civilization without the fastidious conservatism of the primitive.

Thus, in the absence of strict expectations driven home through powerful intersocial agreements on codes of conduct, the anarcho-communist, desirous of a permissive society, still faces the issue of what to do with the antisocial and possibly belligerent renegade, who, according to the rules of his society, has a right to the social product created and produced with or even against his input!

The anarcho-libertarians renounce any axiomatic assumption of man's nature – and thereby will gladly consider man's dispositions to deliberate evil – but they reject the need for a single mechanism to ensure harmony, particularly one that demands a monopoly of coercion and force within its area. They prefer to deduce the rules and principles of anarchy from the laws of human action and the principles of catallactics (market exchanges). For the anarcho-libertarian, man does not require a costly, monopolistic state to oversee or to plan his affairs, nor need he worry about having to surrender his own right of self-defence to a single organization that will typically turn around and abuse him: he can shop around and purchase defence or protection services on the competitive market. All the governmental apparatus of legislation and regulation that socialists and conservatives believe as indispensable for the smooth running of society, and which should accordingly be held only by the state, the anarcho-libertarian rejects. Neither does man need to change: all that is needed to be understood is that because man acts and seeks to better his affairs he will engage in contracts that will reduce the costs of insecurity and vulnerability – if he lives in a culture that is generally peaceful and cooperative, his security costs will be less relative to a man living in a more belligerent and untrustworthy culture or next to one (see private security below).

SOCIETY

It has already been established that the anarchist is not an advocate of the anchorite existence. Much anarchist thought, especially from the nineteenth and early twentieth centuries, stems from socialists, communists and syndicalists who look forward to an era of collectivism in which individuals are tied together by an overwhelming feeling of solidarity, which the state prevents from emerging. Without the state, people will be free to embrace the social life that they wish for, but, in the writings of most of the collectivist-oriented anarchists, this will be a life of moral and economic equality. In the most optimistic readings, there will be no prejudice or class or gender distinctions: no irreconcilable conflict will exist in the anarchist society, for conflict and antagonisms only emerge when some individuals are given privileged positions to intervene in others' lives; since the state deprives people of peaceful methods of resolution or introduces highly inefficient mechanisms, conflict and friction resulting from the resulting lack of proper security naturally result. Remove those privileges and all will be on an equal footing.

Anarcho-libertarians disagree with the egalitarian optimism of the Left: somewhat more conservative at heart, they recognize the perennial need for the intersocial prejudices that the conservative upholds as being useful for ensuring the formation and support of moral orders; different generations and genders will always have dissimilar values and mores, and the spontaneous society which anarchists seek to unleash may not lead to a homogeneously moral society. The anarcho-libertarian looks forward to a free world, but also one in which he may enjoy the freedom to exclude others from his private clubs or contracts, a freedom that the Left traditionally despairs of, but which the Right underlines that it is a man's prerogative to choose his company and associates. Irrational prejudices such as bigotry and racism are, moreover, costly for the individual actor to enact: it is relatively more expensive, say, for a racist to patronize his preferred shops or only work for people of his religion; so, let a man follow his irrationality if he so chooses, but also let him shoulder the cost of his prejudices.

Robert Nozick presented a caricature of anarchy that has its logical appeal and which has provoked much debate: so long as members are free to leave their societies, it does not matter what kind of society a people form – some may wish to uphold a feudal order, others a religious or cooperative commune, some may wish the unfettered rule of individualism, others the rule of the general will of the people.[10] Societies will survive like private clubs – so long as they attract and maintain members. But Nozick's characterization of anarchy has come under severe attack from anarcho-libertarians, for he posits the need for an overarching minimal state to ensure that no particular society imprisons members against their will by denying them the right of exit.

The specifics of the anarchic society will, despite the collectivist-cum-romanticist overtures that anarcho-communists have made, be unpredictable. If the anarcho-communist accepts that no force or quasi-state enterprise will be reintroduced to ensure equality of outcome in any human endeavour, the free society will become by definition the thoroughly open society that classical liberals lean towards yet pull back in Hobbesian fear of criminal opportunism or Lockean concern with its inconveniences. General anarchists may point to the creative force of artists, who may embrace 'anarchic' lives even in a statist society, and whose energy and talent display what could be set free once the chains are dropped; here, the anarcho-libertarians follow through and emphasize the productive capacity of relatively free societies, which outstrip collectively organized and planned societies: should absolute freedom be attained, humanity's creativity would know no bounds.

But what, the environmentalist replies, about the destruction of the planet's resources if uncontrolled free-market capitalism is unleashed? Anarcho-libertarians retort that such fears are unfounded: environmental destruction reflects a failure of the state to enforce property rights, either by failing to acknowledge them in the first place (e.g., fisheries) or failing to defend them from unlawful exploitation. Private property owners have an incentive not to pollute their neighbours' land, for they could sue for damages; but there is no incentive for the pollution of commonly held land, or land or resource rights protected by government, for if all own it then all may use or abuse the land as they please. Carson drew attention to the effects of pollutions and artificial fertilizers in the 1960s; but as long as the production of waste is subsidized by tax-funded refuse collection or encouraged by restrictive directives on how customers must be sold products, or farmers are subsidized to increase productivity regardless of consumption, then there will be higher levels of effluence and use of artificial fertilizers than otherwise. At this point, the anarcho-libertarian radically departs from the utopian vision of the anarcho-communist who envisages a green world without property rights, for without them, waste and resource exploitation are inevitable.

What, asks the socialist (and the paternalistic conservative), will happen to the poor in this anarchic state? The anarcho-communists believe that all will be provided for, but their economic understanding of production and distribution, when expanded upon, is at times naïve and often absent: resources for all do not suddenly appear out of nowhere, they require producing (and continually producing), even if that production is the mere harvesting of fruit from trees. Activities, gradations of value and use, necessarily enter into the equations. Some, drawing heavily on experiences of nineteenth-century or Third World poverty, claim that the mere distribution of the wealth and resources of the rich will suffice to end poverty. How, firstly, is this to be effected except through the imposition of force (taxation is enforced), which the anarchist allegedly rejects, and secondly, even if the wealth of the richest few were distributed equally and voluntarily (on an evangelical crusade 'to begin society anew'), that may temporarily give the poorest in the world a few extra dollars for a week, but what happens in the following week? Wealth results from production, and the more productive a person and society are, the more riches for all are created: wealth does not emanate from the conspicuous consumption of the few but from their productive capacity either as investors or owners of capital funds or equipment – a law that is as true for the rich as for the poor, but which is often ignored in much political thinking.

The anarcho-libertarian typically possesses a much more robust understanding of the principles of economics, which cannot be ignored by political philosophy, although the result may be disturbing to cherished views. The market system of private property and voluntary exchange that the anarcho-libertarian supports does ensure a tendency towards the most efficient use of resources in a constantly changing and adapting process. Change emanates from the altering values of people's desires as they relate to *both* production (i.e., a desire to work more, or less) *and* consumption; without private property and freedom of exchange there can be no economic calculation, and whilst the anarcho-communist accepts the need or use of trade, he rejects money and private property, which effectively would restrain trading and production patterns to the level of the playground. The anarcho-libertarian argues that since economic calculation will be more efficient in distributing resources, people will generally become wealthier than under any form of mixed or planned society. The poor will become richer as they have done in the freer societies over the past two centuries.

The socialist (and others) may justly demand what will happen to the poor who do not earn enough on the free market? Either they rely on private charity or they die, says Ted Honderich.[11] But is that a fair retort? The anti-statist could easily reply that in a centrally controlled society the poor either have to rely on state charity or die – or even 'and die', given the lower quality services of a mono-poly provider; but more importantly, the curtailing and even prohib-ition of wealth-making creativity that characterizes the free society, lowers the ability of families and individuals to purchase health and care resources. Evidently, the poorer in freer societies have greater access to health resources compared to unfree societies. When socialists give up attacking capitalism's wealth-producing capacity (and even Marx was indubitably admiring and hoped socialism could take over the productive capacity of capitalism without any deleterious effects on production), they have to revert to questions of justice: it is not right for some to earn more than others, while others go without. Justice demands economic as well as moral equal-ity – here the anarcho-communist re-enters and proclaims that that is what his anarchy will be like. The anarcho-libertarian response is that to assure an equality of outcome in which all receive the same would require an application of coercion and force inimical to the anarchist's designs. It is a powerful retort. A society can only be just if the freedom of each is maximized and the future left open so that those who seek to flourish may do so under the constraints of the laws of nature and of the market-place. I may be a great artist, but I will make no money if the public do not appreciate my art – and surely, it would be contrary to anarchist principles to enforce a redis-tribution of income from unappreciative philistines to support me.

But what of rules of social interaction? The anarchist does not reject rules *per se* but does reject legislation – the artificial rules of government imposed on the people. A ruleless society to anarchists would be a dangerous place; even the greatest 'egoistic individual-ists' such as Max Stirner claim the need for guiding rules. Others envisage that moral experts will naturally emerge in society; these will be men and women to whom people will turn to resolve crises or difficult situations; the evidence of natural elites in this regard is strong. Fascinatingly, the Master of Foxhounds (MFH) in England acted as a natural local counsellor and adviser to rural peoples, for his position required diplomatic connections around the hunting country with landowners and farmers; traditionally, folk were more likely to turn to the honest MFH than the usually corrupt MP. Similarly, within the community, children are dependent upon family for learning, young adults upon their elders – wisdom is itself unevenly distributed, which means that counsellors should be expected in society – these can be sociable authorities in matters moral and cultural or counsellors and guides who offer their services, just as today we turn to financial or legal advice and expect to pay for it.

Anarchists envisage authority without state, but when it is tied to the power and violence of the state, it is to be rejected. Authority corrupts human society and its individual members. It does so by first corrupting the nature of the man or woman using power, distorting their attempts at influencing others by empowering them to coerce others into following their policies, setting man against man; it corrupts the targets of authority by weakening their status into chattels or slaves to be ordered around, taxed, or forced into exchanges they would not normally agree to. Authority, for the anarchist, is distinguishable from the effects of wisdom and of the soft pressures of social interaction and guiding etiquette which anarchists believe are as necessary for peace as other political philosophies. A man should be free to follow his conscience and be free to encourage others to do so as well, but he has no right to impose his vision of the good on another. Relations should be characterized by voluntary interaction and the encouragement of the good, and, conversely, the disapprobation of unsociable activities. While some in the community may rise above others for their wisdom and expertise, and perhaps their ability to resolve conflict, they should not put on the garb and mysticism of kings. As we approach anarchy, the need for wisdom and moral authority to be chained to the institutions of coercion will fade and, as Woodcock reports, 'we shall reach a society where wisdom can be transmitted without the intervention of any institution, the society of moral men living in just relations – or, as we may say in modern phraseology, the society of pure anarchy'.[12]

STATE

The anarchist rejects the state as an unjustifiable organ of coercion and violence, blaming it for the horrors of war and subjugation of most of humanity throughout most of human history. Anarchism is, in the words of the early twentieth-century anarchist Emma Goldman, 'the theory that all forms of government rest on violence and are therefore wrong and harmful, as well as unnecessary'.[13] Arising from bullying belligerence and policy of murder, torture, imprisonment and enslavement, the state can only be supported by a force of arms, and concomitantly by the acquiescence of the people in accepting their lowly role as chattels of the governing classes. Accordingly, anarchists of all persuasions are extremely critical of the state and argue for its complete abolition.

The anarchist raises an important question when he asks, why do we need a state? 'A man has enough to do to look after himself without undertaking also to provide for the other citizens', quipped the Ancient Greek Aristippus. Socrates' dismissal of early Greek anarchism is that a man will either be a non-citizen, taking up none of the burdens of the state and thereby be a foreigner in his own town, or he will be ruled and have to pick up those burdens of citizenship: in other words, the anarchic life is impossible because that is not what life is like. The retort is immensely weak however, resting on a circular argument that we need a state because we have a state and we have a state because we obviously need one. But what other reason could there be? A state is necessary to avoid predation from others and to offer protection for the citizens, replies the typical chorus; but that predation results from empowering some individuals with the institutional capacity to take from and hence prey upon others in the first place: take that power away the anarchist replies, and civilians will ease themselves away from the discriminatory and rapacious thieving of governments. They will be able to pursue lives as they see fit, co-operating and assisting after their own fashion, than having a fashion foisted upon them. It is not people who corrupt the morals of others, but governments.

While the anarcho-communist vision of the future draws heavily on Marx's utopian musings on the end of socialism in the historicist (inevitable) process of capitalism – revolution – socialism – communism, anarchists reject the need for a heavily armed proletarian state as an intermediate step. But they disagree on how long cultures will need to adjust to the lack of government. Proudhon thought that once property is justly distributed to small-scale producers – he rejected communal ownership – this would be sufficient to encourage the state to wither away. And while some believe the death of the state will be sufficient to allow human society to flourish, others still believe that our nature must change for it to work. Kropotkin encourages a vision of mutual aid and solidarity in which members of the anarchic commune live off what they put into the social pool; without private property, the commune will work on 'from each according to his abilities, to each according to his needs', but if moral suasion does not encourage an idler to work, then, Kropotkin advises, he should 'go and look for other conditions elsewhere in the wide world, or else seek adherents and organise with them on novel principles. We prefer our own.'[14] The stabbing query remains though: what ought they to do if the idler does not wish to leave, or if the man is mentally incapable of understanding the need for cooperation? Small societies living very close to subsistence level cannot afford the charity that advanced civilizations can afford for care of the deficient and weak.

On the anarcho-libertarian side, no radical overhaul is believed necessary, for people will naturally and spontaneously converge on to mutually binding and benefiting rules: that is, the anarcho-libertarian believes that the freedom gained will be thoroughly sufficient for a society to produce all of its own commercial services, importing from other groups when necessary.

Much evidence does support the cooperative nature of humanity, and history-books often underplay the relatively peaceful arrangements that evolve and are sustained compared to the more obvious imprint that war has on life. Without the state, there will be peace on earth, concludes the anarchist. However, we may raise the problem that not all wars originate in state policy. Primitive wars, religious wars and ritualistic wars all exist below the political horizon in which the state monopolizes the forces of war and its declaration. Perhaps the belief that the state is the sole source of all strife is overly optimistic; after all, why do states come into existence in the first place? This requires serious attention from the anarchist.

Firstly, the existence of a human institution does not imply that it is the outcome of natural or voluntaristic choices. Analogously, Charles Goodhart (once chief adviser to the Bank of England whose name bears a law: Goodhart's Law suggests that any social statistic targeted by state policy will lose its relevance by virtue of being targeted) has argued that the central banks would have emerged independently of any legislation which in fact brought them into existence: a fallacious argument. That they did not emerge prior to active and protecting legislation partly refutes his argument, but that they also required secondary protection to force other free market institutions into their sphere completes the refutation. The fact that central banks were the product of legislation (and typically were created to serve the interests of the Crown by paying off its debt in cheaper paper bills) does not refute the argument that the state may have arisen naturally as monopolistic protection agency. Nozick claims that the minimal state will be the outcome of an 'invisible hand' process in which just as individuals seek to place their trust in a local security firm, so too will security firms place their trust and need for arbitration in another, third-party firm, which will develop naturally into a minimal state.

Secondly, the anarchist contends that opponents rely on a Hobbesian view of human nature which is neither historically supportable nor morally defensible. The Hobbesian view of life is that it is 'solitary, poor, nasty, brutish and short', in which a state is the inevitable outcome of man's fear of his neighbour's predation. The state is thus deployed to ensure that there is peace within its boundaries – a peace to be guaranteed at whatever cost. Freedoms become conditional upon the state's securing the peace, so if the freedom of contract or movement interferes with the peace of society as a whole, it should be curtailed. The guiding reasons behind Hobbes's thinking is that without the state and its apparatus of coercion there would be civil war, which is the worst condition in which humanity can find itself. Here anarchists face the rebuttal of all other theorists: even classical liberals and Objectivists recoil at the anarchist dream of peaceful interaction *sans état*. Hobbes's arguments are thoroughly rejected by the anarchist, as similarly, the anarchist rejects Locke's vision that the uncertainty and costs of knowing and implementing the law that he associates with anarchy prompts people to set up an overarching legislative body which they empower to assure citizens of the law and to enforce it. For the anarchist, this is the justification of the aggressor or the ruling party, and neither Hobbes's necessary nor Locke's pragmatic origins to the state give a good philosophical argument.

Hobbes's conception of the pre-governmental state of nature can be rejected on empirical and logical grounds. Empirically, most human interaction, the anarchist can confidently assert, is peaceful, and although communist anarchists would disagree (but more of them later), private property and exchange lead to peaceful interaction between peoples of different backgrounds, abilities and access to resources. Yet war also figures largely in human accounts, and it is this that the Hobbesian – whether a conservative, classical liberal, socialist or plain realist – fears. Objectivists decry that anarchism entails, in Peikoff's words, 'the view that every man should defend himself by using physical force against others whenever he feels like it'.[15] Accordingly, it is the ever-present threat of aggression that drives man to form a protective agency or to purchase protection services; but, the anarchist replies, does that have to be a monopoly agency which secures forcibly its dues for protection through taxes, and why would that ensure what Peikoff demands as 'objective standards of justice, crime, or proof'?[16] Once an organization gains the power to take resources from the people, it will inevitably seek to expand its jurisdiction of power whilst reneging to some extent or other on its protection. It has no incentive to be efficient either in the purchasing or deployment of security services and it has an excellent incentive to expand its net of taxpayers to secure even more funding for the classes of people who emerge to serve the government in its various functions. It certainly has no incentive to act justly; if the state does, it does so incidentally to its monopolistic and inefficiently self-serving purposes, the anarchist retorts.

Any government function can be supplied by private persons engaging in mutually beneficial trades, the anarcho-libertarian argues, so there is no reason for setting up government protection or insurance services in the first place. In one of the most interesting and not easily dismissed arguments of recent political philosophy, it has been argued that private individuals may wish to employ an insurance company to secure their property and to pay out if it is attacked or damaged by others, just as people can take out insurance and hire private security firms to patrol industrial and residential streets. To critics, such arrangements either display the failing of the state or an unjustifiable expansion of private sources of force and defence. Typically, they encourage it to re-secure its monopoly by either banning private security firms (which is as similarly malicious as prohibiting alternative medicine to the state-sponsored health service!) or by raising taxes on the citizenry to pay for more (inefficient) policing services.

Private policing is often summarily dismissed. Rand follows the usual critique of exploring a scenario of two men, one accusing the other of robbery, who call on their respective agencies to sort out the issue. Neither agency will accept the validity of the charge or recognize the other authority: 'What happens then? You take it from there.'[17] Presumably, we are to imagine that the agencies will fight, for that is what states would do, drawing funds through coerced taxation – and the domestic clash easily magnifies to the international clash, and this is precisely the point the anarchist is making, and Rand (a champion of capitalism) misses the important principle that characterizes free market exchange: private agencies have a great incentive to keep their costs low but also to ensure that justice is done for their clients. Defence companies will not wish to take on the criminally minded, for that would involve having to pay out higher costs for compensation incurred; such folk would become increasingly economically and socially isolated, thereby helping to solve the problem of the 'evil' men in our midst. Such companies would face great incentives to reduce the potential for costly combat and to resolve issues smoothly, just as insurance companies act to exchange and resolve claims; they would also charge higher premiums or refuse cover for people who act irrationally or without mindfulness of others. Individuals or groups of people seeking to wage aggressive war or violence against neighbours are not likely to secure insurance protection, whereas those defending their homes and property will do, and the peaceful will put more resources into defence.

Compare that to the statist model, the anarchist demands. A single security provider, the sovereign state, taxes both victims and criminals alike, and whether it does a good job or not or uses its resources effectively is not of its concern. Being a monopoly, it will tend to provide a poor-quality service at a high price, just as Western police forces do: low-crime but relatively richer areas are taxed proportionally more than high-crime but poorer areas, thus effecting a distribution of criminal resources via this implicit subsidy. (Compare the absurdity of older and more careful drivers cross-subsidizing the insurance premiums of younger and less careful drivers.) More importantly, the state can now expand its realm of intervention both domestically and internationally and its actions are not related to the costs it will incur, for other people (taxpayers) will foot the bill. The perverse incentive that state monopoly over defence and security creates goes a long way in explaining the history of war: not only are the funds easily drawn upon – the only limit being a domestic rebellion from onerous taxation, which has dwindled substantially in the West since the government monopolization of money and the abandonment of convertible currencies as well as an easy tax-base in the guise of corporation tax (businesses not possessing any extra votes for the taxes levied on them).

Unsurprisingly, the logic of the private security model has an enormous appeal to the anarchist of the libertarian persuasion, yet we must also consider its impact on the communist theory, for it depends on the existence and continuation of private property which the communist seeks to abolish. Could the abolition of property be sustained and peace still be secured?

If anarchy could be brought about through the peaceful or violent overthrow of the state, it has be asked why private property would disappear. Proudhon himself rejected its abandonment as utopian and, arguably, often the visionaries of communist anarchies are either silent or highly romantic about the nature of life that will unfold; some retreat to syndicalism – the idea that those presently working the resources will become their owner/care-takers; but what if they wish to trade in their resources to work elsewhere? After all, anarchism implies that we will be free to truck and trade. Otherwise, if no boundaries exist to secure individuals or small groups rights of access and control over 'their' resources again, what can stop another individual or group from also claiming access to the same resources? Even if for a moment we reject the temptation to parade the Hobbesian vision of vicious predators waiting to steal a chance to violate others' holdings, and accept a vision of individuals willing to agree on the use and distribution of a resource (and ignoring how that resource may actually be produced with no one in managerial control), the holders or present occupiers will face increasing costs of production and distribution if others similarly seek access. Without some mechanism of rationing access, the resource will soon be depleted or not produced or distributed efficiently.

If we seek the best answer possible, the communist anarchist may reply that while admitting the unequal distribution of resources, under present conditions human skills are only unequally distributed because of the fractious nature of existing social arrangements: private property creates iniquities that warp human nature away from its natural communal and sociable tendencies driving differences between people, as those who possess access to privately controlled resources are better able to invest in their children's education and skills, thereby perpetuating inequalities. In other words, the anarcho-communist seeks an alteration to human nature, not into a radically different species, which we may easily reject as visionary excesses, but a change acting through a radical overhaul of the culture into which man is born. The rage that anarchists on the Left unleash on the 'system' or the 'machine' is a rage motivated by realizing conditions are not as we would wish them; it is like a child's tantrum except the logic and influence of the rationalization are more biting and more devastatingly effective. The raging anarchist seeks to destroy all that does not fit into his immediate intellectual remit; he becomes a barbarian tearing at the contrivances and ethics he sees all around. However, we re-encounter his desire to reduce the artificial world of capitalist civilization to ruins in the statist philosophy of engineering society for the better: both wish to change human nature, it is just that the former seeks to do it more rapidly than the latter, and both aim at the equality of man amongst men.

Does the communo-anarchist's impatience for revolution and upheaval make sense? Evidently, humans differ in the expectations of self and other because of the culture in which they are brought up, and patently the moral and political expectations of the culture impinge on the individual's moral and social development. So, if humans are to be changed, and arguably for the better from the anarcho-communist position, then culture and all the institutions and apparatus that support it must be rejected. This is Marx's ultimate vision: when the state withers away, it will leave a classless anarchy in which each individual may freely pursue whatever course of production and action he wishes. But if we demand a little more from the anarcho-communist's vision, we will find there is a guiding standard drawn heavily from the golden-age legends reaching back into ancient times, of small, self-sufficient societies whose products were shared equally and for whose members life was contented and authentic. It is a vision that we pick up in some of the environmentalist literature.

However, it may be countered that the dream has its costs: several millions, if not billions, of people would be 'surplus' to political requirements and must somehow disappear. Demographic fears permeate the thinking of most political theories for a variety of reasons (environmental impact, production and distribution problems, dilution of racial or moral 'purities', etc.), but beyond the fear is an intractable biological and economic law that states that the size of a population is governed by its ability to support itself. Human population has expanded because of a successful expansion of its ability to produce resources required to support a growing population; conversely, the vision of a low-productive society necessitates a small population. What will happen to the millions who cannot thereby be supported by anarcho-communist production? They must die from starvation or be killed – and proponents of such visions rarely deign to believe themselves included in the fated.

But the connection to small-scale societies is not a logical one for the anarcho-communist. Proudhon and others believe that workers should free themselves from unequally distributed private property as well as from government but retain their capitalist production processes: i.e., they should not destroy the factories and offices they work in! They dream that life would be good, as modern production would not be rejected and competition would be replaced by mutuality and cooperation; the problems of production and control outlined above have not, however, impressed any serious economist, just as answering 'somehow' to a physicist on how to get a satellite into space. This leaves the anarcho-communist retreating to the utopian vision of small communities living decidedly close to nature – with all its implications.

INTERNATIONAL RELATIONS

War is the product of the state and its usurpation of coercion and force to assure its own interests; in gaining a monopoly on force, the state enslaves its people, whom it was meant to protect, and the enslavement of the people is a sure declaration of war on them. Classical liberals recognize this much, but reject tipping their logic past the minimalist state borders to which their implications take them. Despite the militant wing's bellicose desire to overthrow the rapacious and thieving state, a goal that some believe justifies armed defence and even attack and rebellion against the state (from *both* sides of anarchism it has to be stressed), anarchists look forward to a peaceful earth of cooperation across nominal borders.

All varieties of anarchism look upon national borders as political artifices, drawn by governments and resulting from wars and treaties that rarely reflect the wishes of the local people, who would prefer to be left to their own devices to get on with trading, exchanging and communicating with whomever they see fit, rather than be subject to interventions or distortionary taxes or prohibitions on various commodities and services. In contrast to much of state history, voluntary transactions and interactions between peoples of different cultures have been predominantly peaceful: European exploration and the expansion that became synonymous with imperialism was preceded, on the whole, by peaceful interaction and trade. When Portuguese traders first made their way down the west coast of Africa, after initial hostilities stemming from mutual suspicion and fear, both parties soon settled down to a convivial trade, which was disturbed only by the state-building principles of both kingdoms to secure monopolies on the taxes from the trade; fur-traders to Canada explored peaceably and learned local languages and customs, until the British government sought to impose a mercantile monopoly for the Hudson Bay Company. Often, the anarchist relates, evidence favours non-state interaction and thereby holds up a powerful foil to statism of all hues.

Conservatives may worry about the influx of culturally disturbing immigrants, ignoring much of human history in the process, but claiming that present institutions or practices ought to be defended against the values of incoming peoples, whose culture and beliefs may be radically different from those of the local population. Take away the state subsidies to migration, the anarchist replies, and who shall come shall come because they seek their natural home, just as the locality's ancestors once did. The anarcho-communist may have difficulty in resolving potential resource conflicts as new people enter, but the anarcho-libertarian will argue that the newcomers must engage the voluntary market to secure land or rent property; they will drive up the price of land and property in desirable areas, which will act to establish a new equilibrium not just of prices but also of cultural interaction – all done peacefully without intervention demanding that a certain quota of land be put aside for the immigrants (ghettoization), or that no land may be sold to them, etc. The anarcho-libertarian cannot see any problem in mass immigration, except in so far as present incentives to move are subsidized and distorted by welfare policies, taxes and state-induced wars.

We are left asking: is the vision so unrealistic, when the realism of the state has been so brutal and repressive?

NOTES

1 Peter Kropotkin, quoted in Ivan Avakumović and George Woodcock, *The Anarchist Prince: A Biographical Study of Peter Kropotkin* (London: T.V. Boardman, 1950), p. 209.
2 Jacques Pierre Brissot, quoted in George Woodcock, *Anarchism: A History of Libertarian Ideas and Movements* (Cleveland, OH: World Publishing, 1962), pp. 10–11.
3 Thomas Carlyle, *On Heroes, Hero-Worship and the Heroic in History* (New York: Frederick Stokes, 1888), p. 138.
4 Pierre Joseph Proudhon, quoted in Peter Marshall, *Demanding the Impossible* (London: Collins/Fontana, 1993), p. xvii.
5 Ayn Rand, *Atlas Shrugged* (New York: Signet, 1961).
6 Kropotkin, quoted in Avakumović and Woodcock, *The Anarchist Prince*, p. 322.
7 Ibid.
8 Friedrich von Hayek, *The Fatal Conceit: The Errors of Socialism* (London: Routledge, 1990), *passim*.
9 Ayn Rand, *The Fountainhead* (London: HarperCollins, 1961).
10 Robert Nozick, *Anarchy, State and Utopia* (New York: Basic Books, 1974).
11 Ted Honderich, *Conservatism* (Harmondsworth: Penguin, 1990), p. 97.
12 Kropotkin, quoted in Avakumović and Woodcock, *The Anarchist Prince*, p. 324.
13 Emma Goldman, *Anarchism and other Essays* (New York: Mother Earth Publishing, 1911), p. 56.
14 Kropotkin, quoted in Avakumović and Woodcock, *The Anarchist Prince*, p. 324.
15 Leonard Peikoff, *Objectivism: The Philosophy of Ayn Rand* (New York: Meridian, 1993), p. 371–2.
16 Ibid., p. 372.
17 Ayn Rand, *The Virtue of Selfishness* (New York: New American Library, 1964).

CHAPTER 9

ENVIRONMENTALISM

Environmentalism presents what can be considered as an attitude towards political visions, and may be compared to realism, in that both possess adherents whose beliefs stretch across the philosophical spectrum. Yet it would be superficial to claim that either is merely a political attitude and not a complete philosophy in its own right: a coherent philosophy can certainly be created from the wide-ranging conceptions under both banners. Thus, while a 'green' consciousness has spread through the major political parties of the West, and is increasingly part of the political culture of the citizenry, the precepts drawn from modern as well as ancient thinking can form a powerful ideology.

In contrast to the other ideologies presented in this book, environmentalism stands separately and distinctly for removing man from the centre of politics and replacing him with nature or the planet – generally speaking, his environment. Proponents refer to ecosophy (Naess's wisdom of the ecosphere) or deep ecology – the study of the natural metaphysical relationship between nature and man, emphasizing that man does not stand apart from nature. The planet provides the origin of all life in which man is inextricably bound, but the web of life is recognized as being fragile. This in itself is not a radical or deep political thought: the chance of life existing in the universe is, as far as we can presently tell, infinitesimally small and since there have been several mass extinctions in the past when the earth's atmosphere was affected by impacting meteors or exploding volcanoes, we become all too aware of life's vulnerability. As we advance our knowledge of the past and the effects that we currently have on the planet, our concern for the environment has understandably increased. But environmentalism demands more than just a nod to our ecological impact as found in the ideas of Jefferson or Thoreau: the earth and its multiplicity of environments (biosphere, biomes) should take precedence over anything that man can or should do.

This may seem a surprising or a critical claim, yet the overthrow of anthropocentric politics is what environmentalism seeks. Some supporters of environmentalism such as Passmore may not fully agree with the relegation of humanity either morally or politically, and prefer, like social democrats who baulk at the prospect of complete nationalization, to mix environmental elements with other philosophies. But we are concerned here not with the contradictions or inconsistencies that form the mainstay of everyday political life and commonplace thinking but with the essence or core philosophical ideas of the ideology. What does the ideology logically entail if we let the principles speak for themselves, and we do not allow our own peculiarities and wishes to mar their progress?

Environmentalism thus stands awkwardly in the pantheon of political philosophies, in maintaining that the dignity of man or of his society should be sacrificed to any supra-social or supra-human value such as the animal kingdom or the planet. Yet we may understand the environmentalists' denigration of man as similar to the demotion of society by anarchists, of individuals by socialists, or of peaceful relations by realists. The demotion of all human values and even human life itself should not be a bar to political thinking; after all, 'fundamentalists' of different religions often espouse policies inimical to cooperation and peace between peoples, and make antagonistic policies a way of life, and war more likely. Moreover, the environmentalist will retort that the demotion of man is not required because man is hated (although in some environmentalist quarters that conclusion is not held back), but because man has disrupted the natural equilibrium of the planet; his impact has, typically considered in the modern era, been thoroughly negative. Pollution, overpopulation and exploitation of resources on hitherto unknown scales leaves man with too much power, and that power (often seen, as in Marxism, as economic) and its effects must be countered before it is 'too late'. By that, the environmentalist implies that the earth will enter a dangerous phase of climate change, or that there will be mass extinctions or other calamities. This secular vision of impending disaster complements the theology of millenarianism and no doubt taps into the same ancient emotional roots that humanity must atone for its sentience, pride, technology and progress. For the environmentalist, the disequilibrium fostered by man must be addressed politically, ethically and legally. The main philosophical foundations upon which modern civilization is built must be examined and rejected when they lead to a presumptuous destruction of the environment.

Many environmentalist sentiments have a long history reaching back into the dim cultural perception that our ancestors had 'lost something' when they settled down into increasingly complicated civil societies: a prior 'golden age', often synonymous with man's pre-historic 'innocence' and closeness to nature. Such atavism maintains a strong grip on human imagination, as does the corollary thought that we have lost an idyllic beginning by advancing our technology and correspondingly inflating our hubris (pride). That golden age has often been translated into a new vision for the future in the various utopian tracts that have been produced over the centuries of explicit philosophizing: such tracts range from extolling the natural peacefulness of man, before advanced civilization twisted his morals into aggression, competition and war, to those that assert a mythical past of animal and human equality in which no predation occurred by any species upon any other. The latter presents a historically false picture of the past, yet its legendary undertones can certainly be read in some 'animal rights' literature or even in the great satires upon man's inhumanity to man in which men turn to vegetarianism and war disappears, or they release animals from domesticity and even inter-species aggression ends. Politically, regardless of whether they recall a golden and environmentally friendly past, or the ancient philosophical threads that disdain either man or his achievements or both, the environmentalists champion a new golden age of peaceful coexistence and clean living, and argue that a political apparatus – usually, but not necessarily, the state – is to be used to enact that vision.

Historically, the modern environmentalist movement can trace its origins to Romanticism, which emerged in the late eighteenth century. Romanticism sought, generally speaking, to remind Western man of the greatness of nature and the limits of his control over it. Romanticists rejected the characterization of the 'Age of Reason' in which, as its critics argued, the indefinable and incommensurable values of emotion and natural beauty had been rejected in favour of the application of the mind and Newtonian mathematics to life and the universe. The Romanticists sought to draw our attention to the ineffable sublimity of the world and to realize that despite the technological inroads that human scientific and engineering endeavour could make, nature always had to be obeyed. Scientists knew this – after all, they were dealing with nature's laws every day and were therefore more aware of their own limitations than non-scientific critics. But a fearful thread ran through a broad range of concerns that were levelled against science and progress, which caught intellectual and popular imagination, that man may tamper with and unleash forces beyond his control, for which he would have to pay dearly, either with the loss of his soul or materially with his life or the lives of others.

The engineering and industrial society developing out of the scientific revolution prompted fears of a Moloch-like god devouring the lives of simple folk and driving the inventors and industrialists into satanic pursuits of knowledge and wealth; for their own sake, it is implied, rather than for the sake of something else. In early romantic writings that something else was the soul or conscience of man, or the idyllic image of the noble savage, the vision of a prehistoric man, unencumbered by modern civilization, or any trappings of civilization at all, who lived close to nature. We read of such idylls today – in sympathetic anthropological accounts of touring journalists in search of Eden and the noble savages of the Amazonian rainforest, the North American plains, or the jungles of Borneo, who are heralded as better people than modern man.

Modern environmentalism presents a collection of ideas from which a coherent political philosophy can be produced: one that alters political values to assert the primacy of the planet over that of humanity. Like many ideologies, it splits into particular variations on a theme, but one particular *idée fixe* is that of the romantic ideal of a better life for man lived closer to nature – removing the artificiality of civilization and returning to a simpler way of life.

Yet what is better in the rudimentary life of the barely economically developed? Some exude a jealousy for the proximity to the flows of natural life with its alleged simplicity; others wistfully regret the strong cultural bonds such peoples possess that have been lost in the advance of civilization. The complaints of the latter we can hear in the other political philosophies – the conservative who grieves for the loss of longstanding traditions, the socialist who mourns the collapse of communal property, the anarchist who bemoans the loss of perfect freedom – for those complaints can justly govern anthropocentric political visions. But the former ideal – that envy of the non-civilized state of nature, of life lived fully in the heart of nature, typically lived by the few, struggling and defining themselves as naturally as possible as individuals and as collectives – forms a core environmentalist principle. Man remains, but advanced civilization is renounced for being thoroughly exploitative of nature's bounty, for being destructive of nature's beauty and for cultivating competitive and bellicose tendencies that inevitably spill out into social and international violence.

Much that is paraded under the environmentalist banner is logically and scientifically confusing. It is not because the philosophy is new that confusion reigns. Adherents throw extrapolations into arguments as facts with little knowledge of scientific method; we are asked to accept on faith obvious conclusions drawn from weak data (to 'believe in' global warming instead of understanding potential causes); or clear implications of general trends from single events are asserted (a hurricane is evidence of man's destruction of the planet). This is not good science. For the philosopher, all things ought to be questioned and questioned deeply, never accepting at face value *alleged* scientific assertions or emotive ejaculations concerning man's destructiveness and implied innate evil.

The language of environmentalism has overtaken the language of socialism and libertarianism, and that should not be ignored or underestimated. But popularity, often stemming from state-funded research or unscientific and deep cultural fears of what may come to be promulgated by the media, is no guarantor of philosophical validity or truth. Millenarians have frequently appeared doom-saying; the problem we face is sifting out the wheat from the chaff, the evidence from the concoctions and the wild extrapolations from statistical trends.

Politically, our duty is to explore the particular premises upon which environmentalism is built, and to question not just what is being implied but also what political vision it logically entails. To bow our heads to the green men in deference to their putative custodianship of the planet is to reject philosophy, and to reject philosophy is to condemn our future to a myopic life of instinct and emotion, which may sound more natural to followers of Rousseau, but which in practice tends to violence and destruction of man and the planet.

MAN

For the environmentalist, man is at once an animal species no better, biologically speaking, than any other species; he also stands apart, however, from all other species by virtue of his rational capacity, and it is this ability that presents the environmentalist with a grave dilemma: should man's mind be upheld and cherished as the potential saviour of the planet from the problems his species has created or faces, or should it be condemned outright as being the originator of those problems? The division plagues not just environmentalism, for man's mind patently can unleash great benefits to himself and his environment as well as great costs – he may turn his intelligence just as much to war as to peaceful interaction.

Generally speaking, environmentalists remain sceptical of man's mental abilities to resolve the problems he is creating by virtue of living. They look back to a cleaner and less cluttered world, when humanity's numbers were barely a million or so and scattered across the world. These environmentalists imply such images in their criticism of the densely populated cities – or at least we can infer that is what they imply. Although few may explicate that the prehistoric vision is what they see as best for man, many may take on the trappings of early culture in their dress (but rarely employ sincerely the harsher ethic that such an existence would entail); others may perceive that man's golden age lay in the medieval period, before the growth of sprawling cities, and dovetail their thinking with socialists for whom the guild system was the epitome of small groups of operatives working together for the common good (that the dream does not reflect the reality is another matter). In the city, man is far removed from his natural environment and therefore severed from the impact that his producing and consuming has on the planet. Immersed in the great nexus of international market exchange, he loses touch with the natural flows of life, and his rites and rituals, once so intimately part of the great life-cycle, are so far stretched from their roots as to make them meaningless to modern participants. For progressively minded philosophers, such advances may not amount to anything deleterious but simply reflect a changing or advancing culture. For the environmentalist, however, they are indicative of man's loss of his natural roots – hence, the dream that man may use his mind to resolve the problems of his environment is an arrogant and contrived dream: the vision, let's say, of the urbanite far removed from the green vistas of life which he desires to shape according to his own mental images of what they should look like (which fields should be conserved, which species protected) and not leave them to their own devices.

The unleashing of reason – of logic and science – frightens the anti-intellectual environmentalist who sees in its result nothing but destruction. Man is thus not to be trusted; his thinking takes him away from the interplay of life and death and hence away from his true interests. These values are defined by the nature of his biological species – minus his mind, that is. Yet there are those who cherish humanity's powerful tool, which has evidently enabled men to lift themselves out of a vulnerable tribal existence to that of being a highly successful species. After all, from a grand biological perspective, any species that expands its numbers and its longevity must be doing something right: if red squirrels were seen to adapt to the incursion of greys and their numbers increased, we would cheer them on. However, the worry amongst most environmentalists is how far we can let humanity proceed unchecked. Is man to be trusted to calm his reproductive drive and the consequent impact of higher numbers on his environment, and is he, more broadly speaking, to be trusted to diminish that impact by choosing a way of life that will complement the needs of nature rather than conflict with them? Optimists within the environmentalist camp accept that man can change his values and therefore turn his mind to the needs of nature, whereas the pessimists hold no such hope. Thinkers across the range of environmentalist political philosophy assert different solutions for the mental dilemma humanity faces. Some claim that a *laissez-faire* attitude will be sufficient to secure a better and greener future for man; if left to their own devices – and typically without government intervention in their choices – people will converge naturally on an environmentally friendly view of life. The economic consequences of depleting resources and of polluting their neighbours' lands will ensure that environmental problems will diminish to reasonable (natural) levels. However, pessimists argue that left to his own devices man is rapacious and myopic – he needs secure direction from powerful governments and their agencies, without which he will trash the planet and sow the seeds of his own destruction. The political solution thus emerges: man must be forced to be more natural.

It follows that man's life evolves best (i.e., most naturally) when it is as close to the land as possible. Here environmentalism connects with the politics of blood and soil – of toiling on the land (in what might be called an eco-niche), generation after generation, being shaped ethically, culturally and politically by the environment of forest, mountain, desert, tundra or jungle. Contented is the man who works the same land as his ancestors and conversely how unhappy is the man who is removed from the land of his ancestors and finds himself living in a high-rise apartment. Happiness – or the virtuous life – can only be attained by the man who lives closest to nature, who engages consciously (and thus authentically) with the environment around him. Practically, he should thus seek to cultivate the land around him in a manner that is in harmony with the landscape: in other words, to the extent that the environmentalist permits a moral vision of man working the earth, he should farm on a small scale, seeking to mix his crops and stock rather than rely on a single product, and he should set aside areas to retain a natural wilderness to encourage biodiversity. The vision of the small-holding complements the aesthetics of many environmentalists who berate man's contrived urban living – and it certainly drives the dream of many Westerners who look upon the countryside as their natural abode.

SOCIETY

Human society is an aggregation of individuals, and political thinkers often focus on the group rather than the individual for their analysis and exploration of political dreams and goals. Politics for such thinkers (indeed most political thinkers) involves looking at how the group may best live – either because their policies will ensure the best lives of the individual members or the best potential for the group as a whole regardless of its impact on certain individuals.

As we have seen, the environmentalist inverts politics. Eco-politics should not involve the conception of society standing alone and independent of the environment, but should begin with fully recognizing man's close connections to his natural state. Anything above and beyond the basic human drives is to be shunned or ignored in defining an eco-politics, for that is when the distortions of our values enter and we turn our back on the planet and its protective biosphere, viewing it, at worst, as something dispensable.

Released from the strong tie to the soil and the natural cycle, the group is likely to magnify the myopia of the individual, permitting individual members to ignore effects that they may have through free-riding on the assumed less destructive actions of others. The workings of the market – human interaction in production and exchange – may generate environmental costs that are not borne by the traders, and which, if unchecked, may slowly build up to catastrophic levels. This is when politics, as it is traditionally understood as the employment of power for collective ends, may be harnessed to guide society in its choices and to enforce taxes upon producers and consumers that reflect the unseen costs of environmental damage.

Not all environmentalists reject science and progress – some such as Passmore acknowledge that science and technology enable humanity to live an environmentally cleaner existence, and typically go on to demand that the state should encourage behaviour – production and consumption – that will support biodiversity or a reduction in noxious gases and other effluence. But then again, some misanthropic environmentalists cannot but see humanity as being the cause of all the earth's problems (or at least those that can be directly traceable to human action) and argue that the planet would be better off without man. But whom, we must ask: which men and women should either kill themselves or stop reproducing? Unless the advocate has committed suicide, or at least presents a sincere intention to do so, to save the planet from himself and thereby dissipate his molecules harmlessly (i.e., without conscience or sentience to bother them) back into the world, we can only conjecture that such people imply in their wishes that *other* people ought to give up their lives, so that the few, the truly green few should inherit the custody of the earth as it was meant to be. With any such proposal we may ask why the many should sacrifice themselves for the sake of the few (or the few for the majority), and what gives this elite the moral supremacy to demand such sacrifice? Custody of the planet may be the vision that such environmentalists invoke, either explicitly or implicitly, that the planet will be better looked after in *their* hands than in the hands of the multitudes who now devastate the planet in pursuit of their own self-interest. But if the pursuit of self-interest is rejected in favour of environmental guardianship, we must push our enquiry and ask what, or whom, is the ultimate beneficiary? The answer that the misanthropic environmentalist proposes can only be the planet – it is for the planet that millions must sacrifice their lives: they must die, so that the planet may live.

The argument may seem extreme to those who prefer to uphold human life (each and every individual) as being intensely precious, yet its format is ancient. In the past, the gods were to be appeased by human sacrifice and many of those gods were gods of the natural orders – the sun, the moon, the woods, the rivers, etc. Men, women and children were to give their lives up to the earth, so the earth may return them a bountiful harvest or secure them from the ravaging vengeance of the angry sea or wind gods. But the misanthropic environmentalist can retort that the ancients, who lived closer to nature, were right in the demands for restricting human advancement, or pride, or even population: a hurricane or tsunami are quickly mustered as evidence of man's abuse of the planet, for even if such events cannot be traced directly to man, the impact on lives certainly can. However, hurricanes which peter out in mid-ocean are assuredly less indicative of man's culpability, and with all arguments for sacrificing victims, a bolder justification of the victims' lack of moral worth must be proposed.

Most demands for sacrifice relate to ameliorating human affairs: communists sought the blood of capitalists, whom they believed were living parasitically on workers; revolutionary anarchists desired to kill those in authority; pagans of many cultures believed the wives and slaves of the king or hero had to be sacrificed to ensure their service in the other world; or people were to be killed to appease or feed their gods. But the misanthropic environmentalist rekindles an ancient belief in the inherent sinful or evil nature of man and cloaks it in quasi-scientific language. Perhaps that would mean that anyone may be sacrificed to ensure the survival of the planet and that this type of environmentalist would not lament the deaths of thousands in manmade disasters (and sometimes a gleeful smugness is evident in their descriptions of such disasters); nonetheless, moral thinkers would certainly challenge the direct or indirect killing of any people, especially children, whom most would agree cannot be held culpable in any way for their parents' destruction of the planet.

From the extraordinary position of misanthropic environmentalists who envisage a world without man (or at least a part of the present population), most environmentalists would reject any policy of killing people, but would accept some form of control or regulation of human activity for greener ends. Controls still imply the need for sacrifice – a demand that all people, or some, relinquish present living standards or choices, in favour of the perceived interests of the planet. The adjective 'perceived' has to be added, for it is specific people with particular philosophical ideas creating particular values that they believe others should abide by. Yet values do not spring from the earth itself – it is upon our interpretation of the facts around us that we build our thoughts: we perceive an entity, think of it as beautiful or useful, and impose upon it a value. Sometimes that value may ascend to sacred status – we ought never to touch or to adulterate the entity, for it is 'holy'. Many cultures have promoted 'sacred groves' that may not to be violated and which are accessible only to a priestly class, and modern environmentalist demands echo those commands in barring access to economic exploitation or human residence: in so arguing, they seek to impose an objective or intrinsic value upon a particular environment.

Political visions of prohibiting access to environments emanate from people, for human beings are the only political species on the planet. There may be some disagreement about being the only cultural species, as some of the higher animals are able to learn socially and pass on such learning to offspring, but humanity is the only species capable of claiming 'we should put the planet first' or 'we should not reproduce' or 'we should conserve this ancient forest from human predation' – no other species thinks or acts like that. Values are purely subjective in origin – or intrasubjective – in that they are the product of thinking and sentient beings; but against the subjectivity of value, environmentalists stress that values are intrinsic – that certain entities or actions are valuable in themselves with or without human evaluation. Thus a lake may be said to possess intrinsic value above and beyond any human use for it, and regardless of whether humans could gain any advantage from it whatsoever.

In the long run, environmentalist visions converge on a sustainable existence, with human society living in harmony with nature. Society should become sufficiently self-directed to ensure that it does not pollute the environment or kill animals wantonly. Yet a gross division emerges in environmentalism: should human society remain, intellectually speaking, separate from the rest of the animal kingdom, or should its prerogatives and rights be accorded to other animals? In some respects, the question of 'animal rights' belongs to ethics: what kind of life ought we to live, asks the ethicist, and we may ask to spell out what is meant by 'we'. The definition of 'moral personhood' (the defining criterion of ethical existence) ought to be expanded beyond the human species, according to animal rights thinkers, which obviously impacts on how politics is viewed. Animal rights advocates (who may or may not be environmentalists) demand a wholesale review of our definitions of politics, law and ethics. It is presumptuous for a single species, a minor one on a small branch of nature's broad and diverse evolutionary tree, to assume hegemony over the rest of the world: animals ought to be brought within normal ethics, or man ought to be ejected from his arrogant position and all speciesist laws and morals (e.g., our right to domesticate, eat, or kill other animals) cast aside.

Thinking about this, a disparity emerges in the environmentalist movement between those who propose a vision of man reconnecting with his natural environment and those who baulk at the prospect of, for example, hunting: often the forceful ethic and corresponding political dimension of animal rights intrudes into the daily working of environmentalism. (To study nature requires an active and potentially disturbing presence, which worries some environmentalists.) To return to a state of nature closer to the natural rhythms of life would certainly entail an embracing of the hunt with its rites of life, death and killing. The rites and rituals emerge from the deep recesses of prehistory, and seek to remind hunters and followers of the deep ecology of the chase. However, the urban mindset, so far removed from the soil and the reasons, customs and values of farming and hunting, rarely connects its own perception of environmentalism with the bucolic vestiges beyond the suburbs. Partly, that disparity is sustained by the belief that all violence will end once man returns to arcadia and a strict non-intervention in natural affairs, but often it is sustained by a driving emotional attachment to love life in all its guises, regardless of any inconsistencies that may develop in arguing for arcadia and for animal rights.

Thus environmentalist society must explain the membership of that society, something that the other philosophies do not have to resolve – for the anarchist, the conservative, the socialist, etc., that society is human. If we remove the ambiguity by pushing through the misanthropic environmentalist philosophy to clarify the logical conclusions to be drawn from its premises, we may end up with a world *without* man. For such an environmentalist, the planet comes before man. If we disappeared, the world would 'be better off'. The brutality of such a stark conclusion may appeal to few environmentalists, leaving the rest to argue over the ambiguity of social membership: should it include animals as full members, or just exclude property ownership of them? Or do we retain an anthropocentric ethic and assert man's right to live off the planet just as we accept the fox's right to live off the duck, grouse, pheasant, etc?. At such a juncture the philosopher may baulk – if man's position is denigrated to equate to that of the rest of the animal kingdom (assumedly with no gradation between wolves, rats, starlings, flies, snails, etc.), either society must refrain from doing what has been, generally speaking, in its nature and history (predating for meat) or it must be thrown back into the wilderness to survive on a par with the rest of the animal kingdom – and live according to primordial drives of blood-lust and rapacity.

GOVERNMENT

Government is simultaneously a despised artifice and a potential vehicle for environmentalist policies.

Free market environmentalists of both the libertarian and anarchist variety argue strongly that much environmental destruction is caused by too much state activity (after all, the state has little incentive not to create environmental costs), and/or by a lack of property rights. The latter thesis provides a powerful argument that few recognize, mainly because property is seen as the bastion of capitalist society and capitalism is portrayed as the resource-consuming beast that creates environmental problems in the first place. Theory and evidence show otherwise: when property rights are identified and properly enforced, environmental destruction is minimized, as owners have an incentive to keep waste and costs low. Some may complain that the imposition of a property right on the land is a contrivance to be avoided in the first place, for the land would not be then exploited, but the absence of a property right is no guarantee that the land would not be used and abused: communal ownership or a lack of ownership permits overproduction should people become interested in the land's resources, for there is no incentive to ensure sustainability or environmentally effective use by its users. Private ownership entails a thoroughly different attitude and therefore use: an owner of a timber plot faces a range of incentives (based on what other people would want to give him for his resources or for the land itself) and he will tend to choose what best reflects his interest in the land. That may mean denuding the land of timber in favour of building houses, but as a manager of the land, he has to ensure that the land's value provides him with a source of value (not necessarily income as such) over a period of time. If he does not take care of his plot, its value (derived from what others would exchange for it) will drop relative to other prices; if he overexploits the land, he reduces his own ability to earn a return in the future. The property-owner has to be sensitive to the land's use now and in the future and faces distinct incentives to conserve and manage it well.

Other environmentalists disagree. The argument for common ownership fails on economic principles (laws of human action that wishful thinking cannot alter), so the argument against private ownership turns on the need for active government intervention. Private owners may ensure that their needs are met now and in the future, and private ownership may thus far be an effective vehicle for conserving the environment and its resources, but even landowners do not look that far into the future or take into consideration the wider ecological impact their activity may imply. The free market environmentalist may accept the landowner's decision to clear a forest for a building-site, but the interventionist will demand a greater justification. There is no guarantee, he will retort, that the private owner understands or that the price mechanism takes into account the wider environmental or long-term impact (such as depletion of the ozone) of his decision. Government and its traditional apparatus of coercion must therefore intervene in private decisions to impose upon owners the 'true' environmental cost of any action – taxing those who use certain resources and subsidizing those whose actions are deemed more 'environmentally friendly'.

The free market advocate will reply that the third-person perspective of what constitutes a proper evaluation of resource use is arbitrary, and represents a violation of voluntary exchange, and builds into the price mechanism improper distortions that can only lead to a worse use of resources and therefore greater environmental destruction than otherwise would take place. For example, subsidizing technologically expensive alternatives to carbon-based fuels encourages industry to go down paths that it would not have taken, and forces consumers to pay more (through the taxes raised to subsidize the pet environmentally friendly projects) and thereby reduce expenditures on devices that they may have bought to reduce their own waste. The intricate web and the interdependency of prices means that any intervention into voluntary choice will create unintended and often unwanted effects. Similarly, the introduction of 'environmental pricing', taxes or subsidies that are based on alleged scientific reports on the effects of human choice upon the environment, can be exposed as arbitrary and politically motivated decisions that again create unwanted effects. To secure a landscape from development, environmental institutions impose prohibitions or taxes – but upon what grounds are the officials' estimates and decrees established? California prohibits off-shore drilling for oil, says the cynic, so America becomes increasingly dependent on supplies from the Middle East and gets involved in its affairs to secure resources it could easily tap into in its own backyard. More pertinently, why is this landscape chosen as sacrosanct, or that animal's environment to be saved and not another's? The sceptic may note the traditional political processes involved – the lobbying and backroom deals that are far removed from 'scientific evidence' (i.e., arbitrary economic assessments by third parties), but it can also be asked why 'scientific evidence' should only incorporate the welfare of a forest or a snail but not people.

The environmentalist, we have seen, rejects the emphasis on human society, so it will be right, in his eyes, to ignore human welfare or to relegate it below that of the voiceless animal kingdom which man all too readily subjugates. The historic advance of the modern state into human affairs therefore provides a useful vehicle to impose upon individual and societal choice an environmental manifesto, and so environmentalism fits easily into statism – the political philosophy of assuming the validity and political and moral efficacy of state action. The only barrier to advancement of a green agenda becomes the particular political processes that restrain green policies: voting systems that underrepresent environmentalist parties, for example, or even the lack of voting power in the animal kingdom, and therefore the need for impartial human representatives of the animal voice. Ancient rites of the hunt may have evoked the spirit and voice of the prey – or the spirits of the wood – but that has been all but been lost in the cacophony of modernity, so their voices must be given fair representation in the social contract: government must redress the present imbalance in favour of the planet.

INTERNATIONAL RELATIONS

An interesting element emerges from environmentalism regarding international relations. In general, environmentalists place little hope in traditional or mainstream statist politics. They seek to gain the support of international agencies – both voluntary and governmental – to secure environmental policies, such as agreement on climate change. National efforts to alter carbon emissions, for example, can only fail in the absence of collective effort: CO_2 emissions, they remind us, do not respect national borders.

In their particular critique, the great producers of the world are singled out as creating the worst problems (which usually translates as the West being at fault for producing too much of everything and creating a 'throwaway society'); these countries must lead the way in agreeing to combine legislation and codes to reduce emissions. Proponents of 'Third World' development reject the need for controls arguing that they need to produce pollution, just as the West has done, in order to develop economically, before they can afford cleaner energy solutions. At this juncture, summits are held, emission quotas are haggled over and sceptics suspect that the winners are usually the conference delegates and hosts rather than the planet; environmentalists may argue that they are necessary to raise political consciousness, and although rarely rising to their expectations, do a service in reminding people of the need to think about man's effect on the environment.

However, environmentalism also possesses a nationalistic side. The romanticist idyll of generations toiling on the same landscape, being moulded by the land and mixing their blood with the soil, lends itself to nationalistic sentiments of the pureness of blood and race. It is not surprising to find that Hitler and his National Socialists were environmentalists, for they peddled the Teutonic myths of the love of environment, animals, vegetarianism, and the corresponding blood-and-soil duet. The purity of the race was deemed intimately linked with the purity of the landscape, from which foreigners were to be barred. The Nazis possessed no monopoly on such thinking – it has a deep history that prevails (subconsciously perhaps) in blood-and-soil myths; interestingly, there is presently a Libertarian National Socialist Green Party – the confusion of titles designed to market to all potential converts, no doubt, but whose policies demand individual autonomy, collective ownership, separate homelands for different peoples and a green agenda.

Usually modern environmentalism is frustrated by state policies and state borders – it generally echoes the anarchist's and libertarian's criticism of the artificiality of political borders – and activists seek to fight the planet's cause on an international rather than just a local scale, while mustering resources 'to green' political and cultural ideas.

CHAPTER 10

APPLIED POLITICAL PHILOSOPHY

The application of philosophy to politics is where we encounter political ideas and their impact. Politics surrounds us – most head-lines involve politicians and their ideas on how people ought to live their lives; often they disagree and accentuate the nuances between them but periodically more radical ideas are brought to the fore and sometimes they manage to shift the entire paradigm of debate – such was the Whig ascendancy of the eighteenth century, the social reform movement of the early nineteenth, the socialist movement of the mid to late nineteenth century, the various forms of totalitari-anism in the first half of the twentieth century, and the liberalism of the post-war period.

What motivates any human action is a desire to change one set of circumstances for another, whatever those circumstances may be. The goals and ambitions we form hinge upon ideas, but a person acting alone or in a group may effect that change in two fundamen-tally different ways – peacefully or violently, and politicians must choose between the two. Peacefully means encouraging the volun-tary assistance of others whether in exchange, gifting or mutual assistance on a common project. Violently means deploying force or its threat to effect a change in processes or outcomes. That is, I can encourage you to help in my project by appealing to your own inter-ests by offering remuneration or other rewards or by appealing to our friendship or communal benefits that will accrue if we help each other; or I can threaten to beat you up, torture or kill you, take your property or income away, or constrain you against your will if you do not work for the project.

The choice between peace and violence is indeed stark but think of any project and consider whether it has an underlying application of force (e.g., taxes or threats of imprisonment). But many people encourage a confusion of overlapping terms to argue in favour of force with words of peace: you should give up your time, property, energy, life for reasons of 'equality' or 'justice' or 'environment' or 'God' or 'the State' or 'the Queen' or 'the country'. Many lives have been lost and property confiscated in the name of such abstracts, whether we like to hear about them or not. Confusing the terms is a common ploy, one the Romans were quite adept at (enter a country to 'broker a peace deal' between two belligerents and end up master of both). It is also a ruse that has not disappeared from human discourse – some may even sincerely believe in the abstracts to which they demand that others bend the knee, but whether they follow through themselves is a matter of political biography and the judgements of sincerity or hypocrisy.

When it is pointed out to political thinkers and activists that their project involves a subtle or not so subtle threat of force, the reaction is often indignant and one is denounced as immoral or thoughtless or barbaric for some reason – can one truly be against the state or its interests, one's race, God, the environment, or the great banners or equality, justice and freedom? But the distinction between the two methods of human interaction is there, regardless of the emotional pain it may cause some to have their policies laid out as violent intrusions. While the indignant can be judged as hypocritical or thoughtless, the more honest enthusiasts may accept that violence is a justified means to achieve some noble or moral goal (arguing that the end justifies the means), which returns us to the realm of thinking about and examining carefully the grounds upon which violence is to be justified, against whom, in what measures and for how long. Defending violent means for their own sake is very difficult, but defending them for an overarching goal becomes more understandable, if difficult to assess in terms of the costs and benefits.

Politics may thus proceed peacefully or violently. Leaders or vocal thinkers may encourage us to work for particular causes such as defending our territory or building a bridge or celebrating the past or honouring sportsmen and women; or they may presume to use the power of the state to force such projects upon us against our will; or at least against the will of those who would prefer not to cooperate. Such is the stark contrast that we must accept: then we choose accordingly – peace or violence. There is no in-between in means deployed.

The breadth of force that is employed to secure cooperation increases from libertarianism through conservatism, statism and socialism – that is, the libertarian demands state action in very few areas (police, courts, military – all securing life and property), whereas the socialist believes it to be necessary in all areas of production, distribution and consumption. While the breadth of political action increases with the advance of the state into social affairs, the concentration of force need not alter at all. The intensity of the imposition of a fine or of the locking away of a citizen or of an execution do not change as such, except that in the more totalitarian (extreme statist, however construed) systems arbitrary measures are often deployed to instil fear across the entire population, so that the stopping of a citizen may or may not involve his arrest, and an arrest may or may not entail an execution depending on the whims of the officials involved. In such societies, life is controlled to its fullest by political processes: nothing is to escape the vigilance of the authorities, who maintain their grip on the people through division and fear.

Once we leave the stateless polity of the anarchists, who rely on communal morals, or elders spontaneously evolving morals, or even private security companies to keep the peace, the balance between securing the good state and providing so much power that officials may be tempted to abuse their prerogative becomes the driving aim of much political philosophy. The Platonic tradition derived from his *Republic* stresses the need for a thorough and equal education for the citizens, which eventually divides them into three main social strata; the highest strata will run the polity, the middle will defend it, while the lowest strata will provide for it. Control over everybody's actions and strict boundaries on the permissible, will, for Plato, provide for a strong and healthy polity. The utopian elements that are part of the *Republic* nonetheless provide a lasting vision of political thinkers' designs down through the centuries: the dream of a better society motivates many a plan. But dissenters proclaim the horror of permitting the one (monarchy), the few (oligarchy), or the many (democracy) to rule on behalf of anyone else – the one or few over the many, the many over the few. The ancients were aware of the dangers involved in all the known political systems of the day – supporters claiming that the other systems necessarily collapsed into tyranny.

The modern labels for the philosophies that are examined in this work (Statism, Realism, Conservatism, Socialism, Libertarianism,

Liberalism, Anarchism and Environmentalism) seek to explain how the good life may be promoted through political change. They are not quite the same as the Ancient Greek ideals, as societies and economies have changed enormously since then. Nonetheless, each idealism has its supporters who believe that the others must collapse into chaos or tyranny, so we face the archetypal Charybdis and Scylla between which modern statesmen and theoreticians seek to steer their polities. Radical thinkers reject the metaphor however: the dilemma or the implicit fear besetting politics is imaginary, a device like Marx's religion acting as the opium of the people to keep the faith in the existence of the state. Thus the anarchist reminds us to assail the assumptions on which we base our own political theory, for assumptions can be dangerous when unchallenged.

Securing the peace is precisely the state's purpose for many thinkers, but detractors will complain that it is the state that generates war and violence in the first place by imposing regulations, demands and taxes that necessarily disturb the peace. But there will always be people who will exploit their fellows by stealing, abusing, threatening and fighting; why else, Thomas Hobbes asks, do we lock our doors at night and take precautions against our neighbour's trespass? Thus we need a state to secure our lives and property. Without property, we would not need a state, Rousseau retorts, for property – the distinction of 'mine and thine' – separates man artificially from his neighbour. Without property, there would be economic chaos, reply the libertarians and anarcho-libertarians, and economic chaos would keep the poor poor and the powerful rich. And so it goes, as Kurt Vonnegut would say, shrugging for the many who become dizzy at this point.

Dizziness is however a powerful tool to induce apathy in people – especially voters. If people are apathetic, they are less likely to challenge the status quo and established political elites are less likely to lose power. Thus the need to think and to be critical (rather than be just negative) of political thought, thinking through arguments and their implications. The stakes, as many people in the world find, are high – peace or war, cooperation or violence.

In this last chapter I shall accordingly be taking a critical look at several topics that fire current debate to show how we can raise some inquiries: the nature of law; the problem of war; the rise of globalization; internationalism, nationalism and secession. Much of the critique is mainstream – the kinds of notions that philosophers are trained to consider, but some of it is less so and thereby may probe readers' cherished beliefs. Philosophy, a thankless task at times, seeks, in its love of wisdom, to keep the mind sharp – if a cherished belief is challenged, you are free to uphold it regardless, or you are free to consider it deeply; and either return to it gratified in your justification or reject it as a superficiality that does not accord with other beliefs you may possess.

LAW

The rule of law is the attempt to secure consistency and coherency in the application of formalized codes through a community. A distinction can, however, be drawn between legislation and law which has interesting political repercussions.

Consider this theory: a core element of life in a community is the emergence of expected codes of conduct that rarely need to be explicated (e.g, as expounded by Montesquieu, Hume, and Hayek). So much interaction takes place without the need for written rules that our attention needs to be drawn to those processes that assist rule formation – the implied mutual benefits of cooperation and the unstated costs of non-compliance. Social interaction would thus produce commonly understood rules through an ongoing process of convergence – action, exchange, avoidance, association, education, all serve to promote a continuous contract of expected behaviour. Children learn those expectations swiftly and generally cooperate with the broad rules of social life, unless there are extraneous incentives not to; similarly with adults – compliance with the unwritten expectations of life is less costly than non-compliance, and the incentive structures they face go a long way in explaining why most people abide by the rules and only a few renege on them. But what happens when people do renege on the law?

For the anarchist, the voluntary rule of law as governed by social expectation is sufficient to secure peace. The problem that arises for critics is what should one do with the man who does not believe in peace, who seeks to undermine the benefits that the rest of the population enjoys, who aims to wreck social cohesion through violence and intimidation? The anarchist would prefer ostracism – forceful if necessary – arguing that he must not be welcome in their community. Anarchism (especially the left-wing variety) presumes that membership is conditional upon abiding by the generally expected rules of conduct, which seems understandable. (But what strength does a moral demand possess, if not backed by force? Or is that a straw man argument, for if the renegade purchases property and lives peacefully among his enemies, then surely he may justifiably be left in peace or ignored as people see fit.) Those of other ethical persuasions may accordingly deem the general rules intolerable: for instance, we may all implicitly agree that punching another person is unacceptable (outside a sports ring that is) and that the aggressor should atone or compensate his victim or be ousted from the community; but not wearing a niqab veil is just as customarily offensive to others – should such an offence merit ostracism? For some it should: the non-compliant citizen is always free to leave to find less intolerant lands. Others denounce the imposition of particular values on individuals as an invasion of their individual rights to property and lifestyle, which when held as the 'trump card' override the value of any umbrage some may take: I may thus be as obnoxious as I wish, so long, the argument goes, as I do no physical harm. Even in the pure property based rule and interaction of anarcho-libertarianism, individual differences and disagreements will not disappear – why would a political system be presumed to be able to change human nature? That needs consideration, for if human nature cannot be changed then we must search for that social and political system best suited to the limited range of human potential – a very Aristotelian quest indeed.

Statist thinkers approach law differently. The law is what the state enacts, not what the people implicitly converge on: what is permitted is permitted by decree, rather than any notions of freedom of action and of morality independent of the state. The law, that is 'acts of legislation', is described as positive law, whereas constitutional law prescribes how the state's apparatus and its officials should work and what their limits and remits should be. However, as the state expands, its jurisdiction necessarily intervenes more in non-political affairs until politicians typically begin to see their role as defining through legislation how people ought to live in the minutiae of their daily lives. This the libertarian baulks at, for he prefers the state to remain tightly limited to criminal and foreign affairs; the conservatives accept some intrusion of legislation especially in matters of morality (e.g., ages of consent); environmentalists applaud planet and animal defending laws; and the socialist sees politics as reaching into commercial matters and forcing a continuous redistribution of income from the relatively more productive to the relatively less productive. Interestingly, realists keep a pragmatic eye on legislation – as Machiavelli instructed his Prince, government should not intervene in the traditional liberties of the people otherwise it will lose its power base should they revolt, so the law should reflect whatever requirement sustains the establishment and its interests.

Thus how a society is to run depends on how the law is viewed by the various theories. Anarchists believe there is no need for anything greater than customary rules, whereas most theorists side with Hobbes and assume that in the absence of codified laws on conduct and state powers to proscribe and to punish, life would be intolerably violent and uncertain.

But to return to the argument that divides legislation from law. If legislation differs from the law, it may be justly rejected and the state's officers resisted. Many philosophers may accept such a division but then differ on how to respond to a growing wedge between perceived morals, which may be held as universal or customary but prior to any political legislation, and the legislation passed by a political body. If such a potential wedge is admitted, then we must ask if resistance becomes justifiable and to what extent? Is merely raising one's voice sufficient? Rarely so, history teaches us. So should people turn to violence and disorder to show their displeasure or fear of losing their rights? History apparently shows the effectiveness of such rebellions, but, conservatives warn, a closer look will find a mixed empirical bag – more restrictive governments often follow revolutions. Freedom of expression and voting are the hallmarks of liberal democracy, but, as John Stuart Mill would argue, they rarely remain sufficient bulwarks against the tyranny of the majority. Should each individual bear arms? (While there is evidence that private gun ownership tends to reduce violent crime, there is apparently no guarantee that it would also protect citizens from a gradually encroaching government as some Americans tend to believe.)

Arguably, the greatest defence against state legislation violating commonly held laws are ideas – but the expression of critical opinion requires a supporting cultural and political framework, and if a political philosophy seeks to restrain criticism, then it lends itself to a totalitarian disposition in which legislation becomes arbitrary and destructive. Some of the greatest thinkers warned of the totalitarian leanings of arbitrary legislation, voices we could do well to listen to in an era of legal multiplicity.

The separation of law from legislation presents an intriguing position from which to judge and discuss acts of Parliament or Congress, but the political philosophy of law continues into other realms to ask such questions as: when a crime is committed, should the criminal recompense his victim or society? Do individual citizens retain a right to self-defence or revenge? May a person be put to death for his or her crimes? On a higher plane, we can ask whether law is a reflection of reason or consensus, fiat or human nature?

WAR

War undoubtedly is violent and uncertain. It is an open-ended conflict, or threat of conflict, by opposing sides, which can only see that the aggressive overthrow and defeat of the other can resolve their initial quarrel. Most thinkers claim war to involve groups of people who merge together into armies to fight – but John Locke argues that war begins with one man settling a design of violence (or fraud) upon another. This avoids ascertaining the number of violent participants which constitute a war, but it does not help to distinguish between duels and family feuds. For the individualist, this does not matter: that an individual shoots at me in a battle or in a duel still constitutes a murderous attack on my life. Collectivists, on the other hand, of all political persuasions worry less about the life of the individual than the continuity of the group – their focus is more on the total that fight and die.

The explanations of war are found in the particular philosophies of each theory. Statists, conservatives, and most libertarians believe war originates where there is an absence of government (or effective government), whereas socialists generally claim war to arise from property and class relations, but then they divide on whether or not war is necessary to purify society of the culture of property and class division (as Marxists tend to argue for). Anarchists blame the institution of government, for government is necessarily invasive and coercive regardless whether its violence is enacted on the domestic or international front. Environmentalists charge humanity as a whole as waging war on the planet (and sometimes stress war's environmental impact over the impact on humanity), and claim war's origins to be peculiarly human – that is, a product of our (genetic) nature, and which acts to blight our existence on earth.

Can there be any justification for initiating aggression against another human being? For libertarians and anarchists the initiation of aggression destroys the implied peace between men and threatens the moral sanctity of the individual; and rights theorists emphasize that certain rights (such as the right to life and the pursuit of happiness) are inalienable, which means that no other individual or government apparatus may take them away. The moral inviolability of life therefore justifies stopping aggressors (and therefore rejects an absolute pacifism), but can it extend to physically punishing or killing them in turn? Logistically, the area is complex: Hobbesians deny that a man's right (even that of a criminal's) to self-preservation can be taken from him, while Lockeans claim that the initiation of aggression forfeits an aggressor of any right to life and he may be disposed of as the defender sees fit – he may be justly enslaved or killed. Conservatives temper the justification of self-defence with the need for a collective or cultural concept of punishment: the aggressor may deserve punishment, but that punishment should be decided by the impartial officials of the state, not by revengeful individuals; some libertarians accept the usefulness of impartiality; but others stress that most arbitration and the securing of damages will emerge in the market place with insurance companies negotiating claims (as they presently do in many areas of civil damage) rather than in the state's organs.

Clausewitz, a realist, argued that war is the continuation of politics by other means. That is, he assumes that political processes are not inherently warlike (which the anarchist rejects), but that all wars are a justifiable extension of politics into other realms of choice backed by extraordinary state powers – the armed forces. War is thus governed by political decision-making, hence the generals are subject to political goals and the broad strategies of their political masters. But often in history warriors have taken up the political reins and blurred the distinction between military and political interests to create a realist's dream of military rule. This many thinkers cannot accept – the men of violence should remain separate from the political processes: they enact the rule and force of law both within and without the polity, but they should not rise to the executive office unless they remove their military garb, and cut all their connections to the armed forces.

Outside, or complementary to, the great political ideologies, we find just war theorists, who note how expectations of common conduct emerge in warfare regardless of political intent or codification of rules. Even in continuous protracted violence individuals recognize mutually benefiting rules that they obey through implicit understandings with the enemy – such rules evolve into powerful cultural codes whose breach incurs severe disapprobation (often clothed in terms of 'honour'). Such processes again give credence to the anarchist conception of life, a philosophy that tends to be quickly dismissed but which retains a fascination for those who do study it: in rejecting states and artificial borders, individuals and their communities would be free to evolve their own forms of behaviour and codes of conduct, and those codes will continue to evolve over generations and across interacting peoples. So long as there are no artificial impediments to intercourse, there should be no reason for concerted or persistent violence to break out, and the rare occasions in which an individual or gang sought to impose its will aggressively upon citizens could be met with cooperative defence and punishment by those concerned.

Critics of war may remind us of the power of irrational drives that overwhelm the attempt to secure peace through freedom. Tribalism – the adherence to the group and its implied and explicated aims – is a most influential force in human life; it produces a grip on the mind of the individual, providing him with a powerful sense of belonging and hence identity. When the trappings and apparel of the tribe are dropped, the individual may act rationally (i.e., peacefully) towards all he meets, but the adorning of tribal garments and the consequent focusing of the mind on the status and honour of the tribe diminishes his ability to act independently. Philosophically, we each may espouse dogmas but they become potentially anti-social and even conducive to aggression and evil once they are framed by group identity and action.

The antidote, liberals and libertarians proclaim, is in the freeing of man from men – the realization of choice and the expansion of freedom to choose a life other than that of an immediate surrounding group. Cultural pluralism encourages toleration and the acceptance of dissent (in behaviour and in thought), and plurality expands with the advancement of voluntaristic exchange – in other words, with markets, art, music, literature, love, and other forms of interpersonal interaction and exchange. When the state (for it can only be the state) panders to particular interest groups it fosters economic and national tribalism, pitting certain producers or consumers against others, reducing the normal complexities and overlapping matrices of free exchange to the warlike posture of two (or more) groups facing each other with apparently irreconcilable differences that only violence (pushing the politics of the situation into other means) can resolve. The open society of classical liberalism is pluralistic because it permits individuals to forge relationships on many different levels with others of their choosing. But for some that plurality, so embraced by humanists from the sixteenth century onward, drives people away from the customary rules and expectations that have held their culture in place, giving people a ready identity and often a common purpose, and if war is to be risked for the identity of the group then that is a permissible risk. (Michael Ignatieff's work on 'blood and belonging' is especially apt here.)

When we look critically at war, the philosopher must evaluate the governing ideas behind the war: what apparently justifies the violence (justice, self-defence, human rights) is in turn open to analysis. If war is to be waged to defend a nation, what is it about the nation that is worth defending? (Would you fight for your President, Prime Minister, the Inland Revenue, the mass media?) If it is a war of justice, what conception of justice is being proposed, or if for human rights, not only must we ask whether it is right to contravene some people's rights to defend others (after all, in war people die) but also what kind of rights are presumed? To what extent, if at all, must a woman subjugate herself to others' values? Is it better to fight and die for one's country (and think of Wilfred Owen's war poems) or to survive? What is honour and should it play a role in personal decisions? The questions begin to unfold with a rapidity that must be checked here in favour of the reader turning to more appropriate works.

GLOBALIZATION

A phenomenon that cannot be avoided in political philosophy is the increased global nature of economics, culture, and hence political interaction. What is important to consider is how the different political theories react to what is generally agreed to be a force of change beyond the reach of traditional political apparatuses. The global market in produce and services is enormous; and makes all trading nations highly interdependent upon one another. That interdependency is at once a cause for praise and for concern – as international trade has always been.

It is a fact that resources are unevenly distributed around the world, just as skills are unevenly distributed across a population. In the labour market, it has long been recognized that specialization permits people to earn higher returns and also provides the greatest public benefits. The freer and more open societies engage in a division and specialization of labour and production that the ancients recognized as being more productive and hence more beneficial than assigning employment arbitrarily regardless of aptitude or interest. It took more thought to understand that it is more mutually beneficial to trade with specialists than to enslave them, although the Nazis and Soviets ignored that ancient lesson much to their ultimate cost. The same is true of resource access, which is, in many respects, a reflection of specialized labour (e.g., good coffee growers tend to be found in good coffee growing areas).

The propaganda of special interest groups (and there are many) notwithstanding, the economic principle of comparative advantage clarifies how nations may mutually benefit from trade, even if one nation possesses more resources in all areas of production than the others. Some consider that the principle of comparative trade is a 'dogma' or a faith – it is not: while particular economic circumstances complicate the picture, it remains *apodictically* true that trading nations benefit from trade by specialising in that which they are relatively better at producing. Just as a lawyer who types quicker than her secretary can maximize her earnings by concentrating on the higher paying legal work, so too can the secretary earn more: and more importantly, specialization increases joint productivity. Similarly, nations can enjoy higher returns by specializing in producing those products or services that they possess a comparative advantage in. It is not necessary to take an economics degree to understand the principle of comparative advantage, for it is comprehensible in all that we do and in all that surrounds us in market economies – we benefit when we purchase the services of specialists. However, economic principles are often the first casualties in political discourse when both proponents and opponents discuss globalization. This would be risible were the laws of physics jettisoned to argue over famine in the Sudan, but economic illiteracy is considered to be no bar to discussing the same subject. Philosophers are at times particularly prone to expounding ignorantly on economics, but because of a general economic illiteracy, they are not seen to make the gaffes that would expose their ignorance should they preach on medicine or chemistry without having studied those areas.

Thus, when we turn our attention to the globalization phenomenon, we must recognize the principles of international human action that will govern human affairs regardless of national, continental, Western, Eastern, Southern, racial or religious sentiments or interests on the subject. When trade is free (truly free and without subsidy, control, quota or tax), producers will concentrate on producing those products and services that they are best at (by virtue of their cultural or individual skills, or by virtue of access to desired resources) and consumers (i.e., producers of other products) will benefit greatly from exchange. Total world wealth tends to increase as people specialize. In a world without barriers to migration, people will move away from poorly resourced areas and places of low productivity to areas of higher returns, thereby producing a tendency to equalize world incomes. But the states' barriers to migration stop that; we see the effects of migration within countries, where people are free to move from one area to another and most people in the West would find it highly unacceptable to stop a woman from moving to another city to earn a higher income: but the present international community limits the natural migration of peoples. Nonetheless, as David Ricardo explained, even when labour is not mobile across nations, the principle of comparative advantage can still uphold that widely differing nations may benefit from specialization and trade. That is the principle behind free trade: even with migration barriers, trade tends to produce more.

Some do not like it, but before they can advance their dislike, they must comprehend the principles involved: I may not *like* gravity and would prefer to fly unaided, but it is a fact of my existence – similarly with the principle of comparative advantage and free exchange.

The principle of comparative advantage is logically irrefutable. Some may point to particular economies not seemingly benefiting from freedom of trade, but then we must ask: were they losing a particular specialization at the time? Were demand or supply conditions changing (i.e., consumer or producer preferences)? Were technological innovations occurring elsewhere to attract workers from their initial specialization? Were the critics trying to protect their own production or interest groups? Sometimes it is difficult to understand the principles involved when human action and choice is in ceaseless flux and spread across the decisions of millions, but the underlying principles remain.

Having understood that, the critic of globalization can therefore proceed authentically and *honestly*. If he wishes his nation to tax imports of Japanese cars or to impose quotas on Chinese brassieres he must acknowledge that his nation's people will be made *worse off* as a result. Domestic car and underwear producers may be worse off under free trade, for they have to compete with cheaper foreign imports, but consumers will save and thus have more resources to spend on other services. That others can make such products cheaper cannot be wished away. Nevertheless, that protection damages a nation's wealth is not a sufficient reason to avoid imposing a tariff. Being authentic here means explaining that this tariff will make you poorer; that it will protect relatively inefficient producers at the cost of your household budget; but that we think it necessary to sacrifice your wealth to support this particular branch of industry. Perhaps the honest message might not sell, but at least it will not be wrapped in a host of economic fallacies and confusions that border on downright lies.

When French youth rioted in the Spring of 2006 against attempts to liberalize labour laws, we must understand that they were fighting to protect their wages against competition from the masses of unemployed in the cities, who, given the chance of employment, would drive wages below the 'acceptable' rates for middle class students. So the unemployed remain unemployed and socially volatile (as the previous November's riots exposed), while those in work retain their privileges.

Now, if the critic of globalization wishes to proceed, he must seek other justifications for impoverishing the many while privileging the few. For instance, he may argue that trade disturbs cultural purity and that a nation or people have a right to secure their cultural inheritance from foreign influence. The statist theoreticians will justify such intervention by virtue of political representation – if the majority (or whatever mechanism serves to produce representation) demand protection from foreign culture, legislation should be enacted to protect the people. The 'liberal' (i.e., social democrat hanging on to classical liberal principles) will baulk at the imposition of majority will on a minority and the socialist may tie himself up in wondering which producer class (or nationality) to defend, but the anarcho-libertarian will dismiss such a justification as entailing an indefensible intrusion into individual choice: if young French people prefer to listen to British or American rock, that is their freedom – to impose quotas of French content upon their radio stations violates the liberty of radio stations to choose their music according to the tastes of their listeners.

Why should a woman not buy Chinese made underwear for half the price of European made underwear? Some explain that the Chinese run sweat shops, which means that they employ people for less 'acceptable' wages (acceptable to the critic, that is). How would *not* buying produce from the Chinese encourage sweat shop wages to rise? Or why is it presumed that a Chinese worker cannot make a decision regarding whom to work for, under what conditions, and at what wage? Why should the European manufacturers be supported by the consumer? Is it a form of patriotism to wear EU underwear? The economic analysis can extend beyond this (and become even more rhetorical!): it gets us thinking, but other thinkers have sought to provide a broader justification of nationalist protection against globalization.

Realists will assert that a nation weakens itself by becoming interdependent on foreign nations that may in time become enemies. It would be a false economy, they assert, to purchase tanks and weaponry from a potential enemy and thereby reduce the domestic arms industry. The argument is appealing and often used around wartime to secure protection for domestic weapons producers. Turning it around however shows how it too can be undermined: should the soldiers fighting battles be forced to bear substandard and/or more expensive arms? What general would wish that upon his troops? As long as a nation does not cut off its trade routes, it should have no fear of getting access to the products it wishes to purchase; it is the cutting off of trade routes in the name of military strategy or protecting domestic producers that inevitably lowers an army's ability to fight (or the domestic population to feed itself), as various generals have found to their cost.

Globalization implies increased interdependency in the world and from most perspectives that can only bring about good things, as many philosophers in the classical liberal and humanist veins have argued: better understanding of foreign peoples through trade; reduced frequency of famines; quicker help in times of natural disasters; reduced tribalism or nationalism; and improved wealth for the world. Opponents, when they do not rely on emotive assertions and when they do not misunderstand the economics of the international trade, resort to moral or cultural justifications for securing or maintaining the barriers between peoples, but we can also see how the movement towards increased interdependency undermines many traditional political conceptions.

The polity has generally been understood as a local legislative and executive power, held by one, few, or many. The local nature of its remit clashes with the international outlook of traders and migrants who are constantly seeking better living standards and this inevitably increases with globalization: good access to high value resources will attract incomers and thereby destabilize the local culture and nature of politics (as many conservative thinkers stress), whereas high local taxes will drive traders away; or if the polity forbids them egress, trade is driven underground. Only extremely totalitarian societies have managed to prohibit the natural disposition to migrate to better areas and markets with higher returns: but the more that they impose controls on civilians, the more likely the governing classes are to become corruptible, as the temptations of abusing official power increases correspondingly, and conflict and civil war become more likely.

If a great many of the civilians' lives – cultural and economic – are outward looking (enjoying the music or better electronics of another country), the polity can only become increasingly parochial looking. Certain societies eschew foreign or modern contact as part of their cultural upbringing, just as an individual in a free society may avoid styles of popular music or dress: as long as they are free to choose their avoidance, liberals and libertarians allow that there can be no moral problem. But the issue grows to the extent that political processes arrogate that choice and limit or forbid such freedom. As it raises barriers to free exchange and even free association, the political unit falls out of step with the dynamic outside world – its people become poorer both materially and spiritually; a tribalism is imposed to defend its culture while the rest of the world becomes increasingly cosmopolitan. There are many examples of countries shutting borders to foreign influence, and the decision to avoid what is often seen as the detrimental effects of free trade is understandable from a patronizing perspective (not sarcastically meant). But if the right of exit is simultaneously removed, then a stronger justification of the imprisonment of an entire nation must be forthcoming. While we can leave that to ethicists to consider, the converse should also be noted: throughout human history, people have migrated to make a better life for themselves (as we see within nations or customs unions such as the EU), yet over the past century barriers have risen across Western nations to make migration harder or even impossible. Special interest groups (especially unions) demand controls or prohibitions on free immigration to protect their wages. Each country has its own particular codes violating the principle of freedom of movement across polities – in particular, over the last century the West has acted to make migration from poorer countries difficult. The impact on the world – as environmentalists should note – is more disastrous.

Assume that the world is warming and that this climatic change will impinge upon the ability of many coastal peoples to survive as sea waters rise. The anarchist, the free-market libertarian and the economically literate environmentalist will understand that those affected will wish to seek life and employment elsewhere, even swapping higher wages but higher risk for lower wages and lower risks. Global warming may open up new farming opportunities in presently cooler nations, for example, to which climate refugees may wish to move. However, trade and migration barriers will stop their influx, prompting them to remain in relatively more populous areas where they will be unable to earn a higher living. This will prolong their poverty unnecessarily, and any disaster befalling them (natural or manmade) arguably must sit on the consciences of those who refuse entry. When migrant populations are bottlenecked, social tensions arise from their frustrations – they may become dependent upon charitable aid to sustain their material existence, but sooner or later political radicals will demand action against those who frustrate their lives. In such places, men of violence can always find willing conscripts.

The gravest indictment of globalization is that it is not the result of a level playing field. Well-financed governments consort with large tax-paying companies to secure markets in a manner not dissimilar to the mercantilist protectionists of the eighteenth century, who acknowledged the benefits of increased trade, but who believed that one nation's gain was another's loss. Mercantilists thus promoted nationalistic trading – securing monopolies with foreign markets by armed force and then taxing the artificially bloated companies through monopoly grants. Many of the eighteenth century's wars involving Britain and France can be understood in this light. Today, the relationships between companies and governments are less easily detected, but critics capably point them out – what is sometimes ignored is that such relationships will always flourish when states act to privilege some markets or traders at the expense of freedom of exchange. In this respect, globalization is not a flourishing of open trade and free migration, but the advancement of domestic politics on to the international stage, and critics rightly note how the political machinations of large economies (or their established elites) interfere with the domestic programmes of small nations and even justify military intervention (aggressive war and occupation).

INTERNATIONALISM AND NATIONALISM

To avoid an increasing parochialism in the face of obvious globalization of markets and culture, countries may amalgamate power in federal systems, pooling taxes and sharing jurisdictions. Such is the European Union, which was anticipated by the United States of America; however, where the latter produced an explicit federation, the former has yet to form a fully agreed political body. The everyday politics of the EU creates intriguing as well as disconcerting stories – of corruption and unaccountable enforcement of power against the ideal of international cooperation to smooth out exchange and legislation between member states. The original postulate behind the EU was to ensure peace between member states – nations that had, after all, waged severe and protracted wars for many centuries. To supporters, it has succeeded in removing the seeds of war between, say, the Germans and the French, but for opponents it has failed to resolve more pressing concerns on the environment or external relations with other nations, getting involved in protracted trade wars to the detriment of the world's poor or subsidizing economic or political programmes in non-EU nations (e.g., Palestine).

Philosophically, if we rise above the particular issues facing the EU, we can envisage the potential of an overarching polity that may possess the power and relevance to tackle the incidental effects of globalization. This argument implies that only big government, or supranational institutions can rise to meet the challenges of a global market – sorting out immigration concerns by distributing migrants across several nations, reducing currency market fluctuations by forming a common currency, protecting the environment with common standards and ensuring member states do not pollute their neighbours with impunity, and, from a realist perspective, providing sufficient military might to redress any perceived imbalances in the global order (which was one of the main motives behind the EU – to form an independent bulwark between the USA and the Soviet Union during the Cold War).

What dominates such thinking is the assumption that big is better, or that force of numbers matters in political philosophy. The realist will certainly propose the expansion of governmental jurisdiction to include more people and more resources (and higher salaries for officials), adjusting the proposition to acknowledge that vast jurisdictions also tend to lose political cohesion and may engender rebellion, especially if they encompass disparate peoples. The history of empires is replete with increasing demands upon distant populations who eventually were aggrieved enough to rebel, putting further demands on other subject peoples and in turn sowing further rebellious seeds. Imperialism still attracts supporters, who believe that the only way of securing international peace (or agreement on certain problems such as migration or environmental issues) is to impose a political unity on tribal peoples, regardless which continent they reside in. Otherwise, national values will take precedence and undermine the chances of peace or environmental accords.

Institutions such as the United Nations present another forum for international cooperation. The UN seeks members' agreement on common codes of international conduct in peace and increasingly in and after war – ensuring war's legitimacy through international concord, establishing war crimes trials for instance, and reporting on and trying to halt the proliferation of weapons of mass destruction. Its predecessor, the League of Nations, is generally agreed to have failed in backing up its mandate with requisite force or consistency; the UN has similarly suffered a history of inconsistent policies, failing to intervene in some conflicts and embarrassing itself in others, and the fact that its Security Council members include an autonomous upper chamber of decision-making superpowers renders the equality of all nations somewhat dubious.

Against the drive to create international bodies stand the nationalists and secessionists. Firstly, nationalists emphasize the difficulties in forming a legitimate mandate for authority across national borders, and while these borders are understood to be artifices of history, they do represent legitimizing boundaries for political activity – that which takes place within being the proper jurisdiction of the state. The UN seeks to recognize the territorial integrity and inviolability of states' borders, and while the ideal of the international community is that of coming to the defence of any member-states being attacked, the reality of international politics and the skewed nature of the Security Council's separable national interests make the body morally partial; nation-states can only look after their own interests, for they know them better than distant neighbours or international delegates attending foreign conferences.

The point has much merit, but the nationalist still faces the advance of global markets and increased need for free migration around the world to alleviate overpopulation and poverty. On the liberal-statist end of the nationalist spectrum, proponents welcome the competition between states for resources and talent – for if one nation raises taxes to pay for a burgeoning welfare state, companies and labour are likely to migrate to lower-tax countries. Such competition acts to keep states from imposing locally debilitating restrictions on their economies – so long as they do not act in unison to depreciate their currencies, that is. Currency depreciation acts to mask the true cost of statist and socialist regulations, taxes and growing state debts – it is a commonly used tool, accompanied by fine-sounding 'economic' language but which involves nothing less than defrauding current money-holders through the printing of fiduciary money. Those ignorant of monetary matters and the simple but devastating device of monetary inflation should learn of its principles and effects and should check any nation's recent monetary data (e.g., in *The Economist*) to get a glimpse of how frequently central banks turn to the printing presses to protect their national governments (or the EU) from political follies. (Recent data put 'narrow money' growth in the US at 4.7%, which represents the creation of $53 *billion* of notes, coins, and cheque deposits: such monetary inflation has dire effects). Presently, the major economies (USA, Japan, the EU, Britain) try to inflate their currencies at similar rates, which acts to keep cross-exchange rates similar but devalues their currencies with respect to other nations' currencies or to the price of gold or other assets. The student of politics, who may be aware of the devastating hyperinflation of Weimar Germany but less aware of the continued use of the policy, should not underestimate the role that inflation has played in political history, and the political theorist cannot afford to ignore the cheap and deceptive mechanism of masking otherwise politically questionable or highly expensive acts.

Nationalism – the dominant political philosophy of the nineteenth and early twentieth centuries – seeks to maintain political processes within the borders of the state. In its realist variant, nationalists will seek to impose their will on their neighbours to secure their passivity or to be militarily powerful to ensure their own defence; in the libertarian version, the size and borders of the state are of no concern, for the libertarian state will permit free migration and freedom of exchange – it does not matter who should own what resources, so long as people are free to exchange with the owners. The conservative views the state as the embodiment of the people's will or deepest values, ensuring for them not just security and the rule of law but also a vital sense of identity that at once transcends locality in the sense of identity being formed by how others see you, but which does not get lost in vague cosmopolitan abstractions. But such identities and hence legitimate jurisdictions are rarely uncontested by indigenous populations who have often become tied to a particular state through war, dynastic marriages, or even through administrative oversight or hindsight. Liberal nationalism in the nineteenth century taught the world the right to self-determination and that principle remains a powerful if rarely questioned force in political philosophy and practice: if a woman may determine her own life, then why may not similarly minded folk join together to form their own affairs? It is the stress on 'similarly minded' that sustains nationalistic sentiments and secessionary movements.

SECESSION

Who constitutes a 'people' that deserves the right to determine its own affairs is one of the most exciting applications of political philosophy. In the past that decision, we could generally say, was made for most people through conquest and subjugation. Victors in war imposed their rule upon their victims and demanded their tribute (tax) and obedience, sometimes in return for protection and security (as with the pax romana or pax britannica), but often they merely imposed themselves upon the defeated and lived parasitically off their produce – in so far as it was politically expedient, that is. The Spartans provide the archetypal model in that regard – the defeated tribes (*helots*) whose lands they colonized were put to slave labour, and any sign of rebellion or even mental agility or personal strength was cruelly and swiftly dealt with using whatever ruses and justifications they could think of. It is not surprising that the Nazis possessed a Spartan Brigade.

The principle of self-determination emerged from individualistic libertarian principles, which in turn tapped into ancient forms of individualism, both secular and religious. If the individual owns his own person – and no one else may enslave it or violate it – he should be a freeman (which used to mean the deliciously tempting ideal of a person who does not pay taxes). It follows that he has a right to associate with people of his own choosing and form a free association with them, free in the sense that members retain a right to leave the association if they wish and others are free to join if the existing members (one argument could proceed) accept them. The principle of self-determination developed a momentum from religious thinkers in the wake of the Reformation: the logic was inexorable – a man ought to be free to choose the manner in which he worshipped God, and it was a small step for thinkers to realize that the morally arbitrary fact of one's birthplace should not condemn a man to a life of servitude or taxation and deprivation to a government he did not choose. While anarchists place great emphasis on the individual's right to secure his own self and identity in the absence of any state, libertarians and liberal-leaning conservatives evoked common cultural traits and shared identities between numbers of people as providing pragmatic criteria from which to assert the right to self-determination.

Unsurprisingly, a closer look at any nation's history shows manufactured jurisdictions incorporating often less than willing peoples into subjects. Particular cultures have been ignored in political processes behind the modern nation-states we recognize on political maps: languages have been forbidden, music and dances proscribed, traditional names prohibited, ancient religions banned, all in the name of contriving a uniform political face. Such is the story in my own country of the Welsh and Scots, the Catholic Irish and the Cornish; in France of the Bretons; in Spain of the Basques and Catalans; in Russia/Soviet Union of the Chechens, and so on. It is always valuable for the student of political philosophy to descend from abstract theorizing to examine closely the histories of particular countries, to attain a grasp not just of the complexities of political processes but also of the distinct subcultures that have been forcibly merged into forging the appearance of a unified polity under one government.

Some liberationist causes catch media and international political attention, but often the attachment to a local underdog is highly partial – East Timorese were given recognition and assistance but not Basque separatists. Why? Tibet, so often the subject of Chinese violation, does not gain UN attention and peace-keeping troops. Northern Ireland – as complex as any political situation can be – remained a British-Irish affair (with the odd American President chipping in for the American-Irish vote back home). Such partiality should strike the philosopher as suspicious and in turn should encourage him to question the validity not just of present borders but also of the means by which people identify themselves for determination.

If there is local sentiment for self-determination, why should a plebiscite not be held, and if the majority vote for independence, what could justify ignoring that plea on the part of other nations? A refusal to hold a ballot or a refusal to acknowledge the result can then be presented as justifying acts of self-defence against the occupying state. But how should the legitimate voting population be reasonably delimited? This is intensely problematic in mixed cultures with one culture demanding the retention of the status quo, while another demands separation. If groups are geographically mixed, no easy solution can surely present itself without a migration; however, that presumes that citizenship should be tied to locality, which is not at all necessary. Proponents of virtual states (i.e., internet linked and organized communities) can stress the accidental nature of most state borders and the moral arbitrariness of being born in one particular jurisdiction over another – why not permit individuals to choose freely their own state, regardless of their present situation? That would certainly introduce a wonderful competition in citizenship – some states may demand only wealthy members, others only French-speaking members, others may wish to offer state services to specific religions, others to sexual proclivities, or communal ownership of all goods, or sporting interests, or even offering members collective security services against aggression by others.

(In a sense, such experiments are already under way in inline games, where players from all around the world form new identities and establish virtual communities, some even offering law and policing services within their games. Apparently, the interactions and trades between players are not confined to computers, for they have been known to sell virtual objects or services online through online auction houses.)

The imagination may let fly at the possibilities, but the potential for such virtual states may be limited by geography after all. We live in a particular environment, and that environment provides us with access to resources and benefits and excludes others from it (except through trade). It is presently much more convenient to establish government (if there is to be any government at all) upon geographical lines than virtual cyberspace – the secessionist faces the contingent fact of location, culture, language, people and history being entwined and inseparable. Mixed populations, unless they agree upon secession together, may not have the logistic wherewithal to secede, compared to those populations that can easily identify freedom-seeking members amongst their own.

The secession model presents a counter to traditional, nationally oriented politics and even mainstream political philosophy, both of which presume the existence of states as they are (and thereby ignore the vagaries of human history, never mind the conflicts raging around the globe). It presents perhaps uncomfortable questions for those who prefer not to look too closely at the partiality of liberationist movement support, and it offers the political philosopher much to consider in justifying group identity and forming the criteria to recognize legitimate secession.

In the present political mould, the right to secede is, in all but a few headline cases, sidelined in favour of the existing state's right to enforce membership. Indubitably, much contemporary pressure stems from the USA's own history of forcing the Southern secessionary states to remain within the federation, breaking the constitution of the land and then setting a spurious precedent for American domestic as well as foreign policy outlook. Americans are hardly going to encourage Chechens to secede when they did not permit their own states to secede, and the Russian aggressors against Chechnya are doing exactly what their previous governments have done in ignoring the rights of smaller nations to identify themselves as independent peoples and to determine their own affairs accordingly. The American precedent seemingly presents a difficulty for the European Union, but here the game has often been to undermine the member nation-states in favour of encouraging a regionalism through direct subsidies to older pre-state polities. Thus England disappeared from a European Union official map in 1997: split into several regions that were the focus of EU policy and economic development. Such machinations – and the incentives that they create – are likely to encourage further splintering from the national state model, but no doubt EU proponents and thinkers believe that the divide and conquer policy will leave the EU organs stronger as the nation-states' powers dwindle. However, problems will arise if the Basque region, for instance, seeks independence from the EU too: will its right to self-determination be recognized, or will a Lincolnian policy of membership enforcement be imposed?

The start of a new century is often considered to offer new possibilities. The dates are of course relative to Western culture and the envisioned projects have long histories and momenta that traverse numerically or culturally significant dates with impunity. Nonetheless, the apparent blank book that the century offers awakens our minds to what we may wish to see enacted in the new century. The twentieth century has been characterized as the Age of Extremes by the catchy epithet of Hobsbawm, and the violence and vicious effects of totalitarianism have been used by thinkers to promote a drive for hope, justice, toleration and freedom for the twenty-first. But the Western sphere of influence does not stand alone, nor does it possess a monopoly over the direction that the unfolding actions of billions of people will take. There are obviously competing cultures and religions to the relatively secular vision of the West, but these in turn must resolve into the political philosophies that we have addressed here: a theocracy can theoretically be libertarian or socialist, for instance. The choice lies in the field of ideas – political ideas.

Ideas are not monopolized by intellectuals or political thinkers – influences stem from all walks of life, and in the past century the optimistic, progressive vision of science has encouraged many to embrace the cosmopolitan world of scientific endeavour and advancement; similarly, the ever-increasing market-place with its own cosmopolitan reaches often reduces politics to an aggravating sideline show, in which national leaders' rhetoric is removed from the reality of citizens' lives, although the policy implications remain just as debilitating.

GLOSSARY

This brief summary notes some of the main thinkers in political philosophy, as well as some lesser ones that come to light in the main text.

THE GREEKS

Political philosophy proper begins with the Ancient Greeks and arguably with

Heraclitus (d.480 BC), who left several enigmatic epithets including the comment that war is the father of all things: a favourite phrase for many thinkers who see conflict and war as the cause of social or political change.

Thucydides (460–400 BC) wrote a famous history of the Peloponnesian Wars. His writings and reports of battle speeches are often used by realist thinkers to explain balance-of-power politics.

Aristippus (435–360 BC) was a proponent of Hedonism and subjectivism – the theory that the good is to be found in the pursuit of pleasure and what constitutes pleasure can only be discerned by the individual.

Plato (428–348 BC) retains a commanding grip on modern political thinking. His dialogues include the first systematic theses to deal with the nature of the state, the obligation of the citizen, the limits and jurisdiction of political power and the application of reason to political and social issues. Plato argued for a hierarchical state run by an elite whose members are selected by virtue of their abilities rather than birth or connections. In the *Republic* and the *Laws*, Plato (through his character Socrates, Plato's own mentor until his suicide) goes into detail about how the state should be run, from what children should be taught to what kind of music ought to be proscribed. There are to be three classes of people – the workers, the guardians and the philosopher-kings, each reflecting the particular abilities of the population that fit in with the required nature of the state.

Diogenes the Cynic (412–323 BC) was famed for his ascetic rejection of riches, for a few quips and for having lived in a tub. Cynics questioned social norms and sought an independence of mind.

Aristotle (384–322 BC), Plato's pupil, proclaimed 'man is a political animal' (i.e., the civic life is natural to man). He formulated a realistic story of the development of the polity (family–village–polity) that has attracted much repetition and which becomes an integral element of what is known as the natural law tradition. Social life is thus not only to be expected but also it is morally right: those who shun society (anchorites) and who live outside the *polis* are barbaric and lawless.

The state is a natural entity and some are born to rule over others, but it is not birth alone that secures moral supremacy – good breeding counts too: the formation of good, virtuous character, what once was called gentlemanly behaviour, is fundamental to the goodly citizen and ruler. Politics to Aristotle, like Plato, means creating that system which best fits man's nature. All things aim towards ends and the end that human life ought to aim for is happiness, so government should be about securing those conditions that allow people to pursue their happiness on this earth (rather than in the afterlife).

THE ROMANS

Cicero (106–43 BC) followed Aristotle and Plato in asserting the goal of politics as creating the conditions for the pursuit of the good life, but augmented Greek virtue theory with Stoicism. Stoicism stresses tranquillity of mind and morally active participation in political life and a realization of humility against the backdrop of events over which one has no control. Importantly for politics, the Stoics distinguished between *ius gentium* and *ius naturalae*, thereby presenting the useful distinction between the laws man makes and the laws he is subject to, regardless of his particular cultural affinity – hence the theoretical possibility of an international law is formed: a law of the peoples of the world, to which both Romans and barbarians are subject. The art of politics is a skill to be learned through *doing* politics rather than studying it: an absolute adherence to abstract principles (something we are more familiar with in the modern world) would be considered strange to the Romans who sought a philosophy of *life* over contemplation: hence their virtues were to be tempered according to context, but always to be driven, as Cicero emphasizes, by what is honourable. Continuing the Aristotelian theme, he notes that a communal existence is the best form of life for man, and accordingly the state should be created to reflect man's potential. The state should be directed by the best and should be constituted as a meritocracy – rule of the most capable. Cicero was murdered by Octavian's henchmen.

CHRISTIANITY

St Augustine (AD 354–430), Bishop of Hippo, wrote his major treatise *The City of God* on the cusp of the collapse of Rome (he died while Vandals besieged his city). As the great vision that was once Rome crumbled, its intellectual impact remained, and new thinkers, wedded to Christian theology, sought to replicate the secular city's reach and political monopoly by raising in its stead the Roman Church. Augustine's ambition was to ensure that Christians' faith transcended secular hardship and political troubles. His manifesto was that the Church and the spiritual life should surpass the City of Man (Rome) and that men and women should keep themselves spiritually cleansed. We hear again Plato's voice in a man who sought to justify and explain the nature of the Other World, but who ably welded the general thrust of Platonic philosophy to the Christian theological inheritance that had evolved in the previous three centuries since Christ's death. Moreover, we can also detect Stoical ethics – again merged with Christian thinking and Eastern promise of eternal salvation – stretched beyond the tranquillity of mind into an almost absolute renunciation of this world in favour of retaining the purity of the soul.

St Thomas Aquinas (1225–74) was steeped in the Augustinian philosophy that had sustained the mainstream philosophy of the Church over the preceding centuries, but his innovation was to introduce an Aristotelian logic and conceptual framework (from Aristotle's recently rediscovered works) into Christian theology and to produce a powerful epistemological and metaphysical division between philosophy and theology, which has left a strong philosophical and cultural legacy that sustains both scientists and theologians down to the present day: reason and science for this world, faith and revelation for the next. Since we can know our world using the senses and our rational faculty, Thomas's ethics and political philosophy is more concerned with the ordering of this world, and he remains wedded to the hierarchical vision passed down from the Greeks in which some are designed or born to rule others. Aristotle's aristocratic charge is thus rekindled, and so too is Plato's vision of a rationally governed society. Here is the philosopher's perennial call to statesmen to order their affairs rationally with the Christian addition to save men's souls. Theologians ought thus to become philosopher-kings, or at least advise the secular powers in the pursuit of the holy life.

THE REFORMATION

Desiderius Erasmus (1466–1536), was an influential Dutch humanist who satirized and condemned warfare between Christians and who opposed Martin Luther's denial of freedom of will.

Prior to the Reformation, the division between the Church and the individual secular states (princedoms, dukedoms, kingdoms, republics) had erupted into confusing alliances and the degradation of theological matters into political fighting over territory and tax-rolls. In such an atmosphere it may not seem such a radical leap to reject the morality of the other Kingdom in favour of refocusing political theory on ordering secular affairs rationally as the greats had wished, but it was certainly a radical leap to reject all notions of morality in the pure pursuit of power. Such was the work of **Niccolò Machiavelli** (1469–1527). The 'realist' advice that he wrote to his patron (Lorenzo de' Medici) was not thoroughly new in that realism's history reaches back to Thucydides' stories of the Peloponnesian War and even earlier sages' advice to monarchs on how to survive politically; what was new was Machiavelli's attempt to assess politics coldly in the light of the facts of human nature and political constitutions. Many date *The Prince* as the beginning of modern political philosophy – but closer readings also show an appeal to republicanism as offering the best form of government. However, the appropriate rules of statesmanship are shockingly absent of that command to be reasonable and impartial that we find in the Ancients: the statesman can be as fickle as he likes, renounce treaties and go back on his word, but he can do this only so long as he does not provoke his subjects into rebellion.

Sir Thomas More (1478–1535) penned the influential *Utopia*, describing a society in which reason rules the affairs of the community; poverty and moral evils have been eliminated but so too have property rights.

Michel de Montaigne (1533–92) revived Greek political thinking through his humanist essays: humanity, he maintained, should not be so arrogant in its belief of moral supremacy – man can be stupid and incompetent and morally worse than animals. His revival of Aristotle's economic fallacy that one man's profit is another man's loss influenced later writers. A thorough sceptic, Montaigne adopted the epithet: 'What do I know?' which led to a stoical submission to absolute government and traditional culture and politics.

SEVENTEENTH CENTURY

Following on the heels of Machiavelli, **Thomas Hobbes** (1588–1679) expounded the realist cause. In the state of nature, competition for the same values leads men to fighting and war – the 'warre of all against all', so men seek their self-preservation through the creation of a state. Once the state is formed, it possesses the primary and incontestable power to enforce the peace – and for Hobbes, the best way to ensure that is to remove all potential sources of conflict. Pluralism in religion and learning is thus to be rejected to secure peace; otherwise men's quibbling and arguments will lead society back to the fearful civil war. Only beyond the nation's borders does the anarchic state of nature exist – nations look upon each other as predators and prey, ready to enact force and violence against their neighbours at any time. Much of Hobbes's disquiet is with the unravelling of the polity into disorder and brutal violence – hence the need for a strong state to secure the peace.

Gerrard Winstanley (1609–76) was leader of the small but influential group of Diggers, emerging out of the British Civil Wars (1642–50) to found a shortlived communal and anarchic egalitarian community. The more influential Levellers, led by **John Lilburne** (1614–57), sought a libertarian reform of the British polity and economy based on the principal of self-ownership, private property and religious toleration.

John Locke (1632–1704) asserts the right of the individual to live life as he chooses; in particular he owns himself (and therefore cannot be enslaved to anyone else); government is needed to overcome a few inconveniences of the generally peaceable state of nature such as knowledge of and enforcement of the law, but should keep itself out of the lives of its citizens, who possess inalienable rights to their property and their lives. Aggressors – state or criminal – against property and life may be justly punished, executed or enslaved.

EIGHTEENTH CENTURY

Bernard Mandeville (1670–1733) was a Dutch-born English physician whose satire *The Fable of the Bees* claimed that all social and charitable actions are inherently self-serving. Mandeville influenced later utilitarian philosophers and also Adam Smith.

Jonathan Swift (1667–1745) was a Tory libertarian, whose *Modest Proposal* satirized the quantification methods of William Petty by asserting the need for the rich Irish to eat their children in order to avoid both overpopulation and famine.

Jean-Jacques Rousseau (1712–78) developed the Hobbesian–Lockean theory of the social contract to explain that political societies gain their justification from the approbation of the general will: each individual renounces his or her will in favour of that of the community. The general will cannot but act in the interests of the group and recalcitrants must accordingly be forced to be free, as it is in their interests. Rousseau also championed what became the romanticist image of the noble savage, an idealized depiction of pre-civilized man. His influence, like that of Hegel's, cannot be over-estimated – although he is much easier to understand.

Adam Smith (1723–90) wrote *An Inquiry into the Wealth of Nations*, which was highly influential in discrediting the economic doctrine of mercantilism and reducing government intervention in trade. Smith capably explained the reason why nations grow as people spontaneously (i.e., as if through an 'invisible hand', as he puts it), invest in capital, divide labour and specialize in tasks.

Immanuel Kant (1724–1804) is politically known for his defence of rationalist deontology – duty-bound ethics as explained by reason, but also for his tract on Perpetual Peace, which envisages a future without war as commercial interaction between peoples grows.

Edmund Burke (1729–97) was an Irish-born lawyer who rose to prominence in British politics and who, after an initial libertarian (almost anarchist) youth, penned one of the greatest conservatist tracts *Reflections on the Revolution in France*, in which he rejected the French Revolution and the attempted imposition of rationally designed rules and laws on a complex political culture. The result, he prophesied, would be brutal repression and bloodshed as authorities sought to bind the people in homogeneity.

Thomas Jefferson (1743–1826), 3rd President of the USA, drafted a Lockean-influenced constitution and espoused the benefits of an agrarian-educated democracy with curtailed federal powers.

Jeremy Bentham (1748–1832) founded the Utilitarian movement which asserts that any action or policy ought to secure the greatest good for the greatest number. Many nineteenth-century reformers were influenced by his work.

Alexander Hamilton (1755–1804) was a keen federalist and proponent of strong central government for the USA.

William Godwin (1756–1836) is the forerunner of the modern anarcho-communist movement. A fervent individualist and rationalist, his highly influential *Political Justice* argued that reason and civilization could be supported by the free and altruistic actions of people, so there would be no need for private property.

NINETEENTH CENTURY

G. W. F. Hegel (1770–1831) is the conservative defender of constitutional monarchical statism. His philosophy is hard to understand and commentators naturally differ on the emphasis found therein. Hegel looks upon the state as having to forge its identity in relation to other states and hence as needing to assert itself (violently if necessary) on the international stage. Each state reflects the culture of its people, and their history follows a path of development, maturity and decline. For the most part people reflect their culture, but the great men cast aside normal expectations and bend morality for their own purposes.

David Ricardo (1772–1823) explained the theory of comparative advantage which demolished the Aristotelian–Montaignist theory that one man's gain is another man's loss: Ricardo showed that even when one trading partner possesses advantages in all resources, nations may gain from specializing in that in which they possess a comparative or relative advantage.

Comte de Saint-Simon (1760–1825) and his followers argued for the creation of a socialist commonwealth rationally directed by scientists and industrialists. His works were influential on the growing socialist movement.

Robert Owen (1771–1858) was a Scottish social reformer who used his mills at Lanark to set up a workers' community with housing and schooling. Owen's writings have had a huge impact on British socialism.

Jean Charles Sismondi (1773–1842), initially a supporter of Adam Smith's *laissez-faire* policies, was moved by the social effects of urban expansion to criticize capitalism.

Carl von Clausewitz (1780–1831) was a Prussian military thinker and espouser of the doctrine that war is the continuation of politics by other means. He wrote the famous *Vom Kriege* (*On War*) which, in part, outlines the political nature of war but also its inherent tendency to break free of attempts to control it.

Thomas Carlyle (1795–1881), was a critic of *laissez-faire* policies who argued for a strong paternalistic state led by the best men – statist heroes.

Karl Rodbertus (1805–75) was a German economist who argued that the state should take over all production, but that this should be done without violence.

John Stuart Mill (1806–73), a child prodigy educated by his father James Mill and his friend, the philosopher Jeremy Bentham, became an economist, logician and political thinker. Mill initially argued for a predominantly free society but also developed Bentham's utilitarianism to promote the belief that some values (or pleasures) are more important than others; this led him in later years to accept an increasingly socialist position. His ideas evolved into what is now called 'modern liberalism'.

Max Stirner (1806–56) advocated extreme egoism and the rejection of society, and was to have an influence on Nietzsche.

Pierre Joseph Proudhon (1809–65) proposed mutualism and syndicalism. A highly influential thinker, Proudhon believed that as man developed ethically, government would become superfluous.

Henry David Thoreau (1817–62) was a naturalist and individualist who had an immense impact on American thought. He is best known for *Walden, or Life in the Woods* (1854), an account of his solitary life by Walden Pond.

Karl Marx (1818–83) and his colleague **Friedrich Engels** (1820–95) were founders of the modern communist movement whose impact on the world can never be overestimated. Using a millenarian historicism, Marx argued that humanity was on an ineluctable path in which the class systems that have plagued human society were to disappear following a glorious revolution. However, Marxism divides between those who believe that the revolution is inevitable (and therefore we just need to sit back and await its arrival) and those who believe that revolutionary conditions can be fostered to secure it earlier.

Herbert Spencer (1820–1903) argued for the minimal state and the rejection of all forms of statism. Welfare policies do not help the poor but keep them dependent and corrupt morals. In Lockean tradition, Spencer argued for the complete freedom of the individual, so long as this does not interfere with his neighbour's right to pursue his own freedom.

Heinrich von Treitschke (1834–96) was a Prussian historian, whose anti-Semitic and fervent German nationalism influenced the growth of German militarism in the late nineteenth century.

Friedrich Nietzsche (1844–1900) called for the overthrow of traditional, Christian altruist morality in favour of the superman life-affirming morality of defining oneself independently of others. His writings were misappropriated by the Nazis, which tainted his reputation for mid-twentieth-century readers; however, Nietzsche would have had no sympathy with the anti-Semitic philosophers of Nazism.

TWENTIETH CENTURY

Piotr Kropotkin (1842–1921) was a Russian anarchist who argued that natural human society is, in the absence of the state, cooperative and that groups of people would flourish well enough through customary exchanges of produce if left alone.

Emma Goldman (1869–1940), a Lithuanian-born, American émigrée anarchist writer and activist, was imprisoned by the USA for her advocacy of birth control.

Vladimir Ilich Lenin (1870–1924), an ardent propagandist and political agitator for communism, seized power following the 1917 Russian revolution. He wrote many tracts in the Marxist vein and when in power imposed a full-scale socialist nationalization programme, whose immediate disastrous results led to a pragmatic reacceptance of some private markets. Lenin became an absolute dictator and centralized power sufficiently for the more brutal Stalin to take over and exert his less-than-academic understanding of politics on the Russian people and their subject peoples.

Ludwig von Mises (1881–1973) was an economist and methodological individualist whose influential *Socialism* exposed the logical problems of production and distribution without markets. His early work on money also explained the cause of business cycles resulting from central bank inflation of the money supply. Mises explained the workings of the market in his tome, *Human Action*.

John Maynard Keynes (1883–1946) proposed an economic theory that justified statism. He argued that free market capitalism would periodically fail and would therefore need the guiding hand of large government interference by expert economists to steer it through fiscal and monetary policies. His theories were rehashed into the standard fare of macroeconomic courses.

Nikolai Bukharin (1888–1938), Communist Party member and supporter of slow collectivization and industrialization, was editor of *Pravda* before he fell foul of Stalin and was executed.

Friedrich August von Hayek's (1899–1992) *Road to Serfdom* remains an influential anti-government text in which he argues that the 'third way' of mixed government intervention inevitably leads to increasing controls until full socialism or a state of slavery is reached. Hayek also wrote an erudite exploration of law and its role in free societies.

Karl Popper's (1902–94) studies of epistemology led him to defend the open society against those who would prefer to control it through rationalist programmes of social engineering; he also presented a robust criticism of historicist philosophies such as Marxism.

Jean-Paul Sartre (1905–80) attempted an amalgamation of Marxism and existentialism. His general thrust was to focus on the individual's plight having been thrown into the world. Man is free but everywhere he seeks to find excuses for his behaviour and thus lives inauthentically.

Ayn Rand (1905–82) was a Russian-born American émigrée. Through her popular novels and collections of essays, she formed the Objectivist philosophy. Freedom and the capitalist society of free exchange with its emphasis on economic growth and prosperity possess a moral and metaphysical justification – man must use his mind to understand the universe and his mind can only work in a free society. From this, an ethical defence of capitalism and individualism follows.

Rachel Carson (1907–64) was a zoologist and biologist whose *Silent Spring* is credited with instigating the modern environmentalist movement in America (it had long been alive in Europe and Asia); A critic of pesticides she was influential in the banning of DDT use, despite little scientific evidence of its harm to humans.

George Woodcock (1912–95) was a Canadian writer who produced a thorough and, in turn, influential history of anarchist thought.

Isaiah Berlin (1909–97) was a Russian born émigré who migrated to England following the Bolshevik revolution. A philosopher and historian of ideas, he defended liberalism against historicist and determinist theories of man and explored the differences between 'positive' and 'negative' rights.

John Passmore (1914–2004), an Australian philosopher who pioneered 'applied philosophy', espoused a concern for environmentalism with a respect for rationalism and science.

Eric Hobsbawm (1917–) is an influential Marxist-inspired historian whose penmanship rises above his political biases.

John Rawls (1921–2002) presented a novel approach to social-contract theory, asking us to imagine what people would choose for justice and society if they could strip all social prejudices. In this 'original position', society would agree on each person having a sphere of liberty compatible with others' freedoms but that any inequalities would only be permitted which help those who are worst off in society.

Murray Rothbard (1922–95), economist, historian and critic, developed Mises's critique of socialism to propose an anarcho-capitalist philosophy.

Ted Honderich (1933–) a Canadian-born philosopher, presents a poignant statist attack on Burkean conservatism.

Leonard Peikoff (1933–) acts as Ayn Rand's intellectual heir to her philosophy of Objectivism; his *Ominous Parallels* charts the philosophical underpinnings to the rise of totalitarianism in Nazi Germany and its parallels in postwar American thinking.

Robert Nozick (1938–2002) presented a classic defence of the minimal state in his *Anarchy, State, and Utopia*, which has spawned much critique and contrast with his Harvard contemporary, John Rawls's work.

Tibor Machan (1939–) defends libertarianism as a moral system and argues that states could raise finances without resorting to coercive measures such as taxation.

G. A. Cohen (1941–) is an analytical defender of Marxism and the morality of socialism.

Roger Scruton (1943–) is a modern proponent of conservatism and critic of animal rights theories and modern sexuality.

Hans-Hermann Hoppe (1949–), a student of Jürgen Habermas and Murray Rothbard, proposes ethical and economic defences of anarcho-libertarianism.

Will Kymlicka (1962–) has presented appealing arguments for merging modern liberalism with communitarianism and defends the view that minority group rights can be supported by liberalism.

BIBLIOGRAPHY

Aquinas, Thomas, *Selections from the Summa Theologiae*, trans. Paul E. Sigmund (New York: W. W. Norton & Co., 1988).

Aristotle, *Politics,* trans. T. A. Sinclair (Harmondsworth: Penguin, 1986).

——*Nichomachean Ethics*, trans. David Ross (Oxford: Oxford University Press, 1992).

Augustine, St, *City of God*, trans. Henry Bettenson (Harmondsworth: Penguin, 1984).

Bentham, Jeremy (1789), *Introduction to the Principals of Morals and Legislation*, in *Collected Works of Jeremy Bentham*, ed. H. L. A. Hart and F. Rosen (Oxford: Clarendon Press, 1996).

Bukharin, Nicolai (1934), *How it all began*, trans. George Shriver (Chichester, NY: Columbia University Press, 1998).

Burke, Edmund (1790), *Reflections on the Revolution in France*, ed. Conor Cruise O'Brien (London: Penguin, 1986).

Carson, Rachel (1962), *The Silent Spring* (London: Penguin, 2000).

Cicero, *On Duties*, ed. M. T. Griffin and E. M. Atkins, Cambridge Texts in the History of Political Thought (Cambridge: Cambridge University Press, 1998).

Clausewitz, Carl von (1832), *On War*, trans. J. J. Graham (London: Routledge & Kegan Paul, 1968).

Cohen, G. A., *Self-Ownership, Freedom and Equality* (Cambridge: Cambridge University Press, 1995).

Erasmus, Desiderius (1509), *In Praise of Folly*, in *The Essential Erasmus* (New York: New American Library, 1964).

Godwin, William (1793), *Essay Concerning Political Justice* (Oxford: Oxford University Press, 1971).

Goldman, Emma (1911), *Anarchism and other Essays* (New York: Dover Publications, 1970).

Hamilton, Alexander, John Jay and James Madison (1787–88), *The Federalist Papers* (New York: Random House, 2000).

Hayek, Friedrich (1944), *The Road to Serfdom* (London: Ark Paperbacks, 1986).

——(1960), *The Constitution of Liberty* (London: Routledge & Kegan Paul, 1963).

Hobbes, Thomas (1651), *Leviathan*, ed. Richard Tuck, Cambridge Texts in the History of Political Thought (Cambridge: Cambridge University Press, 1996).

Hobsbawm, Eric, *The Age of Revolutions: Europe 1789–1848* (London: Abacus, 1988).

——*The Age of Extremes: A History of the World, 1914–1991* (London: Pantheon, 1995)

Honderich, Ted, *Conservatism* (London: Penguin, 1990).

Hoppe, Hans-Hermann, *Democracy: The God that Failed* (New Brunswick, NJ: Transaction, 2001).

Ignatieff, Michael, *Blood and Belonging: Journeys into the New Nationalism* (London: Vintage, 1994).

Jefferson, Thomas (1775 onward), *Writings* (New York: Library of America, 1984).

Keynes, John Maynard (1936), *General Theory of Employment, Interest, and Money* (London: Palgrave Macmillan, 1960).

Kropotkin, Piotr (1902), *Mutual Aid* (London: Freedom Press, 1987).

Kymlicka, Will (1989), *Liberalism, Community and Culture* (Oxford: Clarendon Press, 1992).

Lenin, Vladimir (1918), *The State and Revolution*, trans. Robert Service (Harmondsworth: Penguin, 1992).

Lilburne, John (1645), *An Agreement of the Free People of England* (London: Coptic Press, 1967).

Locke, John (1690), *Two Treatises on Government*, ed. Peter Laslett, Cambridge Texts in the History of Political Thought (Cambridge: Cambridge University Press, 1997).

Machiavelli, Niccolò (1532), *The Prince*, ed. Quentin Skinner and Russell Price, Cambridge Texts in the History of Political Thought (Cambridge: Cambridge University Press, 2001).

Marx, Karl and Friedrich Engels (1848), *The Communist Manifesto* (Oxford: Oxford World Classics, 1998).

Mill, John Stuart (1859), *On Liberty* (London: Longmans, Green, 1884).

Mises, Ludwig von (1922), *Socialism*, trans. J. Kahana (Indianapolis, IN: Liberty Classics, 1981).

——(1944), *Human Action* (London: William Hodge, 1949).

Montaigne, Michel de (1580–95), *The Essays*, trans. Charles Cotton Ward (London: Lock, Bowden and Co., 1700).

More, Sir Thomas (1516), *Utopia*, ed. G. M. Logan and Robert M. Adams, Cambridge Texts in the History of Political Thought (Cambridge: Cambridge University Press, 2002).

Naess, Arne, *Ecology, Community and Lifestyle: Outline of an Ecosophy*, trans. David Rothenberg (Cambridge: Cambridge University Press, 1990).

Nietzsche, Friedrich (1883–91), *Thus Spake Zarathustra*, trans. Thomas Common (New York: Modern library, undated).

——(1886), *Beyond Good and Evil*, trans. R. J. Hollingdale (London: Penguin, 2003).

Nozick, Robert (1974), *Anarchy, State and Utopia* (New York: Basic Books, 1974).

Owen, Robert (1813–14), *A New View of Society* (London: Penguin, 1991).

Passmore, John (1974), *Man's Responsibility for Nature* (London: Gerald Duckworth, 1998).

Plato, *Republic*, trans. G. M. A. Grube and Revd C. D. C. Reeve, in *Plato: Complete Works*, ed. John M. Cooper (Indianapolis, IN: Hackett Publishing, 1997).

——, *Laws*, trans. Trevor Saunders, in *Plato: Complete Works*, ed. John M. Cooper (Indianapolis, IN: Hackett, 1997).

Popper, Karl (1945), *The Open Society* (London: Routledge, 1986).

——(1957), *The Poverty of Historicism* (London: Routledge & Kegan Paul, 1961).

Proudhon, Pierre Joseph (1840), *What is Property?* ed. Donald R. Kelley and Bonnie G. Smith, Cambridge Texts in the History of Political Thought (Cambridge: Cambridge University Press, 1994).

Rand, Ayn (1957), *Atlas Shrugged* (New York: Signet, 1961).

——(1964), *The Virtue of Selfishness* (New York: New American Library, 1964).

Rawls, John (1971), *A Theory of Justice* (Oxford: Oxford University Press, 1988).

Ricardo, David (1817), *The Principles of Political Thought and Taxation* (London: Prometheus Books, 1996).

Rodbertus, Karl (1851), *Overproduction and Crises*, trans. Julia Franklin (London: Swann, Sonnenschein, 1898).

Rothbard, Murray (1962), *Man, Economy, and State* (Auburn, AL: Ludwig von Mises Institute, 2001).

——(1982), *The Ethics of Liberty* (New York: New York University Press, 2002).

Rousseau, Jean-Jacques (1762), *Social Contract and Discourses*, trans. G. D. H. Cole (London: Everyman, 1993).

Saint-Simon, Comte de (1825), *The New Christianity*, trans. J. E. Smith (London, 1834).

Sartre, Jean-Paul (1967), *Existentialism and Humanism*, trans. Philip Mairet (New York: Methuen, 1974).

Sismondi, Jean Charles (1819), *New Principles of Political Economy*, in *Selected Writings* (Oxford: Basil Blackwell, 1952).

Smith, Adam (1776), *An Inquiry into the Wealth of Nations*, ed. R. H. Campbell and A. S. Skinner (Indianapolis, IN: Liberty Classics, 1976).

Stirner, Max (1845), *The Ego and his Own* (London: Rebel Press, 1982).

Swift, Jonathan (1729), *A Modest Proposal*, in *Jonathan Swift: Writings* (New York: W. W. Norton & Co., 1980).

Thoreau, Henry (1849, 1854), *On Civil Disobedience* and *Walden* (Harmondsworth: Penguin, 1984).

Treitschke, Heinrich, *Politics*, in *Selections*, trans. Adam Gowans (London: Gowans & Grey, 1914).

Winstanley, Gerrard (1649), *New Law of Righteousness*, ed. Andrew Sharp, Cambridge Texts in the History of Political Thought (Cambridge: Cambridge University Press, 1998).

Woodcock, George, *Anarchism: A History of Libertarian Ideas and Movements* (Cleveland, OH: World Publishing, 1962).

INDEX